Jail Management and Liability Issues

Dale K. Sechrest, D.Crim.
Assistant Professor
Criminal Justice Department
Florida International University
North Miami Campus
North Miami, Florida 33181

and

William C. Collins, J.D.
Attorney at Law
P.O. Box 2316
Olympia, Washington 98507

Coral Gables Publishing Co., Inc.

Interior design by Carlos Ceballo and Roger Denton.

Library of Congress Catalog Card Number: 88-064044

Sechrest, Dale J.; Collins, William C.
Jail Management and Liability Issues

Includes indexes.
1. Corrections—United States. 2. Criminal justice, Administration of—United States. 3. Criminal justice, Personnel—United States. 4. Criminal justice, Prisons—United States. I. Title
HV 8756.SE3J 1989 350.91 88-064044
ISBN 0-938993-05-4

Printed in the United States of America

1 2 3 4 5 6 7 8 9 - 93 92 91 90 89

TABLE OF CONTENTS

Foreword

Reaction was for decades the mode by which we in corrections operated our facilities. Regardless of whether we were reacting to our latest budget from the governing body, to a Supreme Court decision, to a change in statutory law, or to the public and media, our actions were in reaction to an outside stimulus. In short, everyone, except those of us who are the professional practitioners, were deciding our fate for us. However, over about the last 15 years, we in corrections have been exerting ourselves as the professionals we are. Accreditation, greater participation in various professional organizations, as well as long overdue intensive training in every area of our profession have all contributed to our achievements in recent years.

Our work is far from complete, though. The progress we have made has taken us only a short distance down the road to true professionalism. While it is encouraging and uplifting to consider where we have been, it becomes more important now to focus on where we are going.

Certainly, any plan for future personal and professional growth must include education. Education in related areas, such as psychology, sociology, and criminology, has been readily available for years. Only recently, however, have purely correctional educational opportunities become available. With the publication of this text, these opportunities have increased significantly. This "nuts and bolts" text focuses on the least recognized areas of corrections — the local jail. Regardless of whether your jail holds ten inmates or 500 inmates, the information contained herein applies. While monetary resources certainly have a major impact upon your facility, much of what we do administratively can be modified and improved upon without spending a dime. Included in this text is the information necessary to enable us to make positive changes and improvements without the shackles of limited resources.

Therefore, as we, as a profession, have progressed out of a purely reactive mode, it now becomes absolutely necessary that we switch into a proactive mode. We should be planning the future correctional agenda. To do this successfully we must have credibility. Nothing brings credibility faster than a person who is professionally educated in his or her field of endeavor.

Use this text book, then, as a proactive tool in your continued personal and professional growth. In conclusion, be proactive — we were reactive long enough.

M. Wayne Huggins
Sheriff, Fairfax County, Virginia

Preface

If you are taking the time and putting forth the effort to read this book you are demonstrating that you fit into the ever-expanding group of jailers striving for professionalism within our field.

This book provides an excellent guide for your use in cross-checking current levels of training, providing references for additional information, and in leading toward the all important device of preparation.

The world in which we live is rapidly becoming one that recognizes, and urges, prevention. We practice preventative maintenance on our car, on our home, and on our jail facility's mechanical system. We have physical examinations to identify medical problems early. We practice preventative dentistry. We have programs in our communities teaching crime prevention. We practice self-defense to avoid being hurt.

Jail management requires us to practice prevention through sound policies and procedures, selection of good people, training of staff, and consistent, well thought-through responses to a variety of contingencies, all of which demand preparation.

I suggest you use this book as the first step in what I call "the practice of preventative law." Threaded purposely throughout are references to legal issues; some of them are direct topic headings, others are by implication. All of them provide a recognition that we, the managers, must know the law.

I urge you, the administrator, to practice preventative law by doing the following:

- Meet with, and get to know, the attorney who will represent you.
- Determine that person's level of knowledge regarding sound detention practice, not only statutory law as it applies to your jurisdiction, but applicable case law from around the nation.
- Assist your attorney by providing copies of applicable standards, statutes, and case law references.
- As you develop your policies and procedures, pass all drafts through your attorney for evaluation and ask the following questions:

> Do these policies and procedures meet your understanding of the law?
>
> Can you defend me, and are we on solid ground if we follow them?

I urge the line staff members who must follow policy and procedure and write those never-ending, always-required reports, to ask themselves the same two questions in a different way:

> Did I behave in a manner consistent with my understanding of policy, procedure, and law?
>
> Will my actions stand legal testing, and can I be successfully defended in the event of a suit?

At all times, remember the three "P"'s of prevention: planning, preparation, and practice.

Paul E. Bailey
President, American Jail Association

Acknowledgements

The idea for this book was suggested by Judy Sechrest, who believed that much of the information gained over several years in developing standards for accreditation might be useful in a book on jail administration. The addition of sections on liability, contracting for services, and problems of new construction appeared consistent with the overall goals of the text.

Several individuals contributed to the completion of this text. Ilene Bergsmann was kind enough to read the original manuscript and use her writing skills to clarify issues and assist in the overall organization. Ernest G. Reimer, formerly of the California Department of Corrections, read the first draft and made several useful suggestions as to the content and the organization of the text.

Joseph Rowan reviewed the sections on suicides and provided updated figures. Dennis Liebert of the National Institute of Corrections reviewed and commented on issues related to the planning of new facilities and provided information on the opening of new facilities.

Phillip Goldberg read the entire manuscript and applied his particular expertise to the area of fire safety and emergency procedures. John J. Vollmann reviewed the section on riots and disturbances. Ken Kerle and Francis R. "Dick" Ford of the American Jail Association provided their comments regarding the substance of specific chapters.

Nick Pappas, who authored a book on jails for the Department of Justice, provided comments and suggestions, as did Marion Mattingly, Washington Representative of the National Coalition of State Juvenile Justice Advisory Groups, who added important comments on juvenile justice issues.

During the course of writing the book the author was doing research on incident rates in the Dade County Corrections and Rehabilitation Department, Directed by Fred Crawford. This research and related contacts with facility personnel have contributed to the creation of the book. Deputy Director Kevin Hickey, Division Directors Sara Heatherly and Jerry Meece, Frank Brophy, Capt. Charles J. McRay, Jail Bureau Supervisor, Lt. Don Taylor, Lt. Lois Spears, Sgt. Sheila Dixon, Corporals Charles D. McKenzie and James Brannock, and many others in the Department have been very helpful in an ongoing process of reviewing jail operations.

Final responsibility for the content of the text rests with the authors. However, it is most gratifying to know that there are persons in the criminal justice and corrections field who are willing to give of their time and talents to assist in the development of what we hope will be a useful guide for improving jail operations.

Dale K. Sechrest
William C. Collins

Purpose of the Book

This book is designed for the administrator, supervisor, or line staff officer who wants to improve the operation of the local detention facility, or jail, based on accepted current practices. Most of the material is also relevant to the operation of state or federal facilities for sentenced offenders. A smooth jail operation is an asset to the administrator, facility staff, the inmates, and to the community. Ultimately, the community requires protection from the offender as well as protection from the unwarranted and unnecessary lawsuits that may result from poor management of the jail facility. Most local officials, jail administrators, and jail staff operate using practices they believe are humane, just, and efficient. However, there are always areas for improvement, and constant vigilance must be exercised to prevent problems in the facility. Therefore, while this book is targeted at the small to medium-sized jail, administrators and trainers for larger jails should find it useful as a checklist and as a training tool for new staff.

The jail is a potential source of major litigation. While many lawsuits brought against administrators, staff and local officials are frivolous, representing an unwarranted and unnecessary intrusion into local practices, some suits are inevitable because of aging, substandard physical facilities, and jail populations far greater than a facility was designed to hold. Many other types of lawsuits can be avoided simply by following some basic procedures of jail administration. Court intervention should not be necessary or desirable to insure that a facility meets the needs of the offenders and the community. Litigation is a time-consuming and expensive alternative to good administration and management. Unfortunately, too often in recent years, litigation has become the only way to provide for an adequate jail. The American Civil Liberties Union (ACLU) "Jail Litigation Status Report" for 1985, the first such compilation, lists 112 pages of cases encompassing almost every state in the union. Gone are the "good old days" when the sheriff could simply turn the jail over to a trusted but ill-equipped jailer.[1]

The control of local detention facilities and services is changing. Sheriffs in many counties are having their jails turned over to county or city departments of corrections. This has led to greater use of the "detention facility" or "adult local detention facility,"

[1]American Civil Liberties Union, "Jail Litigation Status Report, 1985," (National Jail Project, 1616 P Street, NW, Washington, D.C. 20036).

rather than the more traditional "jail." The actual number of jails decreased from 3,493 in 1978 to 3,338 in 1983, a four percent decline due in part to municipal and county jail consolidation.[2] Still, about 63% of all jails are designed for under 50 beds, a decline from 67% in 1978.[3] Five states have placed their local detention facilities under the management of state correctional services, and state inspection teams are a reality for most detention facility administrators. The possibility of having the county commission turn over the entire operation of the jail to private contractors has become a very real threat. Private contracting, as well as the problems of contracting for specific services, are discussed in chapter six.[4]

The detention facilities of the country are in a crisis. This crisis relates as much to litigation regarding operations as it does to the crowding of inmates in correctional systems in most states. Nationally, occupancy rates for jails rose from 64 percent of capacity to 96 percent of capacity from 1978 to 1985, with increases for large jails of 77 to 96 percent of capacity during this period. Jail administrators report that in 1985, 22 percent of the jail population was being held for other authorities because of crowding in Federal or State prisons or in other local jails.[5]

In 1985 the nation's jails held 256,615 inmates, an increase of 62 percent over 1978's population of 158,394. Nearly three-fourths of this population is held in jails in 362 jurisdictions, which the Bureau of Justice Statistics (BJS) calls jurisdictions "with large jail populations." The BJS reports that occupancy exceeded rated capacity in jails in jurisdictions with large jail populations by two percent in 1984 and six percent in 1985.[6] A 1987 American Jail Association (AJA) survey of jails with over 1,000 inmates confirms this figure for 21 large jails, showing capacities of over 100 percent for 19 of the jails reporting, with four (of the 21) reporting populations over 150% of capacity. One in four of the jails in large jurisdictions

---

[2]Bureau of Justice Statistics, The 1983 Jail Census (November, 1984) 1, 5.

[3]Bureau of Justice Statistics (1984) 6.

[4]See Camille G. and George M. Camp, "Private Sector Involvement in Prison Services and Operations," (National Institute of Corrections, 1984); see also "Private Jail in Bay County, Fla., Makes Inroads For Corrections Firms, but the Jury Is Still Out," Wall Street Journal, 29 Aug. 1986: 40.

[5]Bureau of Justice Statistics, Jail Inmates, 1985 (Washington, D.C.: July, 1987, NCJ-105586) 1.

[6]Jail Inmates, 1985: 2.

were under court order both to reduce population or to improve one or more conditions, e.g., "86% were cited for crowded living units, 58% for recreation facilities, and 54% for medical facilities/services."[7] Increased populations and crowding invite problems such as "increased prisoner and staff tensions, increased wear and tear of facility and equipment, budgetary problems from overtime staffing, and an inability to meet program and service standards."[8] Crowding of cell space itself is sometimes not seen to be as great a problem as that of processing additional numbers of inmates through the detention facility, which produces constraints on prosecutors, judges, public defenders, probation officers, and pretrial services personnel.

Problems of jails were determined by the National Sheriffs' Association (NSA) in 1982 in a survey of 2,664 of the over 3,000 jails they asked to respond.[9] For jails of all sizes the top five "most serious" mentioned were personnel, 45%; modernization, 39%; overcrowding, 30%; recreation, 26%; and, funding, 21%. Personnel was a problem for all sizes of jails (four categories were used). Overcrowding appeared to be a greater problem for larger facilities.[10] The most interesting observation was that, using reported staff to inmate figures, crowding did not appear to be the case in some facilities that reported it. The authors speculate that this meant there probably weren't enough staff on the shifts to properly handle the work load, and that this is a general conditions for jails, coupled with "poverty level wages" that inhibit hiring.[11]

The NSA survey found that training is poor to nonexistent in many states. Many jails are seen as physically depressing, employing untrained staff who see little chance for upward mobility, sometimes asking untrained radio dispatchers to do the jail work, and lacking minimal protection from liability either through proper training or

---

[7] "Mega-Jail Survey," A.J.A. Newsletter Fall, 1987: 2; populations used were for January to June, 1987.

[8] Andy Hall, "Systemwide Strategies to Alleviate Jail Crowding," Research in Brief (Washington, D.C: National Institute of Justice, January, 1987) 2.

[9] Kenneth E. Kerle and Francis R. Ford, The State of Our Nation's Jails (Washington, D.C.: National Sheriffs' Association, August, 1982) 21; the actual number polled is not given, but appears to be about 3,000 with an 89% response rate; see also "Personnel, Not Overcrowding, Is Number One Jail Problem, New NSA Survey Reveals," Corrections Digest (Washington, D.C.: Washington Crime News Service, June 21, 1982) 1.

[10] Washington Crime News Service (June 21, 1982) 225-229.

[11] Washington Crime News Service (June 21, 1982) 230-231.

"punitive damage insurance." They emphasize that jail officers are not "guards," but supervisors of inmates, and as such they must display "initiative, intelligence, tact, and diplomacy.[12] They conclude by citing the need for more (increased) pay, better staff screening and more training, education requirements for employment (exact criteria not stated), ways to provide job enrichment (provide career incentives to defeat turnover), use of internships in corrections (stressing it as a career), greater involvement of jail staff in management decisions (i.e., policy and procedure development), and projecting a better image to the community.[13]

No less distressing are the findings of a 1987 NIC-sponsored study of new small jails (average size 28 beds) constructed in the last ten years. Among other problems, the study indicated high levels of juvenile occupancy (58% house juveniles), staff shortages (60%, with 34% seeing it as a serious or somewhat serious problem), overcrowding (44%), space shortages, maintenance problems, and twelve percent reported that they failed to provide any jail staff, relying instead on ratio dispatchers, electronic surveillance, or other unspecified means to supervise inmates.[14]

The National Sheriffs' Association 1982 survey expressed the "jail crisis" in terms of the "barrage of lawsuits." They found current court orders in 10.7 percent of all jails they surveyed, and 19.9% indicated they were presently a party in a pending lawsuit. About 28 percent (744) reported a suicide in their jails in the past five years, a major source of lawsuits. They concluded with recommendations for improvements that should help remedy the situation in the nation's jails, if these problems are addressed.

A 1986 estimate of law suits is that one in three jails is under court order or has lawsuits pending in Federal Court under Section 1983 of the Civil Rights Act of 1871, with another survey revealing that 42 percent of the jails constructed since 1975 had "problems"

---

[12]Washington Crime News Service (June 21, 1982) 230-232.

[13]Washington Crime News Service 232.

[14]Dennis A. Kimme, The Nature of New Small Jails, Report and Analysis (Champaign, Illinois: Kimme Planning and Architecture, for the National Institute of Corrections, October, 1985) 4-6; this report is summarized in Dennis A. Kimme, "The Nature of New Small Jails: Report and Analysis," American Jails Winter, 1988: 40-51.

with lawsuits.[15]

This book describes the types of practices that local officials and the facility administrator need to establish to maintain and improve operations. Changes suggested in the book may require the improvement of present procedures or may involve requests for additional funds and personnel that are consistent with good practice, as established through local or national standards. By following these practices and procedures, administrators and their respective staff will be implementing improved administration and management practices. Also they will be in a position to avoid personal or organizational liability, prevent and/or control riots and disturbances, manage public criticism, provide for the public safety, and in doing so help ensure their long term employment in a most important area of human services.

Organization of the Book

The book has three major sections. Chapters one through five refer to the management of an existing facility and are directed to all aspects of detention facility operations. They should be read by all persons operating detention facilities. Chapters one through five are relevant to both contracting for services and in the planning, design and construction of new facilities. Chapters six and seven are directed primarily to facility administrators and managers as well as all persons, including public officials, who are involved in the planning and construction of new facilities. Chapter six addresses the special problems found in contracting for services with private non-profit or profit-making organizations. Sometimes contracting can be cost effective and should be considered for various types of ancillary services, such as medical care, food, or programs. Chapter six also provides the basis for an analysis of the benefits or contracting for, or "privatization" of, all facility operations. Chapter seven is specific to the planning, design and construction of a new detention facility. Much of chapter seven, however, is relevant to current operations and to contract services. Chapter eight addresses the goal of reaching for professionalism.

---

[15]Dennis Kimme, Gary M. Bowker, Bruce R. Bounds, Robert Deichman, and Harry L. Baxter, Small Jail Special Issues (Champaign, IL: Kimme Planning and Architecture, for the National Institute of Corrections, February, 1986) 2-1.

CHAPTER ONE: ADMINISTRATION

I. Some Basic Guidelines

The following guidelines offer a first step in understanding the problems faced by the detention facility administrator. The administrator must:

1. Know the law of the jurisdiction, including local and state statutes and case law.

2. Determine, in consultation with legal counsel, personal liability and the liability of the agency and its staff for the management of inmates in a detention facility.

3. Determine, in consultation with legal counsel, specific responsibilities for the supervision of subordinates and potential liability for inadequate supervision and/or lack of staff training.

4. Develop, in consultation with personnel experts, an overall personnel program that will allow for the hiring of the best qualified staff for the facility and will assist in holding those staff accountable for their actions on the job. A pre-service and in-service training program must be developed and implemented for all staff.

5. Develop a record-keeping system that keeps track of inmates on an ongoing basis, and maintain a personnel system that keeps accurate records on staff progress and performance.

6. Develop a management system that looks both inside and outside the system. The Sheriff or Detention Facility Administrator will want to consider the employment of a strong operational person to run the jail while the balance of his/her energies are devoted to the political arena. This may help to ensure cooperation with others and appropriate funding.

7. Establish a system for communicating with the courts, including individual judges, regarding what they expect from the facility and court personnel regarding court scheduling, requests for information, etc.

8. Establish a monitoring system for the agency that will keep administrative staff informed of any immediate or potential problems.

9. Maintain positive communications with the press and the public, as well as with public and private agencies that may be able to assist in evaluating the successes, failures, and problems of managing the jail.

II. Keeping Track of Jail Operations

Two areas of importance are involved: (1) administrative records and budgets, and (2) monitoring facility operations.

Administrative Records. Personnel concerns (hiring, retention, etc.) are discussed in detail in Chapter Three. The concerns here are personnel data, budget information, and inmate records. These records may be kept manually or on automated systems. Even small jails require careful record-keeping, generally as part of the budgeting process. Staff salary summaries, operating costs, and inmate counts are critical to making a case for the annual budget, and they are essential to immediate and long term planning. Staff records may be in the hands of an "outside" personnel department, which may work well if communications are good and you have access to them. This may also be true of budgets that are handled by an accounting department that is part of the larger county or city governmental structure.

No matter where the system is located, you have the responsibility for personnel and fiscal decisions related to the facility and should have immediate and full access to those records. If you control the records (in-house) you may be considering an automated system, although this is not a necessity. An expert in this area notes that automated systems may not be necessary for small jails.[16] If an automated system is being considered, and there are many products and services on the market, there are some key steps that can be followed that are essential to success. First, do not be

---

[16]Allan H. Lammers, "Guideposts To Successful Automation in Jails" American Jails Spring, 1987: 58-62.

stampeded by a high-pressure sales pitch into a system that you do not understand and do not control. Start at the beginning. First master the steps summarized below.

Lammers suggest three basic steps: determining information needs, finding the computer programs ("software") that will meet those needs, and then purchasing or developing the hardware necessary to operate the programs.[17] Try to get a system that you can control yourself, in-house — that is, one which your staff can operate. Do not get locked into paying for "computer runs" outside your agency unless you are well-advised as to their cost and availability. Many administrators have paid the price of buying a computer system without proper counseling. Some administrators have even had trouble with these services within their own governmental structure. Remember, no salesperson sees himself as forcing a system on you — they simply believe in it. In which case, you must be sure that if you adopt their system you have contacted at least three agencies who use it and have found it satisfactory.

In-house microcomputer systems with hard disks have developed to the point that most small jails can do very nicely building a system around them with little outside assistance. However, it is important to dedicate one staff member to this task (who likes it) and to provide that person with a consultant with expertise on the system you adopt. Clerical staff must also be trained in such systems. Some people do not adapt well to microcomputers, even the more "user-friendly" systems. Some people feel they "depersonalize" the working environment. It may be better to use these individuals in the area of word processing, rather than data entry, budgeting, accounts payable, or personnel records. Problems also exist in "down-time," when the system may not be working, and inaccuracies in the system. Confidentiality of the data will also be a concern. Finally, the problem of "computer literacy" must be addressed through training and the development of a commitment to the use of the system.

Monitoring/Auditing Facility Performance. Facility administrators who employ a well-developed, reliable monitoring or auditing system consistently report that it tells them far more about their facility operations than previously used informal feedback mechanisms may have. Again, given the growth of liability in jail operations, what you don't know can hurt you. And it often will.

---

[17]Lammers 60-61.

Consideration must be given to implementing a system to keep track of what is going on in the facility — an ongoing monitoring system. This system will serve several purposes. First, it alerts staff to their responsibilities by defining them in relation to operational criteria. Second, it provides for the determination of compliance with existing laws, local and departmental codes, rules, regulations, directives, standards, and policies. Finally, it forces the administrator to find and use operational criteria for the facility, which can be especially critical if some of the above-mentioned laws, rules, or regulations are not in place for your jurisdiction.

Operational Criteria. Practical operational criteria are available from many sources and have proliferated in the last decade. These include national professional standards, such as those developed by the American Correctional Association (1981, 1984), which have been approved and used by the National Sheriffs' Association. They have been adopted, in part, for the jail and prison standards of the United States Department of Justice. Operations manuals have been developed by the National Sheriffs' Association, and there are numerous sets of state and local standards for jail inspection. The American Correctional Association (ACA) standards can be applied through an ACA accreditation program or through an audit procedure conducted by the National Sheriffs' Association, using the same standards.

A checklist for monitoring and evaluating of your security program is given in chapter two.

III. Understanding Liability

A. The Inmate Rights Movement

Prior to the late 1960's, there were virtually no "inmate rights" and the courts maintained what was known as the "hands off" doctrine. Under this approach, courts would literally go out of their way to avoid having to decide a claim arising out of a jail or prison. The main interest courts had in prisons or jails was in sending people to them, not protecting their rights once they got there. This doctrine began to change as part of the larger civil rights movement of the past two decades, and by the beginning of the 1970's there was an explosion of inmate rights issues. With the birth and growth of the "prisoners' rights" movement, the courts' interest came to include conditions of confinement and inmate rights. Courts across the country, especially federal courts, suddenly opened their doors to inmate complaints. In the ensuing decade, there was probably no facet of jail or prison operation that was not subjected to judicial scrutiny. New areas of litigation were constantly being discovered and new rights were announced on a nearly a daily basis, or so it seemed.

The development of a body of law defining the rights of prisoners and the duties of jailers, and the willingness of the courts to enforce that body of law, has created a tremendous pressure on those responsible for the operation of detention facilities to develop adequate operating policies and procedures and to see that those policies and procedures are followed and enforced. The consequences of not taking these steps are court intervention in the operation of the jail, the possibility of the jail administrator and local officials being found personally liable for the violation of inmate rights, and sometimes even the unit of local government being required to pay damages to the inmate.

Virtually every person working in the detention facility who deals directly or indirectly with offenders is potentially subject to suit. This includes the newest correctional officer up to and including the chief jail administrator and the sheriff, as well as volunteers. Liability extends even outside the facility itself and can, in some situations, include county commissioners, county (or city) administrators and even the unit of local government itself. When a violation of an inmate's constitutional rights is traceable to a policy or practice of a unit of local government such as a city or county, that unit of government itself may be named as a defendant.[18]

Current Status of Rights. There continues to be a great deal of inmate litigation; however, the growth of new rights has slowed as the rights of inmates have become more clearly defined. A number of Supreme Court decisions, while upholding the principle that inmates enjoy the protection of the Constitution, have been considerably more conservative than many lower court decisions and have thus helped to slow the breakneck growth in inmate rights of the 1970's.

---

[18]A concise discussion of the history of inmate litigation and a summary of important cases can be found in Krantz, Sheldon, Corrections and Prisoner's Rights, 2nd Ed. (Nutshell Series, West Publishing Company, 1983) 109-116; see also National Sheriffs' Association, Inmates' Legal Rights, rev. ed. (Alexandria, Virginia: 1987).

As new rights continue to evolve and old general statements of rights are clarified and defined, the bulk of inmate litigation today deals much more with enforcement of existing, clearly defined rights. It is expected that litigation will continue in many areas of inmate rights, and the jail administrator must take steps to keep abreast of developments in the field of correctional law. In fact, administrators of all types of public agencies are required by the courts to keep abreast of new case law relevant to their operations.[19] At the least, this suggests reviewing publications in the field, although much material is written generally and may be of limited use in advising a jail administrator as to legal developments directly relevant to his/her operation.

Perhaps the best approach is for the administrator to have legal counsel available in an advisory capacity on a continuous basis to alert him/her in advance of potential problems, and not just as a "go to court," defensive option. This allows for the evaluation of new case law and a planned response. Realistically, however, this approach may be nearly impossible for smaller jurisdictions. Nonetheless, procedures must be established and others revised to apply new knowledge of the law to the operation of the facility. Good training in detention and corrections operations includes components on legal issues, and available in-house and national training should be required for administrators and staff.

B. Basis of Inmate Suits

Inmates most frequently bring one of two types of suits: civil rights actions brought under a federal statute — 42 United States Code Section 1983, or tort actions that allege damage through some form of negligence by jail officials. By far the more significant of these types of suits has been the civil rights action.

Originally passed by Congress in 1871 to protect blacks in the South from the maraudings of the Ku Klux Klan, the Civil Rights Act was originally known as the Ku Klux Klan Act. Now it has come to be

[19]In Wood v. Strickland, 420 U.S. 308 (1975) the Supreme Court said that an official was not immune from liability if he or she knew or "reasonably should have known" that an act taken would violate "clearly established," "unquestioned" constitutional rights, or if the action was taken with malicious intent to cause a deprivation of constitutional rights or other injury. For a full discussion of liability and immunity see Paul T. Hardy and Devereux Weeks, Personal Liability of Public Officials Under Federal Law, 3rd ed. (U of Georgia: Carl Vinson Institute of Government, 1985).

informally known as "Section 1983," with the resulting "1983 suits," a reference to its being located in section 1983 of Title 42 of the United States Code. The Act provides that:

> "...every person who, under color of any statute, ordinance, regulation, custom, or usage, of any state or territory, subjects, or causes to be subjected, any citizen of the United States or other person within the jurisdiction thereof to the deprivation of any rights, privileges, or immunities secured by the Constitution and laws, shall be liable to the party injured in an action at law, suit in equity, or other proper proceedings for redress."

In other words, the Act says that when someone feels his/her rights under either the federal Constitution or federal statute have been violated by someone acting on behalf of state government (including local government), he/she may sue the alleged wrongdoer for damages, an injunction, or any other form of appropriate relief. The Act only authorizes suits against persons who are acting on behalf of government ("under color of state law").

Four amendments to the U.S. Constitution provide the basis for virtually all inmate suits under the Civil Rights Act. (Almost no inmate civil rights suits are based upon the violation of federal statutes.)

The First Amendment. The First Amendment generally guarantees freedom of speech, religion and the press and the right to petition government for the redress of grievances. It has been the basis for a great deal of litigation regarding inmate religious freedoms: Can hair length be regulated over religious objection? Can inmates engage in religious practices to the same extent as non-prisioners? Are some belief systems to which inmates adhere even religions at all?

Rights of correspondence and communication between inmates and non-inmates also have been the subject of First Amendment litigation, as have visiting issues, censorship of publications, and association.

Generally, the First Amendment rights of inmates are less than those of free people, their reduction being justified by the fact of imprisonment. In deciding the scope of inmate rights under the First

Amendment, courts will try to balance the interest of the inmate (in speech, the free exercise of religion, etc.) against the legitimate interests of the institution, which typically involve security and order in the facility.

Under two 1987 Supreme Court decisions, a restriction imposed by an institution on a right protected by the First Amendment will be upheld if the regulation "is reasonably related to legitimate penological interests."[20] "Legitimate penological interests" are generally seen as including interests of security, order, discipline, and, in some cases, rehabilitation. In making this evaluation, four factors will be important:

1. Is there a valid, rational connection between the regulation and the governmental interest which is offered to justify it?

2. Does the inmate have alternative ways of exercising the restricted right? In other words, if there is a restriction that prevents the inmate from attending a particular religious service, are there other ways in which the inmate is able to exercise his freedom of religion?

3. If the institution accommodates the asserted right, what will the impact of that accommodation be on officers, other inmates, and the overall allocation of prison resources?

4. The absence of ready alternatives will be seen as an indicator of the reasonableness of a regulation.

These points are elaborated upon in Collins Correctional Law 1987. [Hereafter the Collins series will be referenced as Collins 1986 or Collins 1987].[21]

The Fourth Amendment. The Fourth Amendment prohibits the government from conducting unreasonable searches and seizures. From the Fourth Amendment we enjoy "reasonable" expectations of privacy against government intrusion.

---

[20]Turner v. Safely, 107 S.Ct. 2254 (1987); see also O'Lone v. Shabazz, 107 S.Ct. 2400 (1987).

[21]Collins (1987) 2, 26, in relation to Turner and Shabazz.

In applying the Fourth Amendment in the detention facility context, again the courts attempt to balance the interests of the inmate against the security interests of the institution. Clearly, an inmate's expectation of privacy is less than that of a free person. Facility staff can conduct many more types of searches of inmates and their property than they can for non-inmates, and they can do so with little or no specific cause for such searches.

Most Fourth Amendment litigation has been concerned with cell and body searches of inmates, although visitor and staff searches have been the subject of some suits.[22] Fourth Amendment issues being litigated in the mid-1980's include strip searches at the time of booking of persons arrested for minor offenses and the extent to which inmates' privacy interests may protect them from observation by the opposite sex. Most courts have concluded that automatically searching such arrestees is unconstitutional.[23] In one case four women were strip searched at a lockup after arrest on misdemeanor charges. Since they were not "inherently dangerous" the search was seen as unreasonable.[24] An earlier (1982) fourth circuit case provided precedent for this view: "Strip searches of detainees are constitutionally constrained by due process requirements of reasonableness under the circumstances... [Defendant's] strip search bore no ... discernible relationship to security needs at the Detention Center that, when balanced against the ultimate invasion of personal rights involved, ... could reasonably be thought justified. At no time would [defendant] or similar [DWI] detainees be intermingled with the general jail population; her offense, though not a minor traffic offense, was nevertheless one not commonly associated by its very nature with the possession of weapons or contraband...."[25] A similar case occurred in Montgomery County, Maryland in 1983, where "indiscriminate strip searches" of arrestees detained at the jail was found unconstitutional.[26] The scope of the case was narrowed in a subsequent decision stating that searches could be conducted using a

---

[22]Jordan v. Wolke, 450 F. Supp. 213 (E.D. Wis. 1978) found that non-contact visitors would be subject to "pat down" examinations and metal detector searches of their persons.

[23]Giles v. Ackermann, 746 F.2d 614 (9th Cir., 1984); see Weber v. Dell, 804 F.2d 796 (2d Cir. 1986) for a listing of other strip search cases.

[24]See Mary Beth G. v. City of Chicago, 723 F.2d 1263 (7th Cir. 1984).

[25]Logan v. Shealy, 660 F.2d 1007, 1013 (4th Cir. 1981), cert. denied, 355 U.S. 942 (1982).

[26]Smith v. Montgomery County, 573 F.Supp. 604 (D.Md. 1983)

reasonable suspicion standard for felony arrestees or misdemeanants suspected of possessing weapons or contraband — a rejection of a probable cause standard.[27]

Also, in Lusby v. T.G. & Y. Stores, the legality of a jail search was upheld where jail staff had reason to believe that the detainees were carrying drugs, and where a person is lawfully arrested for possession of drugs such a search is generally permissible.[28] Given the overwhelming weight of precedent against automatic strip searches of all arrestees, the jail administrator needs to carefully develop and monitor arrestee strip search policies. A related issue is to what extent inmates' privacy expectations protect them against being observed by staff of the opposite sex while in the nude or using the toilet.[29] Here the trend among courts appears to tolerate at least occasional observation of male inmates in the nude by female officers, as found in Grummet v. Rushen. Since an important governmental interest that weighs against inmate privacy interests in this area is that of equal opportunity for female officers and also since the equal opportunity argument is far weaker for male officers working in female institutions or units, there is a question whether the female officer/male institution cases will apply strongly in a male officer/female institution setting.

Issues of search related to pretrial inmates found in favor of the administration in the Federal Metropolitan Correctional Center in New York City for both visual inspections and body cavity searches subsequent to visits.[30] The court there found, with some hesitancy, that the opportunity to receive contraband justified the intrusiveness of a strip search, even though there was no individual suspicion pertaining to the inmate being searched.

Court tests prior to search are more stringent for correctional officers suspected of carrying contraband: "[I]t is our view that a reasonable suspicion standard should govern strip searches of

---

[27]547 F.Supp. 596 (D.Md. 1986).

[28]749 F.2d 1423, 1433-34 (10th Cir. 1984), vacated on other grounds, 106 S.Ct. 40 (1985); see also Salinas v. Breier, 695 F.2d 1073, 1083 (7th Cir. 1982), cert. denied, U.S. (1984), which allowed strip searches of the wife and four children of a suspected heroin dealer where the court assumed probable cause existed.

[29]Grummet v. Rushen, 779 F.2d 491 (9th Cir., 1985).

[30]Bell v. Wolfish, 441 U.S. 520, 99 S.Ct. 1861 (1979).

correction officers working in correctional facilities.... [W]e believe that, as applied to correction officers, society is prepared to recognize that the expectation of being free from the indignity of warrantless visual body-cavity searches continues to exist even within the confines of correctional facilities. In contrast to the legitimate governmental interests asserted for strip searches, we believe that the governmental interests vis-a-vis visual body-cavity searches are diminished severely.... [W]e hold that before the Department may conduct a visual body-cavity search, it must obtain a search warrant based on probable cause from a judicial officer."[31]

Current issues on the testing of correctional officers' urine for drugs will focus on the right to privacy. A 1987 appeals court case supports random testing of correctional officers only in conditions where they have direct, regular contact (day-to-day) with inmates in medium to maximum security facilities, and the court was concerned that the testing be truly random.[32] This case may not hold up. It now appears clear that "reasonable suspicion," and not "probable cause," will be required to undertake testing. Collins discusses this issue at length based on public employee cases.[33] A Federal District Court in Illinois decided against mandatory drug testing for all jail employees without "reasonable suspicion" that the employees tested are drug abusers. It was seen as an unreasonable search, and arguments regarding prevention of smuggling drugs into the facility and maintaining the public's confidence in the integrity of correctional employees were rejected.[34]

In determining the reasonableness of employee drug testing for law enforcement officers, McEwen et al. indicate that three criteria probably will be used: (1) the justification for the tests, although most can be justified in the "public interest"; (2) the likelihood of employee impairment while on the job, which will require the reasonable suspicion ... of impairment test; and (3) the

---

[31]Security and Law Enforcement Employees, District Council 82 v. Carey, 737 F.2d 187, 204, 208 (2d Cir. 1984).

[32]McDonell v. Hunter, 809 F.2d 1302 (8th Cir. 1987).

[33]Collins (1986) 73-74.

[34] Taylor v. O'Grady, No 86-C-7179 (N.D. Ill. 1987).

reliability of the tests and procedural safeguards.[35] A major issue in all drug testing will be the reliability of the tests themselves. Regarding random testing, McEwen et al. cite a case decided by the New York State Supreme Court that barred the New York City Police Department from conducting random tests in the Organized Crime Unit on the rationale that the tests violated the Fourth Amendment rights of the employees; the decision is on appeal.[36]

Very important in the defense of any search case is that the searches under attack were done professionally, and in accordance with policy. Searches done for purpose of harassment or done in a way which unnecessarily embarrasses or humiliates the inmates are likely to be condemned.

The Eighth Amendment. The Eighth Amendment prohibits "cruel and unusual punishment." While this vague concept may be difficult to define in concrete, specific terms, this has not kept courts from deciding Eighth Amendment issues ranging from officer brutality to issues of failure to protect inmates from one another to the adequacy of the overall conditions of confinement in a jail. When one hears of a jail being declared unconstitutional, it is typically because the conditions in the jail — often due to a combination of serious crowding, decrepit facilities, and poor administration — have been found to be cruel and unusual punishment. Adequacy of medical and mental health care is also an issue that is frequently raised under the Eighth Amendment.

In attempts to correct sweeping violations of the Eighth Amendment, courts have assumed a great deal of control over the administration of jails and have forced changes such as major population reductions and construction of new facilities.

Fourteenth Amendment. The Fourteenth Amendment is the source of a great deal of inmate litigation. There are two separate portions of the Fourteenth Amendment that are the basis for litigation: the due process clause and the equal protection clause. The due process clause prohibits the state from depriving someone of "life, liberty, or

---

[35]J. Thomas McEwen, Barbara Manili, and Edward Connors, Employee Drug Testing Policies in Police Departments, Research in Brief (Washington, D.C.: National Institute of Justice, October, 1986) 5.

[36]McEwen et al.; Philip Caruso, President of P.B.A. v. Benjamin Ward, Police Commissioner, New York State Supreme Court, Part 37, Index No. 12632-86.

property without due process of law." This phrase is significant in two respects. In the first, and most common, when the state makes what can be called a "taking" decision (taking away good time or other privileges, taking away a favored classification status, etc.) the state often must provide the inmate with some form of review or hearing ("process") in order to determine fairly the existence of the factual basis for the decision in question. This is called "procedural due process." Its most common application is in the context of inmate disciplinary proceedings.

Under what is known as "substantive due process," a court may rule that certain types of state action are simply not justifiable, regardless of whatever sorts of procedural protections could be imagined. A common substantive due process issue in the jail context is conditions of confinement for pretrial detainees. Conditions issues for convicted persons are litigated under the Eighth Amendment, which prohibits cruel and unusual punishment. However, the Supreme Court has said that pretrial detainees cannot be "punished" until they are convicted of a crime and therefore are not protected by the Eighth Amendment, which prohibits cruel and unusual punishment. To then protect pretrial detainees from intolerable conditions or confinement, the courts have relied on the Fourteenth Amendment's substantive due process concept instead of the Eighth Amendment. The results of either approach tend to be about the same.

Another important aspect of due process is the right of access to the courts that is recognized as part of the Fourteenth Amendment. This right is discussed in greater detail in Chapter Five (Section II.) Although providing inmates with "meaningful access to the courts" may prove expensive and may place substantial demands on scarce jail space (for example, a complete law library takes up considerable room and increases in size every year), failure to properly deal with the clearly established right of access to the courts can provide a quick ticket to court for the jail administrator.

The second major portion of the Fourteenth Amendment is the equal protection clause. In general terms, this clause requires that groups or classes of persons "similarly situated" should be treated similarly (receive the same treatment, similar benefits, etc.) unless the government can clearly justify treating the two groups differently. A classic example of an equal protection issue is different treatment of persons on the basis of race, still a difficult problem in some jurisdictions. In the corrections context in the mid-1980's a recurring equal protection issue was the different treatment of male and female offenders. Several courts have ruled that disparate treatment of these two groups is not justified and that the two groups should have substantially similar facilities and programs (the concept of "parity").[37]

C. Relief Available to Inmates

Two basic forms of relief are available under the Civil Rights Act — injunctions and damages. In the early years of correctional litigation, injunctions were the most common form of relief awarded. Typically, the court would review a practice or condition of the institution, find it unconstitutional, and enter an order directing the defendants to correct the deficiency or deficiencies.

Damages in civil rights cases comes in three forms: nominal, compensatory, and punitive. Nominal damages are reserved for those cases where a right is violated, but the plaintiff can show no real damage. Nominal damages typically are $1.00. Compensatory damages are awarded to compensate or repay the plaintiff for damages actually sustained. Examples include out-of-pocket costs incurred (such as medical bill or lost wages) and damages for such intangibles as mental anguish. Finally, punitive damages are intended to punish the defendant and "send a message" that the defendant's conduct is not to be tolerated. Punitive damages need bear no relationship to the actual seriousness of the plaintiff's injuries.

Recognizing that government officials cannot be expected to predict the development of constitutional law, the courts were reluctant to award damages against officials who might well be doing the best they can, given the resources available to them. Therefore, a concept of limited immunity against damages was developed called the "good faith defense." This defense has now evolved so that unless the right found to have been violated was "clearly established" in law, no damages can be awarded.[38] Because more and more rights in correctional law are becoming "clearly established" as they are reviewed by the Supreme Court, or at least a number of lower courts reach a consensus on the issue, damages are potentially more and more available to the plaintiff/inmate whose rights are violated in some way.

---

[37] Canterino v. Wilson, 546 F. Supp. 174, 562 F. Supp. 106 (W.D. Ky., 1982, 1983).

[38] Smith v. Wade, 103 S.Ct. 1625 (1983).

For municipalities and other local units of government the good faith defense is not available. Cities and counties can be sued under the Civil Rights Act following the 1978 Supreme Court decision in Monell v. Department of Social Services of the City of New York, which held that if the alleged unconstitutional action involved the execution of a governmental policy or custom the governmental unit could be liable in damages.[39]

Another de facto form of "damages" exists potentially in all litigation under the Civil Rights Act in the form of attorneys' fees. Several years ago Congress passed an amendment to the Civil Rights Act, now codified at 42 U.S.C. Sec. 1988, which allows a court to award a prevailing party in a Civil Rights case attorneys' fees, in addition to whatever other form of relief is ordered.

The attorneys' fees act has been liberally interpreted by the courts in favor of awarding fees to prevailing plaintiffs. And, while fees can be awarded to prevailing defendants, such awards are extremely rare. The fee award often substantially exceeds the value of the judgment itself. In a 1986 case, the Supreme Court approved a fee award of over $245,000 in a case where the damages totalled only $33,000, of which only $13,000 were for violation of the plaintiffs' constitutional rights![40]

The presence of the attorneys' fees issue in a Section 1983 case must always be kept in mind and considered as part of the review of the case for possible settlement. Fighting a relatively insignificant issue just as a matter of principle may lead to a small judgment for the plaintiff and to a sizable award of attorneys' fees to the plaintiff's counsel.

Courts may also cite a party for contempt in an effort to enforce their rulings, although these ruling are rarely enforced. They may also appoint monitors or "special masters" where they feel the sheriff or detention facility administrator requires oversight in following a court order.[41]

---

[39]98 S.Ct. 2018; Collins (1986) 107-110.

[40]City of Riverside v. Rivera, 54 LW 4845 (1986).

[41]Susan Sturm, "Special Masters Aid in Compliance Efforts," Journal, The National Prison Project 6 (Winter, 1985): 9-11; see also Collins (1986) 111-122, regarding consent decrees.

D. Who Is Liable?

To summarize, there are two basic areas of liability: violations of civil rights and tort claims. The former is based on federal statutes and the U.S. Constitution, the latter on local liability laws. You may be liable directly or indirectly. That is, you may be held directly accountable for errors you personally caused, or if you are a supervisor or administrator, you may be held accountable in the courts for the acts of your subordinates and may be indirectly liable. There are two forms of indirect responsibility that apply based on whether the suit is a civil rights action or a tort.

Tort Suits: Respondeat Superior. To be liable under the Civil Rights Act, a defendant must be found to have actually caused the violation. Under tort law an employer may be liable for the actions of his/her employees regardless of whether the employer even knew of the actions, let alone could be said to have "caused" the violation. This concept is called "respondeat superior." It is based generally on the assumption that a party injured as the result of the negligence of another should be able to receive compensation for the injuries. Since an employee may not have enough assets to pay these damages, the employer should, as a matter of public policy, be held liable for the actions of the employee. The theory is that if the employer is liable the employer will have a greater incentive for seeing that the employee does not act negligently. And, of course, the "deep pockets" of the employer usually make it a better target for suits.

Public Agencies: Vicarious Liability. Even though the concept of respondeat superior does not apply to governmental units or supervising officials in Sec. 1983 actions, indirect liability can apply to officials of public agencies.[42] Liability can be imposed on supervisors who may not have been directly involved in the incident that violated the plaintiffs rights. If it can be said the supervisor set in motion a series of events or circumstances that ultimately caused the violation, then liability will reach back to the supervisor. According to Krantz, "it must be demonstrated that [a superior or an employee] knew or reasonably should have known that the action taken by him or someone under his control would violate the rights of the persons involved, or that he took or condoned the action with the malicious intention, to cause a deprivation of

---

[42]Sheldon Krantz, Corrections and Prisoners' Rights, 294. See also Pearl v. Dobbs, 649 F. 2d 608 (8th Cir. 1981).

constitutional right or other injury." In short, there need not be evidence of personal participation, but some "causal connection" must exist between the supervisor's actions and a deprivation of a constitutional right.[43]

This idea has come to be known as "vicarious liability, as opposed to direct liability." Direct liability means a supervisor is held liable for what he does; vicarious liability hold a supervisor liable for what his subordinates do. Del Carmen has attempted to clarify the meaning of vicarious liability as opposed to respondeat superior, indicating that vicarious liability is a much broader term.[44] Vicarious liability is a common concern in a series of "failure to" situations, the most common of which is the failure to train. If the supervisor/employer fails to train the employee properly in, for instance, the proper use of force, and the employee improperly and unconstitutionally uses force against someone, the injured party may be able to show the employer's original failure to train "caused" the injury and therefore successfully sue the employer as well as the employee. Other "failure to" areas include:

> Failure to supervise
>
> Failure to properly direct
>
> Failure to discipline or fire; also referred to as negligent retention.
>
> Failures in the hiring process, i.e., failing to screen out obviously incompetent persons.[45]

The failure to train, supervise, direct, etc., argument can be made either in a Civil Rights (Section 1983) case or in a tort action. A main difference is the burden which the plaintiff must meet. In the civil rights context, the plaintiff must show a "deliberate indifference" to his constitutional rights (for instance, the right to be protected from

---

[43]Krantz, 1984; see also Sims v. Adams, 537 F. 2d 829 (5th Cir. 1976) and Procunier v. Navarette, 434 U.S. 555 (1978).

[44]Rolando del Carmen, Potential Liabilities of Probation and Parole Officers, rev. ed. (Washington, D.C.: National Institute of Justice, August, 1986) 161, 180.

[45]See Rolando del Carmen, "Legal Liabilities and Responsibilities of Corrections Agency Supervisors," Federal Probation September, 1984: 52-65; see also Rolando del Carmen, Potential Liabilities of Probation and Parole Officers rev. ed. (Washington, D.C.: National Institute of Justice, August, 1986) 160-169.

harm under the Eighth Amendment). In a tort action the burden is simply to show the defendants were negligent in some way that resulted in a breach of a duty owed the plaintiff (again, a duty to protect the inmate from unreasonable risk) and that the plaintiff was damaged as a result of the negligence.[46]

E. Prevention Through Policies and Documentation

As issues of inmate rights have grown, the importance of preventive law has grown correspondingly. Detention facility administrators must not only understand what the law is, and what it is becoming, but also must take steps to avoid liability and prepare to defend cases.

The most effective steps to liability avoidance are the development of proper policies and procedures, training of staff in the policies and procedures, and close supervision, monitoring, and auditing of staff to see that the policies are in fact carried out. It is embarrassing, as well as difficult, to defend a case in court where the evidence shows the defendants failed to follow their own policies and procedures. Unfortunately, this is not uncommon.

The key to an able defense is thorough documentation. Good records, particularly logs and detailed incident reports, can be critical to explaining an incident and justifying the actions taken by officers. Remember, a case may not be filed, let alone tried, for years after an incident occurs. If records are not available, the defendants may be unable to recall the details of the incident and thus are seriously prejudiced in their ability to defend themselves.

This brief review of correctional legal issues obviously has not included many of the subtleties that exist in any area of law, nor has it begun to go into the detail needed to describe the scope of inmate rights. Its purpose is only to emphasize the importance of understanding that legal issues play a very important role in modern jail administration and that the facility administrator who downplays the significance of these issues is exposed, along with his staff and employer, to serious liability.

---

[46]There are other differences between the two types of actions. A civil rights action offers a broader range of relief (injunction, damages, declaratory relief) than does a tort (damages only). Attorneys' fees are also available to the successful civil rights plaintiff, whereas they generally are not in a tort action.

Reviews of correctional issues can be found in the following publications:

> Collins: Correctional Law 1986 and 1987 editions. P.O. Box 2316, Olympia, WA 98507. These two books analyze and discuss key correctional issues and developments in 1986 and 1987. Published annually.
>
> Rights of Prisoners (1981) by Gobert and Cohen, Shepard's/McGraw Hill, with annual supplements. This over 500 page text is an excellent review of correctional law, including many case citations.
>
> Constitutional Rights of Prisoners, 3rd edition (1985) by John W. Palmer. Cincinnati: Anderson Publishing Co. This 1,004 page text reviews correctional case law and provides the critical sections of cases in rights areas.
>
> Inmates' Legal Rights (1987) National Sheriffs' Association; and, Legal Responsibility and Authority of Correctional Officers (1987) American Correctional Association. These two booklets provide short summaries of correctional law most important to the administrator and line staff. Inexpensive, they are good training tools in the area of legal issues.
>
> Jail and Prisoner Law Bulletin, Americans for Effective Law Enforcement, 5519 N. Cumberland Ave., Suite 1008, Chicago, Illinois 60656. Monthly summaries of selected court decisions from both state and federal courts ($96.00 per year).
>
> Detention and Corrections Caselaw Catalog, CRS, Inc., P.O. Box 234, Kents Hill, Maine 04349. This large looseleaf work indexes and cross-indexes over 1,000 court decisions in the area of corrections. It is an excellent beginning research tool, and it is updated annually.
>
> Potential Liabilities of Probation and Parole Officers, rev. ed. (1986) by Rolando V. del Carmen, published by the National Institute of Justice. While directed to probation and parole issues, this book contains much useful information on liability issues for criminal justice professionals.

Corrections Compendium, Contact Center, P.O. Box 81826, Lincoln, Nebraska 68501. Monthly publication for corrections professionals, containing summaries of some cases, occasional detailed analyses of legal issues as well as other articles, surveys, etc.

In order to understand the types of suits inmates may file, it may be useful for you to examine various manuals prepared for inmates, such as A Primer for Jail Litigation published by the National Prison Project (of the ACLU) or the Post-Conviction Remedies Self-Help Manual.[47]

IV. Developing Policies and Procedures

There are several good sources of information on the development of policies and procedures, directives, or program statements, as they are known in some agencies. Both the American Correctional Association (ACA) and the National Institute of Corrections (NIC) provide guides to their development as well as manuals of model policies and procedures.[48] These developmental guides suggest full staff participation in the process through the use of committees or task forces. Jails with staff of less than 50 will probably not need to designate diverse committees in order to develop or adapt a set of policies and procedures for their use. The policy and procedures manual, however, can no longer resemble the brief booklet of the past. The manual must be comprehensive, and it must provide sufficient detail to let staff know what is expected of them. One 500-bed jail has a manual of over 600 typed (single-spaced) pages, inclusive of forms. The detention standards and supporting documentation for the State of Maine encompass three volumes, a total of about 500 pages.[49]

---

[47]The National Prison Project, A Primer for Jail Litigation, 1984; 1616 P St., Washington, D.C.20036 ($15.00); Daniel E. Manville, The Post-Convictions Remedies Self-Help Manual, 1983. Oceana Publications, Inc., Dobbs Ferry, NY 10522 ($30.00 with special prices for inmates).

[48]American Correctional Association, Guidelines for the Development of Policies and Procedures for Adult Correctional Institutions and Detention Facilities (College Park, Maryland: American Correctional Association, 1987); Policy and Procedure Manual, Oxford County Jail: A Sample for Small Jails (South Paris, Maine: Oxford County Jail, 1981).

[49]Maine Standards for Jails, Holding Facilities, and Short-Term Detention Areas (Maine Department of Corrections, Effective September 1, 1982).

Policies and related procedures provide clear, concise statements of agency practices. They are based on and must reflect statutes and other sources of legal authority for operating the agency. They summarize and operationalize legislation, court decisions, and executive orders or regulations produced by other county or state departments that must be applied to food services, medical services, emergency equipment, purchasing, and the like. They are also useful in training new staff in methods of operation and upgrading the performance of present staff. Ideally, they will ensure some uniformity in operational procedures and can protect against lawsuits. As a management tool they provide the basis for measurement of staff performance. Finally, a good policy and procedures manual is the starting point for the training program.

Each policy statement should state the accepted position of the agency on an issue directly related to the operation of the organization; it should include what action is to be taken, and/or the standards to be maintained. The source(s) for the policy should be stated. Related procedures should list detailed and sequential actions that must be executed to ensure that the policy is fully implemented. These procedures should clearly indicate to whom the policy is directed, inclusive of job titles, functional units, and perhaps inmates. Relevant times (as for counts), locations (as for posts), modes of communication (as for emergencies), and required forms (as for medical screening) should all be included, as required. Areas of discretion should be identified as well as methods for clarifying situations where no policy exists. In this way responsibility and accountability is established. Generalities should be avoided to the extent possible.

Policies and procedures will be best implemented if they are developed with the involvement of staff from all operational areas. A tested method for policy and procedure development includes eleven basic steps:

1. **Organization of the effort.** Policy and procedures development will be done well only if someone in the agency at a senior staff level is designated to lead the effort. This person must be given adequate staff for the task and provided sufficient time to complete it.

2. **Mission statement.** The development of a realistic and attainable mission statement, or philosophy, that will guide policy and procedure development. This process

might be combined with an effort to define terms for use in policy development.

3. **Identification of topics.** The identification of topic areas for policy and procedures development should include an evaluation of facility operations against the standards of the American Correctional Association, comparisons with policies and procedures of other agencies, the examination of model policies and procedures, identification of current and past operational problems, identification of relevant state and local statutes and administrative rules, federal law, and court orders, and local fire safety, sanitation and building codes.

4. **Staff training.** People hired to perform tasks in corrections sometimes are not good writers, nor do they pretend to be. However, a review of the elements of good policies and procedures will help staff to see what it is they must do to either write the policies or to assist those who will do the writing. An editor can be very useful in training staff to do better writing and can make the final product more readable and understandable.

5. **Task Forces/Working Groups.** Staff can be formed into task forces or working groups to write policies and procedures specific to general areas, such as administration, physical plant, security, support services, or programs. Task forces are usually not necessary in small agencies where a single working group with broad expertise should be able to complete the manual.

6. **Resource documents.** All available resource documents must be collected for use in developing policies and procedures. This includes all existing policies, directives, court orders, and relevant statutes. Legal staff can and should assist in locating and interpreting some of these documents for policy purposes.

7. **Initial drafts for circulation.** Initial drafts, which have been edited, should be circulated to all persons who will have to implement the policies and procedures for their comments and suggestions.

8. **Legal review.** Continuing and final review by legal staff will ensure that policies and procedures are consistent with relevant statutory and case law.

9. **Final documents.** Final documents should be signed by the agency head and placed in a manual that is well-organized and attractive.

10. **Distribution.** After completion of the policy and procedures manual a plan should be devised for its distribution and the circulation of updated material in the future.

11. **Plan for Updating.** A system for updating policies and procedures should be instituted prior to distribution. National standards require an annual review of policy and procedures.

Policies and procedures are of little use unless implemented in practice. Training in the new policies and procedures should be instituted or made part of the regular training program.

CHAPTER TWO: ENSURING FACILITY SAFETY AND SECURITY

I. Critical Concerns in Evaluating Security

The most critical concern in detention facilities is the safety and security of staff and inmates, which are the first areas where self-evaluation must occur. Safety will be addressed more fully later. Security must be all inclusive, but it need not and must not be overpowering. The best security is often that which is so well designed it goes unnoticed and unchallenged. There are many experts on security who can be of assistance in evaluating your facility for security problems, often including the staff of your state inspection service or the staff of the National Institute of Corrections. Nothing, however, can replace knowledge developed by your own staff backed up with ongoing training, expert consultation, regular inspections, and attention to detail in every area of the facility.

Agency Self-Evaluation. Every facility should be subjected to outside inspections. These may be done by state jail inspectors on an annual or periodic basis. American Correctional Association accreditation visits occur every three years, although supplementary audits may occur more often. Some inspections are ordered by the courts. Before subjecting the jail to an outside inspection, it is suggested that jail staff conduct a thorough inspection of the facility and determine possible deficiencies, including new equipment and hardware needs. If not already part of state`law, the services of an experienced person from the state correctional system or the state jail inspection service may be a good first step. If a comprehensive jail inspection report has been done you may want to use it as the basis for the self-evaluation. Ideally, there should be a plan in place to correct deficiencies before a state inspector or judge finds it necessary to require a plan.

A comprehensive, systematic inspection can often lead to the prevention of potentially dangerous situations for both staff and inmates, particularly those that may lead to lawsuits. The inspection must include, at a minimum, an examination of all security and emergency procedures, fire safety planning, food service, sanitation, heating and ventilation systems, and facility maintenance programs. If the inspection is sufficiently thorough it will raise questions for which you have no immediate answers. At this point expert assistance may be most useful for determining the seriousness of problems, especially the urgency of making repairs —

that is, establishing priorities, and helping to decide how deficiencies can be remedied. The following is a listing of potential security hazard areas.

II. A Security Checklist

1. PERIMETER SECURITY:[50] All equipment and procedures should be evaluated with respect to the degree of security necessary and the staff required to provide perimeter security.

    a. Perimeter detection devices: closed-circuit television, microwave, infrared, pressure, sound, laser, etc.[51]

    b. Interior closed-circuit television: location, usefulness.

    c. Perimeter control: need for road or walkway patrols.[52]

    d. Fences and towers (in larger facilities): integrity, effectiveness, is the security level appropriate to the facility?

2. FACILITY INTERIOR: Concerns are tampering, hiding places, and damage.

    a. Surface integrity: ceilings, floors, walls, finishes.

    b. Integrity of doors, locks, steel fixtures.

3. CLOSURES: Concerns are appropriateness to security level, possible damage (quality of work), and tampering.

---

[50]See George Camp and Camille Camp, "Stopping Escapes: Perimeter Security" Research in Brief (Washington, D.C.: National Institute of Justice, March, 1987), for an overview of various types of perimeter security devices and the identification of additional resources.

[51]See Joseph S. Coughlin, "The Use of Electronics in Perimeter Security" Corrections Today July/Aug., 1981: 34-37, and David E. Moore, "Perimeter Security Sensor Dilemma," Corrections Today April, 1986: 130-134.

[52]These patrols should be on the lookout also for drug dropoff points near adjacent properties and roads.

a. Windows: glazing characteristics, framing, molding.[53]

b. Doors (hinge placement or "swing," strength).

c. Specialized closures.

(1) Corridors: safety vestibules and sally ports.

(2) Living areas: entrance/exit areas.

(3) Dining areas: entrance/exit, supply entrances.

(4) Program areas: entrance/exit, equipment that defeats security (barbells, tools, etc.).

4. ELECTRICAL SYSTEMS: Concerns are adequacy of lighting, power failure, and possible failure of components.

a. Security lighting.

b. Emergency lighting and power.

(1) Staff and inmate areas.

(2) Availability of battery packs.

c. Electrical System Controls.

d. Video monitoring systems.

5. COMMUNICATIONS SYSTEM: Concern is reliability, especially in an emergency.

a. Audio and Visual.

(1) General communication.

(2) Security and emergency communications.

---

[53]See Dennis Kimme, "Windows and Glazing: A Summary of 10 Years of Controversy" (Champaign, Illinois: Kimme Planning and Architecture, 1980).

6. PLUMBING SYSTEM: Concerns are tampering and maintenance.

    a. Security fixtures.[54]

    b. Water temperature controls: living units.

    c. Emergency shut-off systems.

7. HEATING, VENTILATION AND AIR CONDITIONING SYSTEMS: Security concerns are related to inmate movement in emergencies due to system failure, fire, etc.; the less movement the better.[55]

    a. Smoke removal (ventilating fans).

    b. Tear gas removal.

8. FACILITY FURNISHINGS: Concerns are fire, ignition sources, and possible fuel sources.

    a. Fire retardant characteristics of furniture and finishes: ceilings, floors, walls, mattresses, desks, tables, chairs, etc.

    b. Fuel: newspapers, curtains, wall decorations, etc.

    c. Control of ignition sources: matches, smoking materials.

9. FIRE SAFETY EQUIPMENT: Concerns are readiness of equipment (batteries, water in wet systems, etc.), placement, quality, and reliability.

    a. Detection.

        (1) Smoke and heat detectors.

        (2) Placement of detection devices.

---

[54]See Pat Ruga, "Trouble-Free Plumbing," Corrections Today April, 1985: 154.

[55]Technical aspects are found in "Standards for Natural and Mechanical Ventilation," American Society of Heating, Refrigerating and Air-Conditioning Engineers, Inc. (ASHRAE Standards Committee, 1973).

(3) Placement of alarms: procedures for activating.

b. Fire Control Systems.

(1) Sprinklers: wet or dry.

(2) Standpipes: hoses, connections.

(3) Shut-off controls.

10. KEY CONTROL

a. Keys availability and compatibility. Are all locks keyed the same?

b. Location of keys in emergency situations: training in their use under emergency situations.

c. Back-up emergency release procedures: manual backup systems, power saws.

11. SPECIALIZED AREAS

a. Visiting areas: search equipment and procedures.

(1) Use of nonintrusive detectors (metal detectors)

(2) Searches for contraband: living/program areas and physical searches.

b. Intake.

(1) Personal property management.

(2) Gun lockers for law enforcement personnel.

c. Special cells: psychiatric and special management cases. Are there dangerous niches, pipes, hardware, towel racks, or sprinkler heads that maybe used in a suicide attempt?

d. Segregation: disciplinary, administrative, protective.

(1) What types of segregation used?

(2) Is there a secure hearing room for classification and disciplinary cases?

e. Dormitories

(1) Is security level appropriate to use?

(2) Is staffing continuous?

f. Control Centers

(1) Security from possible breaches; structural integrity.

(2) Intercom systems: availability and ease of use in communications:

(a) Staff to staff.

(b) Inmate to staff.

g. Armory.

(1) Location outside living/program areas.

(2) Secure access procedures.

h. Vehicular Security.

(1) Location and secure operation of entrance/exit areas.

(2) Inspection procedures for vehicles entering and leaving.

i. Medical and Dental Areas.

(1) Control of dangerous substances.

(2) Control of medical/dental equipment.

j. Food service.

(1) Control of kitchen cutlery and dangerous utensils.

(2) Control of food theft.

k. Recreation.

(1) Security of outside areas.

(2) Equipment use: evaluation of equipment for security, such as barbells, ropes, etc.

l. Work and Industrial Areas.

(1) Equipment control.

(2) Job safety evaluation.

m. Court Areas.

(1) Arraignment areas

(2) Video arraignment equipment (if used)

This inspection should not be a one-time exercise. As indicated in national standards, local inspections must be conducted on schedules consistent with the level of problems that may develop. Security inspections should be daily and weekly, fire sanitation, and safety inspections at least weekly, coupled with monthly or annual outside inspections. All emergency equipment should be tested weekly.

Areas of particular concern in security inspections are windows, locks, and related security barriers. Facility staff must know the failure parameters of glazing and locking devices and develop administrative policy for regular inspection of them. This is discussed in more detail in chapter six, but a simple formula is as follows:[56]

---

[56]Derived from Shelley J. Price and Dale K. Sechrest, "Continuity in Design and Operation," Corrections Today April, 1986: 57.

FUNCTION DESIRED	+ SURVEILLANCE TIME	+ TOOLS AVAILABLE	= COMPONENT SELECTED
Desired purpose of components	Staff surveillance and/or inspection schedules)	Availability of tools/weapons to violate barrier	Materials: requirements/ specifications

Also a matter of increasing concern is the control of flammables, which may include shaving lotions and other substances that have been used to burn out window molding materials. Alarm systems embedded in windows can be cut at the moldings. Fire safety is addressed in more detail in section III.

Such inspections should include examination of areas of facility deterioration and materials that may become weapons. Deterioration may occur, for example, in areas with wood doors where there is heavy inmate traffic. Any place where hardware is used that is not durable is subject to deterioration. Acoustical type ceilings are subject to deterioration, as are ceramic tiles, which may come loose and be fashioned into weapons. "Drop" ceilings may provide access from one area to another, as can wide outside ledges. Other architectural features that may become weapons are metal edging under the doors that holds the carpet, the use of plate glass instead of safety glazing, and the use of the wrong lens material in lighting fixtures. The location of janitor rooms and supply rooms is also an important factor in security, especially where these areas are shared between modules or units.[57]

The availability and use of keys in an emergency are very high on the list of liability issues. Are keys available for locks? How are keys located under emergency conditions? Are they in a central location? Do staff know where they are? Are all locks keyed the same? If keyed differently, are the keys color coded or otherwise identified in relation to the locks they operate?

---

[57]Abstracted from John McGough, memo to the American Institute of Architects Committee on Architects for Justice, May 19, 1986, outlining significant liability issues in the planning and design of justice facilities.

Once deficiencies or problems are identified, develop a systematic plan and priority schedule for remedying them. This plan should include a specific statement of what needs improvement or repair, when it will be done, who will do it and estimates of cost.

About That Exotic Equipment. The subject of new and exotic "state of the art" hardware and equipment will be covered in more detail in chapter seven on construction of new facilities. Suffice it to say that there is no foolproof way to evaluate before installation highly advertised security hardware and equipment to see whether it will work. Ideally, these systems should be evaluated by some state or national source to assist you in proper selection. However, because state agencies, federal authorities, and private groups fear making such comparisons due to the potential for lawsuits based on insufficient testing or inadequate evaluation of all systems, such testing is not done. Vendors would also get upset because such comparisons might influence the purchase of their systems.

The best protection is to look at the identical system in another facility, hopefully close to you, to see how well it works and if it might work in your facility. In doing so you must also determine what skills are required to operate it and how it is maintained, including maintenance costs.

Seeing a system in operation is no guarantee that you can get the same unit. Such systems are constantly being "upgraded" or improved. Such improvements often require that the "bugs" be eliminated before they work as advertised. One such locking system randomly opened cell doors until the problems were solved. If practical, you should contract with the person who is maintaining the system you have seen to oversee the installation of your system. Moreover, subcontractors may not install the exact system called for in the contract. There is more discussion of the need for contract monitoring in the sections on contracting for services (chapter six) and new facility construction (chapter seven).

Video Arraignments. A new procedure in many jurisdictions is the use of video cameras for arraignments. These systems provide much greater efficiency in the use of both judges time and staff time. Transportation costs are cut and security breaches are thereby reduced by keeping inmates in the jail facility and having them interact with the judge over television monitors. Jurisdictions now using video arraignments include Las Vegas, Nevada, and Dade and Orange Counties in Florida. Dade County had the system installed in 1982 at a (then) cost of $40,000. The system is a reported success from the standpoint of both judges and defendants.[58] New York City was not successful with such a system, due apparently to equipment malfunctions. (See chapter seven III.E. on equipment selection in facility construction.)

III. Facility Maintenance and Fire Safety.

You are responsible for the maintenance of the facility. This includes the maintenance of the structural integrity of the building, maintenance of equipment, ensuring adequate space, providing a plan for fire prevention and safety, and for seeing that the facility is adequate to meet any changes in its mission prior to undertaking that mission.

A. Structural Integrity

Facility Maintenance. During your inspection of the facility, you will want to see if the integrity of the structure has been retained through proper staff attention to deficiencies and preventive maintenance. The following steps, essential to these goals and fundamental to the maintenance of a facility, can reduce overall operating costs, ensure a safer facility, and reduce staff problems.

1. **Budgeting and Maintenance.** The budget must be sufficient to staff and maintain the facility consistent with the mission statement developed at the time of construction. Inadequate or insufficient staff supervision leads to property destruction and other security problems, many with liability implications. A facility that is over capacity and not staffed to handle the overload is subject to both management and legal problems. The budget must be adequate for purchasing the supplies, parts and services needed to maintain the physical plant and equipment. Contracts for equipment maintenance must be maintained or alternative sources must be available through city or county agencies.

---

[58]W. Clinton Terry III and Ray Surette, "Video in the Misdemeanor Court: the South Florida Experience," Judicature 69:1 (June-July, 1985) 13-19; see also Craig Burger, "Dade County's New Two Way Audio Video System," paper presented at the American Jail Association, May 5, 1987, Clearwater Beach, Florida.

2. **Emergencies.** Staff must be prepared at all times for emergencies, inclusive of disturbances, fires, escapes, and other unusual events, such as sudden population increases due to local police activity (drug arrests, etc.).

3. **Operational consistency.** Operational policies and procedures must be consistent with the design of the facility. For example, controls on inmate movement, the use of security zones based on proper classification, and the provision of programs all require policies designed to use space consistent with facility design.[59]

4. **Record-keeping.** A record-keeping system and communication plan must be created and kept current order to keep staff informed about the operation and maintenance of equipment. Staff must know the purposes of systems and how they should operate, as well as the purpose of any special design features of the facility.[60]

B. Fire Prevention and Safety

Consistent with the maintenance of the facility is a plan to ensure that it is not destroyed by fire. National fire safety standards and local fire codes are becoming more stringent, and due to a rash of prison and jail fires in the late 1970's most state and local authorities are becoming more stringent in their enforcement practices.

The liability implications of a jail fire are enormous. For example, on November 8, 1982, a fire in the Harrison County Jail in Biloxi, Mississippi, claimed 27 inmate lives, injured 61 persons, including firefighters, police officers, jailers, and inmates. Ten inmates and one jailer were in critical condition. A former mental patient started the fire in a padded cell, igniting highly toxic polyurethane padding (which is now prohibited in national standards). He was apparently handed a lighted cigarette by two women inmates, who died in the ensuing fire. The inmate survived

---

[59]"Security zones deal primarily with varying degrees of reliance on staff presence and/or physical barriers restricting inmate access to the outside, separating different groups of inmates, regulating inmate movement, and controlling the presence and passage of contraband in the institution," in Shelley J. Price and Dale K. Sechrest, "Continuity in Design and Operation," Corrections Today April, 1986: 57.

[60]See Dale K. Sechrest and Shelley J. Price, Correctional Facility Design and Construction Management. (Washington, D.C.: U.S. Government Printing Office, 1985) 73-75.

with minor burns. Smoke knocked out the jailer who had the keys; he could not be located while two trucks were used to pull the bars off the outside windows and open the door to the cell block. A year prior to the fire Representative Trent Lott of Mississippi intervened to stop the U.S. Justice Department from sending federal inspectors to the jail, claiming unnecessary federal intrusion into local affairs.[61]

Fire prevention is an absolute necessity to avoid needless injury and death to inmates, staff and visitors to the facility. This problem is made most difficult by the fact that inmates are notorious tamperers. They will tamper with everything in the living unit, especially in their cells. Suicide-prone inmates will use sprinkler heads, pipes, or any type of hook to attempt to hang themselves. Inmates will want to break off the sprinkler head and adapt it for use as a "stinger" to heat their coffee. Staff generally do not like sprinkler systems because inmates do tamper with them and activate them unnecessarily. Sometimes staff will "temporarily" turn off the water in a "wet" system to prevent tampering, leaving it inactive in a fire. This practice cannot be allowed. If your fire codes require sprinklers, you should consider the newer variety of "sunken" heads that come out of the wall not over 1/4 inch when activated. Some units are made of plastic and cannot be used as stingers.

National Standards. In 1981 the National Fire Protection Association Life Safety Code, NFPA 101 included a section on corrections and detention occupancies for the first time.[62] The standards in the 1985 edition are clearly reflected in ACA standards and other standards for life safety in detention occupancies.[63] ACA Standard 2-5149 is a guide to facility inspection:

> 2-5149: Revised January 1984 (Mandatory). There is documentation by the authority having jurisdiction that the facility complies with the applicable fire safety code(s). A fire alarm and automatic detection system are required as approved by the authority having jurisdiction, or there is a plan for addressing these or other deficiencies within a

---

[61]"Toxic Smoke Blamed in Death Toll," and "Lott Intervened Last Year to Halt Mississippi Jail Inspections," Washington Post, 9-10 Nov. 1982.

[62]National Fire Protection Association, Life Safety Code, NFPA 101 (Quincy, Massachusetts: 1985) Chapters 14 and 15.

[63]ACA Standards 2-5149 to 2-5162 (1981) 41-44 and (1984) 37-40, 84-89; see also National Institute of Corrections, Fire Safety in Correctional Facilities, (Washington, D.C.: 1981).

reasonable time period. The authority approves any variances, exceptions, or equivalencies that do not constitute a serious life safety threat to the occupants of the facility.[64]

Elements of a Fire Protection Plan There are five minimum elements of a sound philosophy of fire protection that, if followed, can provide reasonable certainty that life and property can be protected in the facility. These are (1) detection and notification of a fire, (2) an evacuation plan, (3) proper construction and furnishings, (4) a prevention plan, and (5) staff training.

Before considering these elements, it is understood that a detention facility presents unique problems in fire safety. Both inmates and staff are sometimes prevented from taking action to protect themselves from fire due to secure construction and security measures beyond their control. Inmates cannot evacuate living areas without the assistance of staff, and staff will need immediate assistance to move occupants to safe areas during a fire. The situation is not unlike a hospital, where many patients cannot be easily evacuated. This requires an alternative strategy to evacuation of the facility, and jails, hospitals, and similar facilities must first consider "defending in place," if possible, an option which is discussed below. The first goal under any conditions is to seal off all areas that contain the fire(s) and move inmates who must be moved in small groups, if possible, for security reasons.

It is understood that full compliance with the Life Safety Code is often impractical and sometimes impossible if you are stuck with an existing structure that does not have adequate fire safety features due to its age or poor design. However, ways must be found to compensate for shortcomings in the physical plant, based on the findings and recommendations of the local fire inspector or "authority having jurisdiction."

The five elements of the fire prevention plan are as follows:

1. **Detection, Alarm, and Notification** The first element in a fire protection plan requires that three basic procedures are in place: (1) the detection of the fire, (2) the ability to give a local alarm, and (3) a plan for notification to fire departments. Automatic detection is the rule, which means that a smoke and/or heat detector is activated

---

[64]ACA Standard 2-5149 (1984) 37.

without human intervention that sends an alarm to a control booth or fire station manned 24 hours a day. Some jurisdictions still rely only on the physical presence of an officer 24 hours per day. This is not adequate during sleeping hours when inmates are on lockdown and the supervising officer may be called away from the unit. When inmates have no way out of the facility without assistance there should be smoke detection units wired directly to a central control station that is staffed 24 hours a day. Staff in this control station must have a method for reaching fire departments without delay or interference. The system to be used to summon these units must be dedicated to that purpose, be it radio, telephone, or alarm signal transmitted to a fire station. At the time of the detection of the fire there must also be a local, audible alarm that also alerts occupants to the danger. All staff should have at least 20 hours of training in fire safety and two practice sessions with the self-contained breathing apparatus (SCBA) discussed below under training.

2. **Occupant Protection: Fire Evacuation**. The detection of a fire requires immediate action to protect all occupants of the facility. There are three levels of action that must be considered, consistent with the danger presented:

> **Initial Level**: During the initial stages of the fire, evacuation may not be feasible or desirable. Staff may choose to fight the fire, or "defend in place" without moving the inmates from their living units. However, this strategy places great reliance on the frequency of staff training and fire drills, the maintenance of equipment, and coordinated action to suppress the fire. Empty fire extinguishers, unworkable standpipes, or dry sprinkler systems are simply unacceptable. All extinguishers should be checked monthly, and all staff should know the locations of standpipes and hoses.
>
> **Second Level**: Staff may decide to move inmates horizontally through a smoke barrier and into another smoke compartment, that is, a safe area of refuge. This type of movement is greatly facilitated by having two means of egress from inmate living units, as required by the Life Safety Code.
>
> **Third Level**: In a high rise structure, staff may relocate inmates vertically, or if in a single story structure, move inmates outside.

At all times there must be concern with the location of exits, inmate collection areas, and regular fire drills. ACA Standard 2-4134 (mandatory) states that the facility has exits that are properly positioned, clear and distinctly and permanently marked in order to ensure the timely evacuation of inmates and staff in the event of fire or other emergency. All housing areas and places of assembly for 50 or more persons must have two exits.[65] Housing areas of any size must have two exits; however, this may include one exit out of the unit with two exits (in different directions) from that point on, according to the NFPA. The NFPA Code states that an exit is not necessary for each individual fire compartment or smoke compartment if there is access to an exit through other fire compartments or smoke compartments without passing through the fire compartment of origin (15-2.4.1).[66] While the distances to exits are well established in codes, the use of automatic sprinkler systems change some required distances, but these variances should be confirmed with the authority having jurisdiction, as should all variances from code.

Although fire safety cannot be assured solely on the basis of evacuation from the building, facilities must be designed and constructed with this in mind. This includes properly rated fire doors, smoke evacuation systems, and compartmentalization. For example, power-operated sliding doors or power-operated locks for swinging doors must have a mechanical back-up at a remote location, or be opened manually by key and lock at the door. Door locking systems should be pressure-tested to ensure that they will unlock under the force of several pounds. Safety is enhanced greatly by an approved automatic sprinkler system. In a prison fire in Salem, Oregon, sprinklers were one hundred percent effective in reducing damage to a furniture factory, which sustained $3,000 in damage, while damages to five buildings without sprinklers was $1.2 million.[67] If sprinklers are not used, a smoke or heat detection system is absolutely essential.

---

[65]Correctional Standards Supplement, January, 1988 (College Park, Maryland: American Correctional Association, 1988) 24; standard 2-4234.

[66]NFPA 101.

[67]National Fire Protection Association, "A Study of Penal Institution Fires," (Boston: NFPA No. FR78-1, 1977).

Finally, the evacuation plan must include provisions for visitors and staff. Visiting and staff areas require the same careful consideration given inmate areas.

3. **Proper Construction and Furnishings.** Short of total renovation, you may have to add fire protection features to the building, such as fire-resistant materials, additional doors, fire escapes, and back-up locking release mechanisms. The best protection is recognized to be an automatic sprinkler system. Try to find out if the facility was constructed to include "fire compartments" or fire rated areas or enclosures designed to control the spread of smoke and fire. This construction operates much like water compartments on a ship that are designed to control water movement if damage occurs. These compartments must include fire rated doors and a system for closing ventilation ducts. Also, you may want to consider a smoke evacuation system using your present ventilating system, although these systems are not fully tested and may provide oxygen to an otherwise dying fire. Such systems should be completely tested on a regular schedule.

Interior Furnishings. The type of interior furnishings used in the facility must be controlled, including mattresses, wall furnishings, and inmate possessions. The proper storage of flammable, toxic, and caustic substances is top priority. Polyurethane mattresses that produce deadly chlorine gas, as described in the Mississippi example, is a first concern.[68] All materials using polyurethane, including furnishings such as chairs, produce these deadly toxic fumes when ignited. Vendor claims often state that the covering of chairs, for example, is "ignition-proof." However, at high temperatures nothing is ignition-proof. There are five types of materials used in mattresses: (1) neoprene foam, (2) boric acid treated cotton batting, (3) polyurethane foam, (4) polyvinyl chloride foam, and (5) latex (styrene-butadiene foam rubbers or "SBR"). Neoprene foam and fire retardant treated cotton batting mattresses are safest, and are recommended; however, neoprene is more expensive than treated cotton batting. There are drawbacks to cotton batting mattresses related to their deterioration and sanitation (difficult to sterilize). Security also may be a problem in that it is not as easy to hide things in a solid piece of foam padding as it is in a cotton

---

[68]Many of these issues, along with an analysis of several penal institution fires are found in "A Study of Penal Institution Fires."

mattress.[69]

Wall furnishings also may include polyurethane or other deadly chemicals. Where possible these should be removed. At a minimum you should be aware of the dangers involved in using them, particularly in padded cells. Padded cells with latex (styrene-butadiene) were the origin of two detention facility fires in 1977 resulting in 63 deaths.[70] One of these was the 65-bed Maury County Jail in Tennessee where 34 prisoners and eight visitors died, and 31 other persons were injured. Lost keys, lack of remote exits, no direct alarm system, no evacuation plan, and no "in-house" fire suppression equipment also contributed to the deaths. The use of padded cells is no longer recommended by most detention experts due to the effectiveness of medication in managing violent inmates.

Other types of fuel may be found in the facility. Fuel includes anything that burns, especially materials kept in inmate rooms, such as curtains, waste baskets, wall hangings of any type, books, newspapers and magazines. This is not a valid reason for prohibiting all of these materials; however, it is a valid reason for controlling such materials to the extent reasonable and possible. A competent fire inspector should be consulted regarding appropriate fuel "loads."

4. **Prevention.** The fourth element in a fire protection plan prevention, which includes inspections and programs of prevention with inmates. Inspections must be done as required by state or local codes. They will usually be done by the local fire inspector who should be familiar with the most recent codes and standards. Unfortunately, this sometimes is not the case, and outside assistance must be found to develop a fire prevention and suppression plan. Reliance on an incompetent local fire authority will be no excuse in the case of litigation. How do you know whether your inspector is qualified?

Inspection. As stated in ACA Standards (2-5149, revised) regarding the inspecting authority, "The authority having jurisdiction must be knowledgeable about the requirements of the

---

[69]See Phillip Goldberg, "Avoiding Fast Fires," American Jails Fall, 1987: 46. A study of tests of 10 mattresses is available from Center for Fire Research, National Bureau of Standards, Mail Building 225, Room A-07, Washington, D.C. 20234.

[70]National Fire Protection Association, "II. Fire Safety Bulletin on Penal Institutions," (Boston: National Fire Protection Association, December, 1977).

National Fire Protection Association Life Safety Code."[71] All fire inspectors and "experts" are not competent, even when they are former firefighters. Some former firefighters working as inspectors have not had adequate training in fire prevention and other more technical aspects of fire safety. This includes government officials. You should look into their background and training before relying on their judgment; otherwise, you may be liable for inadequate inspection, should a fire occur. Any who are not familiar with the Life Safety Code should be suspect.

If you are in doubt about qualifications, written evidence of training in fire prevention should be requested, preferably certification from a recognized training source. Many community colleges offer courses in fire safety and prevention that will be acceptable for purposes of meeting the training requirement. Remember, experience only as a firefighter, while relevant, does not fully qualify a person to be a fire prevention officer. Periodic outside inspections from other sources are a good check against a poor inspection.

Prevention Programs. Programs of fire prevention must be conducted with inmates and staff, which should include the proper use of materials and furnishings in the facility. The reasons for institutional fires generally include careless use and disposal of smoking materials, faulty electrical wiring (including circuit breaker panels), spontaneous combustion of improperly stored combustible materials, and arson. Ignition sources must be controlled. The most obvious concern is with inmate use of smoking materials. Smoking may be prohibited in certain areas or confined to certain times when supervision is available. Compliance with electrical safety codes is also critical, as is control of electrical equipment.

There may be as many as five fires per month started with clothing or newspapers in an average sized jail (100-200 beds). As indicated below, a major concern is the build-up of materials in cells such as legal papers, newspapers, magazines and the like. These are fuel for fires. There is some legal support for controlling the collection of such materials where they might represent fire hazards. A general rule is that the more problems found in other areas, such as substandard construction, lack of sprinklers, etc., the more justifiable will be the restrictions placed on combustible materials. But control

---

[71]ACA Standards Supplement (1986) 47.

of combustible materials should not be a ruse for restricting inmates' access to printed materials, photographs, and the like.

Materials Storage. A major concern in prevention is the storage of flammable, toxic, and caustic materials in the facility, inclusive of paint, bleach, dyes, lotions, etc. A model policy regarding control of these substances is found in the Correctional Standards Supplement, January 1988.[72] Staff should be alert to the kinds of substances that may be a problem. Staff office areas may be a source of some of these materials and should be checked regularly. Inmates should not be in possession of more of these substances than they need at any one time, and all quantities used should be accounted for at issue and after use. Storage of these and other combustible substances, such as gasoline, must be in a safe area, preferably a fire rated enclosure with automatic sprinkler devices.

Reporting. A key element in prevention is the reporting of fires in the facility, including the time, place, and general description of the incident and the action taken. An investigation and final report should be completed within 10 days of the incident and forwarded to the jail administrator or Sheriff. Use of such a system will allow remedial action that could prevent serious fires in the future.

5. **Staff Training.** Staff must be adequately trained for any fire prevention or emergency plan to work effectively. Some small cities do not have a full time fire department, which may make staff training even more critical. Detection, alarm, communication, and extinguishing equipment must be available and in operating order. Fire drills must be performed on each shift based on clearly established evacuation routes. The SCBA — self contained breathing apparatus — for staff use in fire emergencies should be standard equipment in all living units. Training in the use of the SCBA is essential, since it can be critical that at least one staff member be able to use the unit to open doors in a fire emergency. Current requirements for continuous or "positive" flow types of SCBA must be observed, as opposed to open-circuit "demand" or "pressure demand" types of units. As noted above, at least two training sessions in the use of SCBA equipment should be required of all staff as part of their initial fire training.

---

[72]American Correctional Association, Correctional Standards Supplement, January, 1988 (College Park, Maryland: 1988) App. B .

C. Changes in Facility Use

A critical consideration in the evaluation of your physical plant is whether it is being used consistent with the mission, or purpose, for which it was built. The primary mission of jails is pretrial detention. You may be asked to participate in various types of programs, such as release on recognizance, pretrial intervention, community release, "weekender" sentences for drunk drivers, and the like. Such requests must be considered in light of the original mission of the facility and the demands of the new program for space, staff, and other resources. Overuse of the facility itself may amount to a critical change in mission due to severe crowding. A suggested alternative is the construction of a jail annex, which is discussed in chapter seven.

The following questions are relevant to both changes in mission and overpopulation of the facility, or crowding:

- Is the physical plant appropriate in responding to the current mission statement?
- Has the mission statement changed, requiring a re-ordering of space? Has security been increased?
- Is the available space used for its intended purpose? Will changes in mission reduce the use of space?
- Does the use of space enhance security and programs? Do changes reduce security and program opportunities?
- Is the facility atmosphere dismal and debilitating for inmates and staff?
- Are staff working conditions a consideration in changing operations?
- Is inmate quality of life considered only in minimal terms?

If new or increased demands are being placed on the facility it will be necessary to request additional resources to meet those demands for the short term. A better solution is to begin a short and long range planning process designed to cope with future needs. All large jails were small at one time. The quality of their current operations has been determined in large part by past planning efforts. Altogether too many of these efforts have been based on crisis management rather than well thought through planning using accurate projections and reliable expertise.

CHAPTER THREE: STAFFING THE FACILITY

I. The Need for Qualified Staff

A. (Re-)Evaluation of All Staff

Qualified and trained staff in all operational areas are the key to a well-run facility. As indicated in chapter two, unqualified and/or poorly trained staff are an invitation to litigation. To determine the quality of staff, evaluate all staff positions beginning with the supervisors. Re-examine their qualifications and training as if you were hiring for that position to see that they meet the minimum requirements for the position. If they do not, plan remedial action, such as additional formal education and/or training in specific areas. If these staff persons cannot or will not take these steps, they may have to be reassigned or considered for termination.

> **WARNING:** Often positions in detention facilities are staffed by friends and family members, particularly in a small facility that enjoys a sense of closeness. Decisions about reassignment or termination can be difficult. However, if you are sued in court due to their carelessness or lack of ability, your relationship with them will not be considered. You personally, the employee, your agency, and/or the jurisdiction will pay.

The answer to this problem lies in an administrative structure that requires continuing review of supervisors' evaluations of individual performance by higher level administrators. Staff should understand that their performance evaluation is not based solely on what the supervisor may say, but that the supervisor's evaluation is subject to scrutiny. This may be more difficult in a small facility, but it is probably more important for that very reason — familiarity breeds informality and lack of attention to assigned duties. Consideration should be given to a policy that does not allow individuals who are related to supervise one another's work in the same facility.

Evaluation of staff performance has become increasingly important as more women have taken jobs as correctional officers. Issues of concern include balancing inmate privacy with equal opportunity for women officers, harassment of women by colleagues, safety on the job, and biased performance evaluations. Collins notes that female officers continue to win their rights to work in male institutions. In the case of a small, rural jail, however, Federal District Court found a bona fide occupational qualification (BFOQ) based on the conclusion that encounters between female officers and male inmates would be embarrassing for both, but this was overturned by the appeals court.[73] Outcomes in several other cases are favorable to female officers working in male facilities, with appropriate adjustments for protecting the modesty of the male inmates. Collins also discusses male officer supervision of female inmates, finding a limited body of caselaw, but favorable to male officer supervision of female inmates.[74]

B. Performance Measurement

Evaluation of staff performance is not only important to the operation of the facility, but it is also covered in law by Title VII of the 1964 Civil Rights Act, as amended (1972).[75] This Act states that employers must validate any personnel techniques that affect an employee's chances for promotion. Therefore, along with the need to find and retain qualified staff is the need to evaluate their performance in a systematic way. There are two methods of evaluating staff performance: individual performance reviews and facility performance evaluation. Experts agree that individual performance measures must be clearly related to job tasks as specified in the job description. Again, evaluating the performance of friends and relatives presents problems for the small jail administrator. The best solution to this problem is to have specific job descriptions that state objective, realistic tasks to be performed. These reduce the need for subjective judgments about performance. It may even be possible or desirable to have an independent governmental agency assist in the development of these job descriptions and even conduct the personnel evaluations themselves, rather than doing it in-house. Some agencies contract with a private firm to perform personnel assessments for hiring and promotion. In any case, the administrator and supervisors will want to be informed about the process and know how to participate in it fully.

One source of information on staff evaluation is the model performance evaluation form in the ACA Guidelines for the

---

[73]See Collins (1986) 33-37, and Collins (1987) 22-24.

[74]Collins (1986) 35-36.

[75]Equal Employment Opportunity Act of 1972, P.L. 93-380, 88 Stat. 514, 20 U.S.C. Sec. 1228 (1976).

Development of Policies and Procedures (hereafter, "ACA Guidelines").[76] An additional source is "A Guide for Improving Performance Appraisal" published by the U.S. Office of Personnel Management.[77] This 28-page booklet provides a plan for setting up a new performance appraisal system or improving a current system. The major problem is in creating a fair system of appraisal. Nonetheless, for management to improve operations ("work-related") decisions must be made that will make better use of staff resources and provide for the personal improvement of staff ("career development"). Decisions about promotion and salary are clearly linked to such appraisals, which make them a subject of much concern. For these reasons, the system must use established performance standards, collect objective, reliable, and valid data and apply it in a consistent way, and provide information for employees about their progress.[78]

A second method of evaluating staff performance is to contract for periodic evaluations of facility operations by experienced professionals from other jails, or from individual consultants or specialists where a need is identified. An example might be the need to do a "job task analysis" for the facility. Such an analysis is often performed to identify task-based performance objectives for specific jobs. These objectives then serve as performance standards for entry-level personnel and provide the basis for a training program for existing staff.[79] An alternative is to submit the facility to accreditation by the American Correctional Association, which uses a team of experienced evaluators to identify all areas of deficiencies based on national standards of performance. It may be preferable to get the accreditation evaluation first and then seek consultation in those areas identified by the accreditation team. Since the Association protects the confidentiality of the information it receives, this allows for the identification and remediation of deficiencies before they become legal or public problems. As indicated above, the process may also provide some protection against legal liability.

---

[76]ACA Guidelines (1987) 63-65.

[77]"A Guide for Improving Performance Appraisal" (Washington, D.C.: U.S. Office of Personnel Management, rev. 1979).

[78]"A Guide for Improving Performance Appraisal" 8.

[79]See JoAnn Barsis and Terry Eisenberg, "Job-Task Analysis, Entry Level Corrections Officer, Volume I. Final Report" (Fairfax, Virginia: Personnel Performance, Inc., Submitted to the Commonwealth of Virginia, Department of Correctional Services, June 30, 1986).

II. Salaries and Benefits

Finding and keeping qualified staff requires salaries and benefits comparable to those paid to other public safety personnel, such as law enforcement and fire departments. Unfortunately, this is not true for many detention facility personnel. Before comparability can be achieved, however, qualifications and training must be similar to those for other public safety positions. Comparable pay is supported in the standards of the ACA and the National Sheriffs' Association: "Compensation and benefits for correctional officers are comparable to those for law enforcement officers working in the same organization," and "Jail salaries and benefits should be comparable to those in police and fire departments in the community."[80]

A. Rewards for Performance

Closely related to both performance measurement and salaries is the need to reward staff for satisfactory performance. Studies show that higher starting salaries for correctional officers are associated with lower levels of attrition. Benton and Rosen found that institutions paying less than $10,000 in 1978-79 had total attrition rates of 31%, while rates were 21% for those paying more than $10,000.[81] This was also true for supervisory officers. Since promotions may be limited, salary scales must allow for "step" increases based on merit, and cost of living adjustments must be included in annual budgets. Non-monetary rewards, or meritorious service awards, may also be effective in rewarding performance, particularly if they are tied into the annual performance evaluation system.

B. Staff Rules of Conduct and Grievances

Many administrators want staff rules of conduct but few relish a staff grievance procedure. Evidence points to the fact that a usable grievance procedure often heads off serious problems and can enhance employee job satisfaction. A successfully implemented grievance system may be a significant tool in maintaining positive relations between management and line staff. A poorly implemented system

---

[80]ACA Standard 2-5058 (1981) 14; National Sheriffs' Association, Handbook on Jail Administration (1974) 19.

[81]F. Warren Benton and Ellen Doree Rosen, "Correctional Employment Attrition: Summary of a National Survey" (The National Center for Public Productivity, John Jay College of Criminal Justice, 1982) 4.

could be the cause for discontent. American Correctional Association standards support a grievance procedure and provide a model for it in the ACA Guidelines.[82] An authoritative source of information on union negotiations, grievance mechanisms, management rights, disciplinary and discharge procedures, no-strike and antidiscriminatory language is found in Weisberger's brief book on public sector collective bargaining agreements.[83]

III. Management Styles: Tradition or Participation?

Most correctional facilities are operated on the "military" model of organization. This model is designed to distribute commands from the top down to achieve immediate results with little or no discussion. Safe and efficient facility operation often requires immediate, unquestioned response, especially when emergencies arise. Also, many correctional officers have retired from the military, and this model is understandable and comfortable for them. There is evidence from the military, however, that they are becoming increasingly involved in participatory management.

Benton and Rosen found that five factors were associated with staff attrition, or loss of staff: benefits and perceived benefits, supervisory style, management practices, job content, and unionization.[84] Lower staff losses were associated with higher salaries, greater participation in decisionmaking, more programs for inmates in the facility, and belonging to a union.[85]

Management Style and Staff Participation. An approach to improving staff performance and the reduction of grievances is the inclusion of the staff in management planning and decisionmaking. Benton and Rosen found that line officer participation in decisionmaking as to post and shift assignments, vacation schedules, and overtime assignments will reduce attrition.[86] It appears that

---

[82]ACA Standards 2-5063, 2-5066 (1981); ACA Guidelines (1987) 76-78.

[83]June Weisberger, Examples of Language and Interpretation in Public Sector Collective Bargaining Agreements: A Guide for Public Officials and Other Interested Parties (Institute of Public Employment Monograph, New York State School of Industrial and Labor Relations, February, 1974).

[84]Benton and Rosen 5-6.

[85]Benton and Rosen 6.

[86] Benton and Rosen 5.

policies and procedures can be discussed in ways that will gain greater support from line staff under normal or emergency conditions. Even with a greater degree of participation, however, staff must understand that in the final analysis they will not run the organization, but that they do have a part to play in how the organization is run.

Unions and other forms of employee organization have forced greater participation in management. The wise administrator will meet this demand by gaining greater staff participation in the development of policies, procedures, rules and regulations, and in delegating responsibility to the degree where he/she is comfortable. The autocratic, traditional administrator will resist and possibly fail to develop new and potentially more effective techniques of management. Also, this administrator may face union negotiators with similar demands, a far more formidable and potentially troublesome force than an employee group seeking more control over decisionmaking.

Students of administrative style discuss the classical, or more traditional, supervision models as non-participatory, requiring leadership from strong and relatively distant administrators. The assumption is that individual workers have an inherent dislike for work and will avoid it when they can. Thus, they must be coerced, controlled, directed, and even threatened with punishment if they do not perform up to standards. This model assumes that decisionmaking is at the top level with clear-cut instructions to the workers, and one-way communication "down" to the workers with only reports coming back. The participatory management model, or behavioral approach, assumes that people will exercise self-direction if they are working toward goals to which they are fully committed. It involves the application of skills and specialized knowledge to completion of a job in a less hierarchical, or "flat," organizational structure. It requires two-way communication, line officer involvement in planning and goal-setting, and the placement of decisionmaking at the most logical level. This approach requires an atmosphere of openness and trust where staff are allowed to make decisions relative to their sphere of responsibility.[87] For example,

---

[87]W. R. Rhodes, "A Behavioral Science Application to Police Management," The Police Chief May 1970 37(5): 46-50; reprinted in Harry W. More, Jr., Criminal Justice Management (St. Paul: West Publishing Company, 1980) 76-77. See also Douglas MacGregor, The Human Side of Enterprise (New York: McGraw-Hill, 1960), or for a more current discussion of managment issues see Nicholas Henry, Public Administration and Public Affairs, 2nd ed. (Englewood Cliffs: Prentice-Hall, 1980) chs. 3 and 4.

the senior detention deputy in charge of a shift is given responsibility for decisions about the management of disciplinary problems in the facility during the shift.

Views vary on the effectiveness of traditional supervision models in relation to "modern" participatory management approaches. In fact, due to the size and proximity of staff in the small facility there may be far more participation in management than for larger facilities. People like to be involved, or feel they are involved, in the decision making process, particularly when their safety is at issue, but this does not mean that they can be allowed to become less productive. Some managers and workers are not able to handle decisionmaking responsibilities, and some administrators are unable to delegate authority, in which case more traditional approaches may be necessary.

Administrators can also be confronted with a bewildering array of management techniques that both use and go beyond the traditional and more current participatory approaches. These techniques are designed to improve management and budgeting, and provide methods for analyzing organizational effectiveness. These include Organization Development (OD), Management by Objectives (MBO), Planning, Programming, and Budgeting (PPB), Program Evaluation (PE), and zero based budgeting. Organization Development (OD) is essentially an analysis of the organization designed to increase organizational effectiveness through planned interventions in organizational processes that stress the integration of individual and organizational goals.[88] Management By Objectives (MBO) is based on a participative management philosophy. Planning, Programming, and Budgeting (PPB) is a planning and control device for comparing programs on the basis of cost and effectiveness.[89]

A comparison of PPB and MBO as management tools can be found in Klingner's Public Personnel Management, along with a

---

[88]See W. Warner Burke, "Organization Development," in Barry Bozeman and Jeffrey Straussman, eds. New Directions in Public Administration (Monterey, CA: Brooks Cole, 1984).

[89]For a discussion of MBO, PPBS and various management styles see National Advisory Commission on Criminal Justice Standards and Goals, Corrections (Washington, D.C.: GPO, 1973) 439-453; reprinted in Harry W. More, Jr., Criminal Justice Management (St. Paul: West Publishing Company, 1980) 247-272. See also Mark L. McConkie, Management by Objectives: A Correctional Perspective (Washington, D.C.: GPO, 1975), also excerpted in part in More at pp. 258-272

discussion of Program Evaluation (PE), which is now a fairly standardized technique used in assessing the overall effectiveness of programs, rather than addressing managerial efficiency in accomplishing fixed objectives.[90] New budgeting systems also appear from time to time, such as the zero-based budgeting popular during the Carter administration, although it no longer seems to be widely used.

In looking at the various systems for improving management and budgeting you should always question the usefulness of these systems for your organization based on its size and level of operations. A possible framework for establishing a management system is suggested in an article on detention facility management by Kiekbusch. He provides a tested "management system" that includes (1) setting of priorities, (2) job descriptions with performance criteria, (3) a performance evaluation system, (4) staff training, and (5) the development of an operational manual with staff participation.[91] Any system of management should include these elements, which are certainly preferable to "management by crisis."

The administrator must constantly be aware that the county commission or board of supervisors will want to improve operations and keep costs down, that staff will want greater security and increased rewards, and that inmates will demand better conditions. Whatever system is used to achieve these goals requires short- and long-range planning, contact with the controlling political entity or entities in setting priorities, some degree of staff participation in organizational decisionmaking, and a system for evaluating performance, both for individuals and for the total organization.

IV. Calculating Shift Coverage

You must make some decisions about the numbers and types of staff needed to operate the facility. Staffing a detention facility is the greatest budget expenditure. It represents the major cost of operating a 24-hour care facility of any kind. In jails, correctional officer's salaries make up approximately 50% of the life cycle operating

---

[90]Donald E. Klingner, Public Personnel Management (Englewood Cliffs: Prentice-Hall, 1980) 214-224.

[91]Richard Kiekbusch, "Management, One Jail's Experience," Corrections Today Aug., 1985: 134-138.

budget; civilian salaries account for 24% of the operating budget.[92] Without the inclusion of construction costs the proportions are slightly higher, meaning that about 70% to 80% of the costs of operating the jail (after construction costs) are personnel costs.

A. The Post

A "post" in a jail or correctional facility is a job defined by its location, duties and time(s) of operation, as opposed to a job description, which may be a more general description of a type of job, such as "detention deputy." It may be fixed, as in a control center, or a "roving" post with an assigned zone of coverage. It may be filled interchangeably by several officers over 24 hour periods. Some posts operate for the entire 168 hours in the week, others for lesser periods of time, depending on the type of position. A "post" is not the same as a "position" in an agency. A person with the "position" of correctional officer or detention deputy works a "post." Determining the needs of a jail begins with calculating the number of posts needed and determining which posts must be staffed during each shift.

B. Shift Coverage

Several publications provide information on the calculation of shift coverage, or "shift relief factor," and should be consulted.[93] A current "Staffing Analysis Workbook" has been published by the National Institute of Corrections, which includes work sheets and formulas for doing a proper staffing analysis in the jail.[94]

The shift relief factor represents the number of staff required to cover each post. For a post requiring 24 hour coverage in three 8-hour shifts estimates are approximately five staff to cover each post. The extra two staff members are needed to make up for regular days off for the three primary people, as well as for holidays, sick time,

---

[92]Dale K. Sechrest and Shelley J. Price. Correctional Facility Design and Construction Management (Washington, D.C.: GPO, 1984) 98.

[93]See F. Warren Benton, Planning and Evaluating Prison and Jail Staffing, vol. 1. (Washington, D.C.: National Institute of Corrections, October, 1981) 30-35 (Volume 2 provides descriptions of the staffing patterns of 20 institutions); see also "Jail Staffing Analysis Forms," (Sacramento: California Youth and Adult Corrections Agency, Board of Corrections, prepared by Farbstein/Williams & Associates, 1981) App. J.

[94]Rod Miller and Dennis Liebert, Staffing Analysis Workbook for Jails (Washington, D.C.: National Institute of Corrections and Community Resources Services, Inc., Kents Hill, Maine, April, 1988).

annual leave, training, days in court, military leave, injuries, union meetings, and the like. The average employee works about 233 days per year; dividing 365 days per year by this figure yields the need for 1.57 staff per eight hours, or 4.71 for a 24 hour period. Variations will occur based on jurisdictional employment practices, such as the definition of a work week, the training time for new officers, and the like. Suggestions for reducing staffing costs are provided in the discussion of shift assignments.

V. Shift Assignments

An overview of shift cycles and shift patterns is found in "Planning and Evaluating Prison and Jail Staffing."[95] Two other publications are relevant and are cited in the bibliography, the Work Schedule Design Handbook and the Staffing Guide for the Federal Prison System.

A. Shift Patterns

The objective of establishing a fixed shift pattern is to provide for necessary post and position coverage and to ensure the completion of necessary work. Considerable attention is devoted to the question of coverage in the NIC Staffing Analysis Workbook and by Benton.[96] Little attention is paid in most analyses to the topic of straight versus rotating shifts. Most facilities work straight shifts where officers come in at the same time each day and get periodic breaks (their "weekends"). Benton indicates that rotation to a new shift time more than every three or four months will affect worker capabilities.[97]

There are two types of shift cycles: the seven day cycle and the six day cycle. The seven day cycle provides for five days on and two off, with holidays off as well. It corresponds most closely with civilian schedules and requires relief workers for holidays, although all employees obviously cannot get their two days off on the weekend. This cycle occurs 52 times per year and generates 261 work days, minus holidays.

---

[95]Benton 35-40.

[96]Benton 35-40.

[97]Benton 38.

The alternative schedule is the six day or "four and two" schedule. This schedule does not allow time off for holidays but rotates employee days off so that different holidays are available in different years. It allows automatically for coverage on holidays. This cycle occurs 61 times per year and generates 244 work days, about five to ten fewer days per year than the seven day cycle, depending on the number of holidays. This difference is offset by requiring half hour longer shifts, reducing leave, requiring overtime, or requiring that the days be made up in training. A variation of this model is the ten hour shift using three shifts, as used in the Pre-Trial Arraignment Facility in Denver, Colorado.

There is no evidence that any particular cycle works better for employees. Generally, the seven day cycle is seen as more advantageous to employees in relating to civilian schedules, and the six day cycle is more convenient to the operation of a 24-hour facility. Neither of these schedules works well for administrative and professional staff who must communicate with other agency employees on regular work week schedule, so often these staff groups work different schedules.

B. Shift Work Variations

Within the shift concept there are a minimum of five variations for consideration by the administrator. Of particular importance is the consideration of the ten-hour shift, which may be more efficient than the traditional eight hour shift, especially for posts that require coverage only during peak periods. For example, inmates are often out of their living units and in areas such as administration, medical, program and outside recreation only ten hours per day. Using two officers to staff two sixteen-hour shifts can be costly and inefficient. Benton estimates savings using ten hour shifts, but much depends on weighing the efficiency of operations in relation to the design of the shifts.

The five shift variations for consideration are:

1. **Four-Ten Plan**: Employees work four ten hour shifts and are off three days. This has the added advantage of providing double coverage at peak periods on certain posts, such as living units or recreation/leisure areas in the evenings, or for allowing time for staff to supervise an eight-hour inmate work crew. For some high stress jobs, however, ten hour shifts may not be advisable.

2. **Flextime:** This schedule requires a core work period of, say, 10:00 a.m. to 3:00 p.m., but allows variations of starting times from 6:00 a.m. to 7:00 p.m. Eight hours per day, forty hours a week is the minimum work period. One advantage is increased time period coverage in such areas as records and intake at no extra cost. A related advantage is more intensive coverage at peak periods of activity. Counselors and other program personnel may need the flexibility to cover evenings. On the negative side, some individuals are not capable of using unsupervised time productively.

3. **Shift Assignment Variations:** This variation involves the assignment of designated employees to particular operations on certain shifts. It may include the use of two shifts of employees on a particular task, such as intake, to cover a 16-hour period. This may involve extra cost, but can relieve congestion, make better use of work space, and provide greater access to staff by inmates. Another variation is called "rotating assignments," which involves rotation from day to evening to night shifts with each shift change. It has many problems. Dangers are in making the shift patterns too variable, such as rotating employees through the shifts too rapidly. As noted above, studies recommend shift hour changes only once every two or three months, if necessary, since worker capabilities often suffer with rapid changes.[98] Quality of staff supervision may also suffer under these conditions.

4. **Part Time Employment:** Persons requiring or desiring a limited work period, such as students and retired persons with appropriate skills, may be ideal for some jobs. They should not be correctional officers. Part time civilian employees can help cover peak demand periods or summer vacation periods. They may also offer highly specialized or unique skills, such as data processing. They may assist in filling positions that are not attractive to full time employees at prevailing wage rates. While these positions can provide cost savings by reducing required benefits, problems may occur with unions and employee groups, and this option must be carefully weighed against the needs and concerns of the full time employees. Additional problems may include

---

[98]Benton, quoting Koosoris, 38.

insurance coverage and the provision of training for these individuals.

5. **Split Shift:** Typical of the hotel and restaurant industry, the split shift has advantages to the supervisor of having more staff available at peak periods. Since this increases the overall daily time commitment of workers, much depends on finding persons who will work such shifts. The area of greatest use is for food service personnel, but transportation staff might also work on this pattern. Students may sometimes find this type of shift work desirable.

These techniques for varying facility coverage can contribute to improved operations. They can place more employees with appropriate skills on the job at the times they are needed. The use of longer shift periods can reduce staff job preparation time, which Benton estimates at 12.5% of shift time for an eight hour shift and 10% for a ten hour shift. Also, the absolute numbers of staff can be reduced through the use of longer shifts, part time help, and split shifts. The reduction of one employee per shift can amount to a $20,000 to $30,000 saving per year. And, these methods can improve employee job satisfaction. For example, employees who are the most productive can be rewarded with the first choice of flextime hours, a valuable no-cost incentive. Or, students working part time or split shifts may be viewed as potential employees upon graduation.

VI. Providing Adequate Staff Coverage

All of the staffing patterns and shift variations considered must be viewed in the light of the 1985 Supreme Court decision in Garcia v. San Antonio Metropolitan Transit Authority, in which the court overturned an earlier ruling that exempted most traditional local government activities from requirements of the Fair Labor Standards Act.[99] This decision meant that overtime pay was mandatory. The immediate result for many jails was the restructuring of schedules to avoid paying mandatory overtime. However, in November of 1985, Congress passed a law that eased the impact of Garcia, allowing compensatory time to be awarded as an option, but requiring it to be given at the rate of 1.5 hours per hour worked. It became effective in April, 1986.

---

[99] 105 S.Ct. 1005 (1985); the overturned case was National League of Cities v. Usery, 426 U.S. 833 (1976).

American Correctional Association standards state that the vacancy rate for staff who work directly with inmates should not exceed an overall average of 10 percent during any 18 month period.[100] Detention facilities should not operate understaffed. The greatest danger is to have staff work two consecutive eight hour shifts. Staff who work beyond their eight hour shift are likely to be tired. They may be prone to errors of judgment that can result in accidents and/or disruptive inmate behavior and possible lawsuits. They may be the victims of burn-out, and their work schedules surely contribute to higher staff turnover in the long run. It is short-sighted to fund overtime, which poorly paid staff often need and request — and unions may demand. As indicated above, it is now even more expensive time in overtime dollars, and it portends potential liability losses.

Overworked staff may also resign, as happened in Pennsylvania, where a correctional officer quit due to hazardous working conditions that involved too few staff and forced overtime and was allowed unemployment benefits.[101] Rather than increase costs, additional positions should be authorized. An understaffed facility must be considered a top priority for increased funding in order to meet required personnel levels. The wise administrator will be on record with the funding agency regarding needed positions.

---

[100] ACA Standard 2-5072 (1981) 17.

[101] Delaware County Prison v. Com. Unemployment Comp. Bd., 455 A.2d 790 (Penn. App. 1983).

CHAPTER FOUR: MANAGING THE INMATE POPULATION

There are several key points of concern in the management of the inmate population, the most important being:

1. Intake and release procedures: legal acceptance and authorized release, identification, managing pretrial inmates; property management (valuables);

2. Security classification: management of medical/mental cases, violent offenders, public inebriates, women and juveniles;

3. Public contact: visitors and attorneys; and,

4. Type of supervision: security levels, methods of supervision (direct contact versus remote surveillance).

I. Intake and Release Procedures

Intake is the booking period for the new inmate. Arrestees who are turned over to the jail generally find it an emotionally stressful and degrading experience. The receiving officer may be the object of hostility, and, as such, must remain businesslike to be effective. A violent incident, attempted escape, or suicide attempt may occur during this period. As indicated elsewhere, searches may be a problem for some categories of arrestee. While release procedures may be less dangerous they may be no less stressful.

Many mistakes are possible at intake and release. These include mistaken identification of persons at intake and release, poor search procedures, and failure to properly screen for medical or mental problems. Some jurisdictions are now experimenting with identification systems that go beyond fingerprints, ie. identification such as taken from a reading of the pattern of the retina of the eye. However, this has not been proven successful to date. In no case should inmates be allowed to take fingerprints or, for that matter, have anything to do with the intake or release process.

Many arrestees do not really belong in a jail. The National Coalition for Jail Reform and other groups have taken the position that public inebriates, the mentally ill and retarded, and juveniles do not belong in adult jails. Many young people are put in jail facilities who should be sent to juvenile detention facilities or taken home. The public inebriate should be in a facility with a program designed for the treatment of alcoholics.

Of the almost seven million admissions to jails each year over 600,000 are seen as mentally ill or retarded, or about 8.6 percent.[102] These individuals should be referred to community agencies as soon as possible after admission.[103] A related problem in the jail is the potential for suicide, which is discussed below. Women, juveniles, drug and alcohol abusers, handicapped persons, mentally ill offenders, and potential suicides are discussed in greater detail below.

There are some categories of offenders who can be released to home without incarceration and managed through agreements with cooperating social agencies. For example, the elderly shoplifter has become an increasingly troublesome problem in many jurisdictions. These are often people with adequate resources who are simply "stretching" their scarce dollars to meet real or imagined needs. In Broward County, Florida, the courts work with the "Area Agency on Aging" to divert elderly offenders, provide them counseling, and arrange restitution. Many times these offenders discover new linkages with their peers in the community. Jail staff should encourage such programs in order to reduce the intake of these individuals.

Intake Medical Screening. Inadequate medical and mental health screening at intake can lead to deaths from diseases such as diabetes or epilepsy, or from drug overdoses or suicides. Professional administrators are recognizing the need to screen out these offenders prior to admission. The jail administrator must learn to negotiate with the law enforcement, medical and social agencies regarding the handling, retention, or diversion of certain types of offenders. Model programs for screening mentally ill offenders can be found in Galveston, Texas; Multnomah County, Oregon; Montgomery County, Pennsylvania; and Dayton County, Ohio.[104] Since these diversion

---

[102]Estimates for prisons are 6% of the total inmate population classified as mentally ill and 2.5 percent mentally retarded; See the Sourcebook on the Mentally Disordered Prisoner (Washington, D.C.: National Institute of Corrections, March, 1985) 15.

[103]See two pamphlets by the National Coalition for Jail Reform: "Jail, The New Mental Institution," and "Look At Your Jail," both undated (c. 1983); they discuss the problems of the 3,493 jails in the U.S., especially as they must receive mentally ill and retarded individuals no longer managed by mental health institutions.

[104]National Coalition for Jail Reform, "Jail, The New Mental Institution" 6-9.

alternatives require community resources and may be seen as "soft on crime," often they will not be popular. A sheriff running for office may find this role runs counter to the tough law enforcement image that must be projected to the public. It is a role perhaps better suited to a board of supervisors or county commissioners who can weigh the budgetary issues in reducing jail populations and divert resources to other programs. At the very least the administrator will want to know the costs of operating the jail in order to recommend alternatives to community representatives (officials) that might be more cost effective, if not more efficient.

Release procedures require careful scrutiny. Procedures must include positive identification of releasees, verification of authority to release (preferably in writing), return of jail property by the inmate, and the return of inmate property with documentation of receipt. There have been occasions when inmates have substituted themselves for the releasee. Proper identification procedures must be established, including a comparison of intake and release fingerprints. Any other method tried should be carefully evaluated before wide use.

II. Security Classification

Inmates coming into the jail are, for the most part, unknown personalities. This is just one among many reasons why the use of single cells is preferable, especially in the early stages of incarceration. Placing a potentially dangerous inmate in a group living situation invites trouble, as may isolating a potential suicide. Increasingly, correctional officers are being sued and sometimes found personally liable for the placement of inmates in situations where they may be injured by other inmates.[105] However, recent cases have led to some confusion about the direction of the court with respect to liability and what constitutes negligence. It appears that negligent deprivations of life, liberty, or property simply cannot violate the due process clause of the Fourteenth Amendment, which is reserved for more serious abuses of power.[106] These abuses appear to be based

---

[105]In Smith v. Wade (461 U.S. 30, 1983) a correctional officer, Wade, was held liable by the U.S. Supreme Court in the amount of $5,000 in punitive damages for "reckless or callous indifference to the federally protected rights of others." Compensatory damages of $25,000 were not appealed; however, $5,000 in punitive damages were awarded to the inmate; see Palmer, 735-740.

[106]See the discussion of Daniels v. Williams 106 S.Ct. 662 (1986) and Davidson v. Cannon, 106 S.Ct. 668 (1986) found elsewhere in this book and in Collins (1986) 4-5, and

largely on "wanton" use of force, or force used "maliciously or sadistically for the very purpose of causing harm.[107] Due to the need to make decisions about the dangerousness and/or potential problems of inmates both for safety and liability reasons, intake and classification have become increasingly important to jail management.

A. Types of Offenders

Offenders arriving at the jail are placed in one of several categories of supervision, with its related housing area. These are included in American Correctional Association standards used in accreditation, and accepted by the National Sheriffs' Association. They call for the separate management of various types of offenders in the jail, as follows:

Male pretrial detainees

Female pretrial detainees

Sentenced males

Unsentenced females

Other classes of detainees, such as witnesses and civil prisoners

Community custody inmates, such as work releasees, weekenders, trusties (sometimes "trusty" is used, but never "trustee")

Special problem inmates, such as alcoholics, narcotic addicts, mentally disturbed, physically handicapped, and persons with communicable diseases

Inmates requiring disciplinary detention

Inmates requiring administrative segregation or protective custody

---

Collins (1987) 13-14, 136. See also Charles H. Whitebread and Christopher Slobogin, Criminal Procedure (New York: The Foundation Press, 1986) 50-51.

[107] Whitley v. Albers, 474 U.S. 89 (1986).

Juveniles, including those whose juvenile status has been waived and those awaiting a juvenile hearing[108]

While these categories of offenders are manageable for large facilities with varied security levels, smaller facilities often have difficulty managing these classifications of offenders separately. Clearly, the first priority are mentally or physically ill offenders who require separation, treatment, and possible removal to another type of facility. Dangerous offenders must be separated from others at all times and kept under close and continuous supervision. Men, women, and juveniles must be separated from one another by sight and sound at all times. Also, sentenced offenders who are awaiting transfer to state or federal facilities should be transferred as soon as possible after sentencing. Unfortunately, this has become a problem in recent times due to the introduction of mandatory sentences and subsequent lack of space in state facilities. This problem may lead to consideration of new facilities or alternative sentencing options, as discussed elsewhere. The numbers of offenders sentenced to time in the facility should be monitored carefully in consideration of the development of a separate facility for them, such as the jail annex described earlier.

Pretrial release programs are found in some medium and larger jail systems, and should be encouraged both as a humane procedure and to keep the jail population down to manageable levels. Pretrial release programs release offenders into the community on their own recognizance ("OR"). Well run programs have very low failure to appear (in court) rates, often well below 5 percent. Failure rates for bonded inmates are higher. Newer forms of community supervision that use electronic monitoring devices may increase the use of pretrial release.

B. Intake Classification: Security, Custody, and Housing

No matter the size of the facility, the following must, at a minimum, be recorded as part of the booking process for each detainee: sex, age (adult-juvenile decision), offense, legal status (pretrial, unsentenced, sentenced awaiting transfer, federal prisoner, etc.), history of violent or disruptive behavior, escape potential, evidence of vulnerability to attack (immaturity, homosexuality, etc.), evidence of a physical problem (potential medical emergency) or mental handicap, evidence

[108]See ACA Standard 2-5354.

of drug or alcohol involvement (withdrawal distress), and evidence of suicidal tendencies. Examples of classification forms are readily available from the National Institute of Corrections, state agencies, or other local detention facilities.[109]

A classification code should be developed to alert staff to the type of offender they will be dealing with. Especially important is the notation of any special needs, such as medications taken, possible drug withdrawal, or special medical condition (diabetes, epilepsy, AIDS, etc.). Training in the "signs and symptoms" of drug abuse, physical problems, or mental disabilities is becoming increasingly used to train booking and classification officers. The management of various special types of offenders (women, juveniles, handicapped, mentally ill, etc.) is discussed below.

Generally, the initial intake classification should be done within four hours of admission to the facility for every person brought to the facility. A classification officer must be on duty 24 hours a day, working in the booking area. This officer's responsibilities and duties must be clearly specified, including the time in which intake is to be completed and the use of any criteria relevant to diversion — bond or release on own recognizance ("OR"). This officer should be aware of laws that allow inmates to be treated by their own physician at their own expense, familiar with prosthetic devices, which can be dangerous weapons, and concerned about communicable diseases, especially in the current period of the AIDS epidemic. He or she must know about available local, state and federal facilities that can house and/or treat some types of detainees. Many potential detainees are diverted to home or other agencies during this period. Alcohol or drug detoxification and treatment programs are good examples of these types of diversion. Estimates of drug abusers in some jurisdictions are as high as 50 percent of admissions, making this a prime area for diversion of offenders. Detainees who are not diverted must undergo additional classification prior to placement in the population.

Custody Classification System. A custody classification and re-classification system must be in place for the management of the various types of offenders described above who are to remain in the

---

[109]For an example of such a form that is not useful, see James Austin and Paul Litsky, <u>Federal Probation</u> March, 1982: 61; this article also discusses the differences between jail and prison classification, noting that jail classification is more limited due to inmates' shorter length of stay.

facility. This process is sometimes discussed as a "security" and "custody" classification process. Security refers to the type of physical (architectural) constraints used; custody refers to the level of supervision required.[110] Such a system is needed in order to determine the level of security necessary to supervise and/or protect offenders in custody, to determine the appropriate housing assignment consistent with administrative needs and legal requirements for the jurisdiction, and to determine the offender's suitability for participation in facility programs. If you operate a large facility, a classification team may complete housing and program assignments. Smaller facilities may simply use a classification officer to make these decisions. In either case, additional information may be required on some inmates prior to a final determination of custody level, such as their offense history, prior to placing them in the general population. If this is the case, pretrial inmates may be held in a "special custody" housing area during a "quarantine" period pending a decision on their housing assignment.

Aside from any special holding period, four major categories of security classification are most often used: maximum, medium, and minimum custody, and segregation (or isolation). Note in these custody definitions that each level includes the physical setting, the type of supervision to be used, and a description of the behavior that leads to the classification:

> **Maximum Custody**: Inmates in maximum custody are housed in a separate area of the facility. They are single-celled and restricted to specific areas of the facility, with movement outside only in the company of an officer. They require constant and direct supervision and control. They are permitted association with the general inmate population in programs and other inmate activities at the discretion of the facility commander or his designee. An inmate in this custody designation is under "close" supervision when he has been involved in recent and numerous episodes of violence to others and there is the belief that it will continue, or there is a suicide potential ("suicide watch" is indicated). This classification includes inmates with (1) a history of aggressive and/or assaultive behavior — e.g., predators and disruptive inmates, (2) a history of escape or attempted escape, (3) a history of severely irrational behavior, and/or

[110]See Robert B. Levinson and J.D. Williams, "Inmate Classification: Security/Custody Considerations," Federal Probation March, 1979: 37.

(4) a need for isolation based on medical or psychological evaluation.

Medium Custody: Inmates in medium custody are housed in the general (major) areas of the facility and do not work outside without constant supervision. They require a moderate amount of control and supervision because they represent a risk of nonviolent offenses, rule infractions, and escape attempts. Movement is generally in view of correctional officers, but less restricted than maximum custody. These inmates participate in available programs and other activities without constant or direct supervision. This classification includes inmates with (1) minor medical and/or psychological problems, (2) local charges pending, (3) holds (detainers) for other agencies in addition to local charges, and/or (4) a criminal history indicating closer supervision than minimum security inmates.

Minimum Custody: These inmates can be housed in dormitories, prerelease, or work release facilities. Inmates in minimum security are not expected to present management problems and can function with little supervision since they are not seen as dangerous or as escape risks. This classification includes inmates with (1) no criminal history or only minor offenses, and/or (2) no history of violent or aggressive behavior. Inmates in this category often are put to work in and around the facility without constant, visual supervision as "trustys" (plural is "trusties," but <u>never</u> "trustees," who are persons responsible for the management of another's property). Recent programs for convicted drunk drivers that incarcerate on weekends only are good examples of minimum custody programs for inmates representing minimal security problems, as noted below.

Segregation. The classification plan must include a segregation area for inmates requiring administrative segregation for their protection or the protection of other inmates and staff, or "protective custody." There also must be an area to house disciplinary segregation cases, where inmates may be held prior to hearings on facility rule violations and held for punishment for specified periods of time when found guilty of rule violations. (See chapter five for additional discussion of conditions in this area.)

The extent of use of these levels of classification will depend on the condition of the physical plant, the supervision philosophy used (direct or remote), and staffing patterns (frequency of patrol and observation). For example, some jail administrators make every effort to avoid the use of protective custody. If over 5 percent of the population is in protective custody it is probably being overused and a review of procedures is required. The worst possible situation is to have inmate classification limited by physical plant constraints. Good examples of how to limit medium and maximum security to those who need it include the creation of minimum security areas or facilities for less serious, minimum security offenders. For example, a separate facility should be created for drunk drivers, who should pay for their incarceration as part of their treatment program. A pre-release facility or work release facility should be part of any jail operation that has over 50 beds.

The Classification System. In developing criteria for custody placements, the U.S. Bureau of Prisons staff are required to weigh equally the history of escapes or attempted escapes and the history of violence as the top two concerns for classification, using seriousness and the time (date) of occurrence of the offense(s) to further evaluate these variables. These criteria are followed by detainers (number, type, and severity), length of sentence expected, and, grouped together — disciplinary reports (type and frequency), prior arrests and commitments (seriousness of prior offenses), and notoriety.[111] Clearly, past criminal history, violence potential, psychological/behavioral problems, and current offense are the primary concerns in custody classification.

More general classification concerns related to the safe housing of inmates include the protection of sex offenders (aggressive and passive), who may require high supervision; the protection of young or naive offenders from sexual attack; awareness of the status of organized crime or drug figures ("drug czars"); knowledge of notorious or high publicity cases; awareness of gang affiliations (potential revenge-seekers); and the identification of informants, some of whom may have prior experience in the facility. The key to safety is awareness and immediate action in managing potential problems. The November, 1987 riots by Mariel Cubans in the federal system at Atlanta, Georgia, and Oakdale, Louisiana underscore the

---

[111] Federal Prison System, Program Statement, "Subject: Security Designation and Custody Classification System," December 1, 1982.

need for immediate action based on political events affecting prisoners.[112]

Benefits of the Classification System. A good classification system can improve management through the reduction of escapes and incidents in the facility. It can assist in creating staff training priorities, allowing better program planning, and in improving planning for future expansion (facility construction or renovation). It can provide useful information to support the budgeting process for the facility, especially where staff are needed to manage difficult populations, or where crisis periods are anticipated, such as that mentioned above for the Federal Bureau of Prisons. Counties and cities may experience similar problems where rock concerts or other scheduled events are to take place. The classification system must also include periodic re-classification for both pretrial and sentenced inmates. As more is known about an individual offender it may be possible to reduce his or her level of security, which makes more secure space available for incoming detainees. The addition of new space may also create opportunities for re-classification of some inmates.

Periodic review of the system will be needed to correct for overclassification, or the overuse of maximum or medium security, a condition that can cause frustration among inmates and staff and cause problems in the facility. A related problem is underclassification of dangerous or troublesome inmates, which can result in escapes, assaults, and other types of internal problems.

C. Special Categories of Detainees

Women. Women detainees present special management problems due to their small numbers in most jails. Women offenders must be separated completely from male offenders and juvenile offenders. Ideally, a separate facility should exist for women prisoners. However, if you are in a jurisdiction with a small to medium-sized population this may not be possible, and it can present a problem for the small jail. When non-dangerous women prisoners must be held in the facility, a room or rooms should be set aside that are separated by sight and sound from the mens' quarters in the jail. Consideration must be given to the special medical and hygienic needs of women. Programs must be developed for women, to include the use of

---

[112]"State Dept. Says It Could Have Delayed News That Sparked Riots," Criminal Justice Newsletter Feb. 15, 1988: 1.

recreation and other facilities on a schedule shared by the male population. There have been a series of federal district court decisions requiring parity of programs for women and men. The concept of parity, or equality of programs and services, if it becomes generally accepted by the courts, will have major implications for jail operations. The most recent edition of the Collins update shows little progress in this area.[113] Dangerous women offenders should be considered for transportation to a larger jail facility in an adjoining county, or housing at a state prison facility if one is nearby and agreeable.

Juveniles. There is considerable sentiment nationally that juveniles do not belong in jail facilities for adults. Although less than one percent of the detained juveniles now reside in adult facilities,[114] some estimates have run as high as half a million juveniles annually being held in adult jails for some time period. Estimates are that only 10 percent of these youths require secure detention.[115] "A shocking consequence of placing juveniles in adult jails is that the rate of suicide per 100,000 youths in jail is 12.5 percent compared with the 1.6 percent rate of suicide in juvenile detention centers."[116]

Questions are often raised, however, about juveniles who are bound over as adults for trial. These persons could be as young as 14, and they may be physically as imposing as an adult offender. Should juveniles be held in facilities designed for adults? The American Correctional Association standards clearly answer in the negative: "... juveniles, who are subject to trial as adults, are separated by sight and sound from adult inmates, although they may be in the same facility structure. Juveniles who are not subject to trial as adults are not housed in the facility."[117] The Juvenile Justice and Delinquency Prevention Act of 1974, as amended, called for removal of juveniles from adult jails by 1985. As of September 1987, 22 states were ineligible for federal funds because of their inability to remove 75

---

[113]See Glover v. Johnson, 476 F.Supp. 1075 (E.D. Mich., 1979); this and other cases are discussed by Collins (1986) 76-79 and Collins (1987) 36-37.

[114]Bureau of Justice Statistics, "Jail Inmates 1984" (Washington, D.C.: Bureau of Justice Statistics, May, 1986) 2.

[115]Corrections Today Nov./Dec., 1981.

[116]Corrections Today Nov./Dec., 1981.

[117]ACA Standard 2-5355.

percent of juveniles from adult jails; Congress may attempt to cut of all funding in 1988 if full (100%) compliance is not reached.[118]

Juveniles belong in separate facilities. They belong in facilities designed to meet their physical, psychological, social, nutritional, educational and recreational needs. Consideration should be given to home detention alternatives or the use of secure community residential centers, if available. Unquestionably, juveniles who are dependent, abused, or neglected must not be in adult jails, or even juvenile detention facilities ("juvenile hall"), but preferably in shelters designed for their care pending a decision about their placement in the community.

The question of whether juveniles may be detained in juvenile detention facilities prior to a hearing has been addressed by the Supreme Court. The Court found that in New York State juveniles posing a "serious risk" of committing a crime (by adult standards) could be detained, consistent with the fact that the stay was limited to seventeen days by statute and that they could wear street clothes, partake in educational and recreational programs, and receive punishment only by room confinement.[119]

There is some case law indicating that housing any juveniles in adult jails may present major legal problems. At least one court has ruled that holding children in jails violates due process.[120] Other courts have ruled that housing juveniles in jails may, depending on the facts of the case, violate the rights of the children.[121] Another legal development that may have a substantial impact on housing juveniles in adult jails is an April, 1987 decision from a federal district court in Iowa in which the judge held that the juveniles held in jails in states which had received funding under the federal Juvenile Justice and Delinquency Prevention Act could sue to enforce the Act's requirements that states receiving funds remove juveniles from adult jails and lock-ups. Prior to this decision it was not clear that juveniles could sue under the Act or whether enforcement of the Act was left solely to the federal government.[122]

---

[118]Crime Control Digest Sept. 21, 1987: 2-3.

[119]Schall v. Martin, 467 U.S. 253 S.Ct. 2403 (1984).

[120]D.B. v. Tewksbury, 545 F.Supp. 896 (D. Ore. 1982).

[121]Swansey v. Elrod, 386 F.Supp. 1138 (N.D. Ill. 1975), Doe v. McFaul, 599 F.Supp 1421 (D. Ohio 1984).

[122]Henderickson v. Griggs, No. 2C 84-3012 (N.D. Iowa April 9, 1987).

Pending the outcome of court decisions, if juveniles are held in a jail that also holds adults the disposition of their cases should proceed as rapidly as possible. They should be separated by sight and sound from adults. Staff supervising juveniles should have special training in the needs and responses of children, and supervision should be quite close. Opportunities for recreation should not be limited, and meals should be planned in consideration of the needs of children. Community social agencies should be consulted regarding special needs, such as education, counseling, and religious needs.

Alcohol and Drug Abusers. It is estimated that 25 to 40 percent of all jail admissions are for an alcohol-related problem — the public inebriate, the alcoholic, and the situational drunk. As many as 80 percent of admissions may be drug abusers. Drug abusers are often generically categorized as "substance abusers." Urine testing in Washington, D.C. and New York City showed about 55 percent of admissions having drug involvement at arrest in 1984 and a figure closer to 70 percent in 1987.[123] The first concern in the case of the alcohol or drug abuser should be his/her medical condition. Ideally, they should be handled in health care facilities, especially if they manifest delirium tremens (the "D.T.'s"), withdrawal symptoms, or other health problems. Drug addicts in withdrawal should be under the supervision of a physician, either in a hospital or, if that is not possible, the jail infirmary. Methadone and other medications can be used in this process.

Handicapped Persons. Handicapped inmates and visitors, including the deaf, blind, and wheelchair handicapped, must be managed in the facility. A handicap differs from a disability in that the latter may be a problem but not present a limitation on major life functions. A handicap is generally defined as an impairment of a major life function, such as deafness, blindness, or paralysis. Handicaps and disabilities are often lumped together, which is unfortunate. As

---

[123]For Manhattan Central Booking in 1984, 56 percent of male arrestees tested positive for opiates, cocaine, PCP or methadone, and dramatic increases were found in cocaine use from 1984 to 1986; in Eric Wish, "Drug Use in Arrestees in Manhattan: The Dramatic Increase in Cocaine from 1984 to 1986" and "Drug Use Forecasting: New York 1984 to 1986, Research in Brief (Washington, D.C.: National Institute of Justice, Feb., 1987). Cf. Mary A. Toberg and Michael P. Kirby, "Drug Use and Pretrial Crime in the District of Columbia," National Institute of Justice Research in Brief (Washington, D.C.: National Institute of Justice, Oct., 1987) in which they found that drug users were detained more frequently and received more stringent conditions of release if not detained.

noted above, a strong classification system is essential to their identification and transfer, as well as to the management of the physically handicapped. Also unfortunate is the fact that mental health problems are often referred to as mental disabilities. Mentally ill or impaired ("disabled") persons should not be in the facility. The concern here is with handicapped persons who require specialized management.

Section 504 of the Rehabilitation Act of 1973 (29 U.S.C. 792) prohibits exclusion of the handicapped from participation, denial of benefit, or discrimination under any program or activity receiving Federal financial assistance. Within the act is a provision requiring handicapped access to most public facilities. These laws are found in the Architectural Barriers Act of 1968, 42 U.S.C. 4151-4157 (Public Law 90-480), which directs the federal government to set an example nationally for accessibility to facilities for all people. The essence of the Act is captured in a booklet entitled Uniform Federal Accessibility Standards.[124] The 88-page UFAS booklet has been adopted by the Departments of Defense and Housing and Urban Development, the U.S. Postal Service, and the General Services Administration. Section 4.1.3(9)(c) includes requirements for correctional facilities (jails, prisons, reformatories, etc.) and states the Standards should apply in the following areas:

> 5 percent of residential units available, or at least one unit, whichever is greater, all common use, visitor use, or areas which may result in employment of physically handicapped persons.

The UFAS handbook covers new and existing construction, provides definitions that are instructive for anyone planning construction of any kind, and has numerous graphics. The standards are consistent with the American National Standards Institute (ANSI) standards for general use. Any consideration of facility renovation or new construction must consider these standards for handicapped access. In addition to these standards, the National Institute of Corrections (NIC) has published a report, "The Alienation of Disabled Inmates."[125] (In this report disability means physical handicap.)

---

[124]Architectural and Transportation Barriers Compliance Board, updated, 1985, originally published in the Federal Register on August 7, 1984 (49 FR 31528). In order to enforce the act for both facilities and programs the ATBCB was created under section 502 of the Rehabilitation Act of 1973 (Public Law 93-112).

[125]Alan S. Kalmanoff, "The Alienation of Disabled Inmates," paper for the National Institute of Corrections (June 2, 1983), 12 pages.

While the NIC report indicates that no significant political movement, legislation, or court rulings are now in existence, it notes that the "legal impact of disability rights on corrections is imminent."[126] On the one hand, the author discusses the need for a special facility or housing block for the handicapped inmate, including TTY phones for the deaf, mobility training for a newly-blind inmate, and consideration of the needs of paraplegics and amputees. On the other hand, he discusses "mainstreaming" or preparation for independent living — trying to get these inmates into the general inmate population rather than special housing that might be discriminatory. This may be less of a dilemma for the small jail where special housing is not available than it will be for the state prison. If available, facilities for sentenced offenders (jail farms, etc.) may allow greater flexibility with this population, and it may be possible to normalize the environment for them. When it is not possible to get the offender back into the community, and there is a choice of facilities, the inmate should be allowed to live with the general population in a "normalized" environment.

Mentally Ill Offenders. Offenders with mental health problems should not be in a jail. As indicated earlier, of the almost seven million admissions to jails each year over 600,000 are seen as mentally ill or retarded (8.6%). These individuals should be referred to community agencies as soon as possible after admission.[127] However, this has become an increasingly common problem with the closure of many mental hospitals as part of the community treatment initiative that swept the mental health field in the 1950's and 1960's. The promised "continuing treatment and support" in the community has not materialized. Many of these patients don't take their medicines or seek out help when they need it. Many of the community agencies to which they turn are not equipped to deal with the chronic mentally ill patient, or the mentally ill and drug-involved criminal (now called "dual diagnosis" cases). Many community mental health professionals are reluctant to deal with criminals, who are often dangerous people.

---

[126]Kalmanoff, 2.

[127]See two pamphlets by the National Coalition for Jail Reform: "Jail, The New Mental Institution," and "Look At Your Jail," both undated (c. 1983); these publications discuss the problems of the 3,493 jails in the U.S., especially as they must receive mentally ill and retarded individuals no longer managed by mental health institutions.

These mentally ill and/or drug-involved individuals are often left to the jail — the agency of last resort, which may only aggravate their problems. The mentally ill and retarded fill the medical and isolation units. They are preyed upon by other inmates, violate the rules, cause destruction, and may attempt suicide. They return to jail at alarmingly high rates. A study by the grand jury in Dade County, Florida found 70 of 100 mentally ill persons released from prison were back in mental hospitals or in jail within two years.[128]

Mentally ill or retarded persons must either be screened out of the jail or treated in it. If you do not have a program in your community to manage mentally ill or retarded offenders, as well as the addicted or alcohol-involved offender, you should be exploring the possibility of starting one. Several examples have been mentioned. Galveston County, Texas, uses a team of sheriffs' deputies trained to work with mentally ill people; this team helps divert these individuals to mental health agencies.[129] A similar program operates in Multnomah County (Portland), Oregon, where a full time mental health counselor works at central jail intake to divert offenders to mental health care.

Pima County, Arizona, decided to provide short-term treatment for mentally ill inmates using trained correctional officers and "corrections specialists" who had good ability to communicate, observe and interpret behavior, intervene in crisis situations, and apply the principles of direct supervision of inmates. Five inexpensive and easily developed programs were initiated: physical exercise, recreation and arts and crafts, hygiene, training in "living skills" (when to know to seek help), and nutrition. While no formal evaluation has been done, inmates appear to be returned to the general population sooner, and liaison with outside mental health agencies in order to assist offenders in need has been improved.[130]

---

[128]Miami Herald, "Jury: Mentally Ill Defendants Are Neglected," 14 Nov. 1985; a related report found a 56% re-arrest rate for persons found not guilty by reason of insanity, Miami Herald, "Study Criticizes Handling of Mentally Ill," 17 May 1985.

[129]Programs in Galveston County, Portland, Montgomery County, Pennsylvania, and Dayton, Ohio are summarized in "Jail, The New Mental Institution," National Coalition for Jail Reform, undated pamphlet (c. 1983).

[130]Frank R. Hecht and Ramon Smithhart, "Management of the Acute and Chronically Mentally Ill Inmate: A New Experience" American Jails Fall, 1987: 10-12.

Montgomery County, Pennsylvania, has a 33-bed psychiatric hospital that provides immediate, short-term care for people with mental health and drug/alcohol emergencies. The program developed as a response to two jail suicides by mentally ill inmates in 1972.[131] A "hotline" is used by law enforcement officers to access this diversion service. Where diversion programs are used they should be supplemented with alternative community placements, such as halfway houses or short term community psychiatric units. The police department in Dayton County, Ohio, has negotiated contracts with three local community mental health centers and hospitals to provide immediate 24-hour a day coverage for their facility for mentally ill offenders. An award-winning program in the Suffolk County Correctional Facility in Riverhead, New York, is described by Filou.[132] The program has been operated for the last nine years by county health services as an accredited outpatient mental health clinic. The facility claims a nationally recognized model for jail suicide prevention that includes special training to selected classification officers and immediate referral when obvious signs of distress are noted. Programs for the mentally ill include hospitalization (civil commitment), where possible, and treatment in the facility, if necessary, counseling, crisis intervention, advocacy and referral, and continuing communication (feedback) between mental health and jail staff. Funding is by the county department of health services which receives a 50% reimbursement from the New York State Office of Mental Hygiene, Local Assistance Program. A case management position is funded by state mental hygiene; the total budget for salaries is $400,000 with about a third of this allocated for employee benefits.[133] Filou emphasizes that the program has created a safer environment for staff and inmates through a constructive, problem-solving approach that has reduced suicides, tensions, and acting out in the facility.

D. The Potential Suicide

An increasingly difficult mental health problem in jails is the suicidal inmate. Of the 303 jail deaths in the year preceding June 30, 1985, 39 percent were suicides, 50 percent natural causes, and 11

---

[131] Bill Curry, "Punishment or Treatment," State Legislatures February, 1985: 27.

[132] Mary B. Filou, "Mental Health Services in a Large County Jail: Suffolk County's Award Winning Program," American Jails Winter, 1988: 52-58.

[133] Filou 56.

percent from other causes (accidents, injuries, etc.).[134] Rates of suicide in jail populations are more than 16 times those for comparable populations in the community. Juvenile suicide attempts are as serious a concern as adult attempts, and they are significantly more likely to occur among juveniles held in adult jails rather than among juveniles held in detention facilities. The rate for juvenile suicides in adult jails has been documented as 4.6 times greater than youths in the general population. [135]

Jail suicides often occur early in the jail stay due to inadequate or nonexistent diagnosis of depression and/or the poor supervision of potential suicides. Procedures for identifying potentially suicidal offenders are covered below. An additional resource is the Jail Suicide Prevention Information Task Force of the National Institute of Corrections. This Task Force can provide information and assistance in this extremely important area of jail operations, including procedures designed to help identify these inmates at admission and to prevent suicide attempts.[136]

Early identification. Any person coming into the police lock-up or jail may be suicidal. Early identification is critical because 29 percent of the suicides take place within three hours of admission, 51 percent within 24 hours. Almost two-thirds of the suicide victims are under the influence of alcohol or drugs at lock-up. Three-fourths are locked up on non-violent charges, and most are young, single, unskilled males. Drunks who commit suicide most often attempt it within 48 hours. Most occur while the victims are in isolated areas. Suicides are accomplished by hanging (96%) with torn bedding (48% of hangings), or their own clothing, other than shoelaces or belts (34%). For this reason hooks, knobs or other hanging devices are to be avoided in all cells.

Recognizing the potential suicide. The potential suicide may be recognized at the time of arrest or at admission, or this behavior

---

[134]Bureau of Justice Statistics,Jail Inmates, 1985 (Washington, D.C.: Bureau of Justice Statistics, July 1987, NCJ-105586) 2.

[135]Community Research Forum, Juvenile Suicide in Adult Jails — Findings from a National Survey of Juveniles in Secure Detention Facilities (Urbana: University of Illinois at Urbana-Champaign, 1983). These and other findings are in "Special Report: Prisoner Suicide," Detention Reporter May, 1986.

[136]Contacts are the National Center on Institutions and Alternatives in Alexandria, Virginia (703) 684-0373 or Juvenile and Criminal Justice International in Roseville, Minnesota (612) 481-9644.

may manifest itself later in the detention period. We are cautioned to be careful of the intoxicated individual who might not be thinking rationally, and there are cautions about the use of isolation. If the inexperienced person is placed in a jail setting without human contact, he or she may attempt suicide. We are told that suicides happen quickly after entry.[137] Therefore, it is imperative that staff be on the alert for potential suicidal behavior at screening. All new admissions must be screened by a health trained staff member, who can be a nurse or a health-trained correctional officer. All arresting officers and jail officers must be trained to recognize signs of potential suicide. What, then, are the first things to look for? What are the most immediate signs of suicide? The most common suicide profile is a person who:

> is age 25-30, single, male, white (except in large urban jails);
>
> is a first time arrestee or has an insignificant history of prior arrests;
>
> is arrested on a minor charge;
>
> is under the influence of alcohol;
>
> is excessively depressed, ashamed, or guilt-ridden over the crime, which may be more serious than normal in the person's mind;
>
> in combination with the above, has no documented history of mental illness or previous suicide attempts.[138]

Where possible, persons who meet this profile should be released, preferably referred to a helping agency. If held, the individual must be watched closely, especially in the early stages of detention. Persons who may not meet the above profile, who may be held in the facility, are persons with evidence of prior suicide attempts, a record of mental illness, a particularly heinous or bizarre crime (torture slaying, mass murder, etc.), and previous prison terms that present the very real possibility of long term incarceration. These persons should be carefully watched from the onset of detention.

---

[137]"Special Focus on: Suicide in Detention Facilities," Detention Reporter Nov., 1983: 5.

[138]Adapted from Joseph R. Rowan, "Almost All Suicides in Jails and Lockups Can Be Prevented If ...," (Roseville, Minnesota: Juvenile and Criminal Justice International, Inc., c. 1985).

Obvious signs of a potential suicide for inmates who have been detained for longer periods are (1) talking about suicide to staff or other inmates (2) a recent record of a prior attempt, (3) puncture or slash marks, or (4) evidence of a recent or current problem accompanied by depression or expressions of hopelessness. More subtle signs include (1) sudden mood swings, (2) sudden changes in habits, such as not shaving, (3) significant weight loss or gain, (4) vague references to death, like "I won't need the rock concert tickets," (5) knowledge (through letter or visit) of a family crisis, (6) giving away possessions to others, and (7) speaking in flat, emotionless tone with lack of feeling for anything.[139]

A recent study of jail suicide prevention in Cincinnati, Ohio, identified suicide "attempters" and "non-attempters," noting that the key discriminating factors were self-reported alcohol/drug abuse, self-reported suicidal thoughts, feelings of hopelessness, and a history of multiple suicide attempts.[140] Ninety-one percent of the substance abusers identified as "attempters" did attempt suicide; however, 54 percent of the "non-attempters" also were substance abusers. As a result of the study, criteria were developed that placed an inmate in a more secure mental health area of the facility if the screening interview found five or more suicide attempts, intoxication at admission, or "suicidal thoughts," i.e., expressed feelings of hopelessness.

Managing the Potential Suicide. The mismanagement (or non-management) of potentially suicidal inmates is one of the biggest areas of jail litigation, both adult and juvenile. There are professional differences regarding the best practices, especially those which use other inmates to watch potential suicides. The first approach, and possibly the most accepted, is to have the potentially suicidal inmate in a suicide-resistant/protrusion-free room or cell where 24 hour staff observation is possible, generally from a control booth. The second option is to use trained volunteers recruited from neighborhood crime watch or other groups with similar goals, or, as a last option, to use an inmate as a suicide watch companion, as does the Federal Bureau of Prisons. In this approach there is no

---

[139]Federal Prison System, Program Statement, "Suicide Prevention Program, No. 6341.1, June 18, 1982. This directive covers staff training in signs and symptoms, referral procedures, and observation (maintenance) procedures.

[140]Bobbie Hopes, "Jail Suicide Prevention: Effective Program Can Save Lives," Corrections Today December, 1986: 64-65.

possibility of physical contact, since the inmate is stationed across the hall, in front of the cell, or in an adjacent cell. A third approach is to place the inmate in a "multi-bed cell or dormitory with other selected inmates who can watch him ..."[141] This approach raises the possibility of inmate mischief, and for that reason is least desirable. No matter what approach is selected, continuous surveillance of the suicide-prone detainee is required.

American Correctional Association standards require screening for suicide, among other types of mental illnesses,[142] and careful observation of prisoners thought to be violent, suicidal, mentally disordered or who demonstrate unusual or bizarre behavior.[143] This certainly means more than every 30 minutes, which is the standard for all high and medium security inmates. Generally, personal observation is required on a continuing basis using one of the options cited in the preceding paragraph. The ACA Standards also require at least one single-occupancy room for seriously ill, mentally disordered, injured, or nonambulatory inmates who are held in the facility that allows continuing observation.[144] This type of cell, and other issues related to suicide prevention, are discussed in more detail in an extensive, 20-chapter Training Curriculum on Suicide Detection and Prevention in Jails and Prisons. This publication addresses many areas of suicide in custody that are not well-addressed elsewhere. It includes a discussion of controversial issues in suicide prevention, the "psychological autopsy" and suicide follow-up support for staff, arresting, and investigative officers (which also deals with the feelings of staff), suicide prevention, and first aid for hanging attempts.[145]

In the Curriculum Rowan and Hayes provide some guidelines for the construction of these types of security cells. However, they first note that overall jail construction which emphasizes a "new-generation," or third generation, supervision style (as discussed later

---

[141]Joseph R. Rowan.

[142]ACA Standard 2-5273.

[143]ACA Standard 2-5174.

[144]ACA Standard 2-5117.

[145]Joseph R. Rowan and Lindsey M. Hayes, Training Curriculum on Suicide Detection and Prevention in Jails and Prisons, developed by Jail Suicide Prevention Information Task Force: National Center on Institutions and Alternatives in cooperation with Juvenile and Criminal Justice International, Inc., with assistance from the National Sheriffs' Association (Washington, D.C.: National Institute of Justice, February, 1988).

in this chapter) is the most important consideration. This type of supervision places all staff in close contact with inmates in the units, allowing them to identify behavior changes more readily based on immediate observation and closer relationships with inmates.[146]

Rowan and Hayes also recommend avoiding isolation for suicide-prone inmates, a situation in which two of every three suicides occur. In addition, special cells can be constructed that reduce the type of fixtures available for completing a suicide by hanging. Glazing (transparent plastic), thin steel plates with holes, or wire mesh can be placed over bars to allow ventilation and increase contact. Large vision panels should replace "peep-holes," and there should be no electrical outlets. Beds should be solid concrete with rounded edges or molded plastic, totally enclosed, as should seating fixtures. They point out that an inmate can commit suicide by lying underneath the bed with the noose tied to the bedsprings — 13 minutes to death. The use of closed-circuit TV and audio monitoring is recommended, with assistance close at hand. An outside view is recommended to reduce disorientation.[147] All fire precautions cited elsewhere must receive special consideration in special cells, especially the use of fire-retardant mattresses (with no seams to be used as cords for hanging). Wall padding is not allowed in many states due to its fire potential, and there are those who say it promotes greater violence in the cell. Foam rubber walls and floors can be used in strip cells, but they are difficult to maintain and will tear. Chapter Seven addresses the construction of jail design in relation to suicide detection and prevention.

The International Association of Chiefs of Police have produced two "Training Keys" targeted at police lockups for use in training staff in the identification and management of the suicide risk. The principles found apply to lockups, jails, or prisons. Also, a "Special Report [on] Prisoner Suicide" can be found in the Detention Reporter. This 54-page report summarizes case law in this area and provides a 15 page "Prisoner Suicide Inventory," which is designed to assess the operational and physical setting of the jail in managing potential suicides. A 2-page booking interview sheet for medical, social and psychological problems is provided that could be very useful in screening for potential suicides.[148]

---

[146]Rowan and Hayes 16-1.

[147]Rowan and Hayes 16-3.

[148]"Special Report, Prisoner Suicide," Detention Reporter April, 1986.

III. Supervision of Inmates

The basic functions of the jail have been identified as pretrial detention, confinement of offenders after sentencing prior to transfer, and the management of sentenced offenders for short sentences, usually misdemeanants. Screening out the physically ill and emotionally disturbed where possible has been discussed, as has the identification of types of offenders and related management problems. This section is concerned with the provision of security within the facility and types of management that may be most effective. The use of facilities for sentenced offenders and prerelease programs will be addressed also.

A. Contact with the Public

While visiting is discussed at length in chapter five, it is mentioned here due to its security implications. Visiting is a major concern of facility security because contact with others can lead to the exchange of contraband where contact is allowed. The U.S. Supreme Court has stated that visiting by relatives and others does not require contact visits.[149] Maintenance of community ties by inmates is, however, a sound management tool used by many detention facilities. Contact visits are a good first step for inmates and their families in helping the inmate to return to the community.

Unless reasonable belief is found to suggest otherwise, attorneys must receive contact visits with their clients. Attorneys need the ability to pass privileged papers to and from inmates. These visits can be observed but not monitored. Visits by media representatives are not privileged and can be denied, although good programs of media contact have been instituted by many agencies, including the Federal Bureau of Prisons.

B. Security and Control

Security and control includes all procedures that ensure the safety and security of staff and inmates in the facility. Variations in types of supervision, required services, and programs all are secondary to maintaining security and order in the facility. The courts at all levels, for the most part, support staff who can demonstrate that they were acting in the interests of the security, order, and safety of

---

[149] Block v. Rutherford, 104 S.Ct. 3227 (1984).

staff and inmates of a correctional facility when they withdrew a particular service or program.

Staffing levels have been addressed in several Federal District Court and a few Appeals Court cases. Rarely, if at all, will the courts specify exact staff to inmate ratios. However, where inmates were subjected to abuse, assault, or mistreatment due to lack of adequate supervision, more staff was ordered.[150] In a Texas jail case the District Court ordered a ratio of 1 officer to 20 inmates to protect inmates and provide adequate security. A ratio of 1 to 30 was seen as inadequate.[151] The jail administration may be held liable for failure to supervise,[152] inadequate supervision,[153] or failure to conduct prisoner checks.[154] The Fifth Circuit has required that: (1) a correctional officer visit each inmate-occupied area once an hour, (2) one officer be present on each floor of the jail at all times,[155] (3) there be some assurance that the number of officers bears a "reasonable relationship to the total number of inmates," and (4) inmate to staff ratios be as high as almost 1:4 in state prisons.[156] Lack of funding, as with other deficiencies, will usually not be a satisfactory explanation for staff deficiencies, as found in the 11th Federal Circuit when the county commissioners were held liable for assault on a prisoner.[157]

Audio and visual surveillance. Based on both professional standards and court decree, reliance on audio or video monitors does not constitute adequate supervision. American Correctional Association standards recommend the use of such equipment primarily in hallways, elevators, corridors, or at points on the security perimeter, such as entrances and exits.[158] Such devices do not

---

[150]Gates v. Collier, 5th Cir., 1974, and Rhem v. Malcolm, S.D.N.Y., 1974.

[151]Alberti v. Sheriff of Harris Co. (1975); See Alberti v. Heard (1984), which required a minimum staffing plan for the jail.

[152]Davis v. Zahradnick (1979).

[153]Redmond v. Baxley (1979) and Campbell v. McGruder (1982).

[154]Griffin v. Smith (1980) and Clappier v. Flynn (1979).

[155]Smith v. Sullivan (1977).

[156]Williams v. Edwards (1977).

[157]Saunders v. Chatham County (1984).

[158] ACA Standard 2-5168.

substitute for staff supervision and personal contact. Although, a Michigan appeals court ordered a case to trial based upon a staff member turning off an audio monitor for a boy who subsequently hanged himself.[159]

Critical Concerns in Maintaining Security. The important concerns for maintaining security and order in institutions have been consistent over time. Reports on the aftermath of riots and disturbances usually cite as causes several activities that are not directly related to staff supervision, design, or hardware, but are nonetheless security matters. Ask yourself the following questions to discover if these issues affect your facility:

- Are officers in the units regularly, and do they remain in contact with the inmate population? Is there constant communication between staff and inmates in order to prevent unrest and potential problems?

- Can officers see the inmates from centralized control booths, around corners, etc.? Do stairways, pillars, doors, toilet shields, or glare from windows obstruct vision? Is security equipment in good repair?

- Are facility rules reasonable and is related disciplinary policy fairly administered?

- Are basic inmate needs met? Is the food good? Are inmates safe from assault? Are they clothed properly? Is medical care available? Can they communicate with family and legal counsel? Can they secure their possessions? Is there hot water for showers? What about soap, toothpaste, and other personal hygiene items? Is there a regular recreation period?

- Is the heating, ventilation, and air conditioning adequate for staff and inmates? Because the risk of disturbances increases in warm weather, should the facility be air conditioned? What are the alternatives if the air conditioning fails?

---

[159] Brewer v. Perrin (1984), Southgate City Jail, Michigan.

- Is the facility functional for daily living and work (for staff and inmates)? Is living space clean and in good condition? Is the facility too noisy in areas where people congregate? Are there areas where inmates can find some privacy (i.e., library, chapel, recreation area, etc.)? Can inmates and staff move through the facility easily? Are stairways or elevators a problem?

- Are there some amenities? Can telephone calls be made from an area with some privacy? (A long telephone cord sometimes helps.) Are smoking materials provided, and is smoking allowed in designated areas? Are there enough radios, television sets, and newspapers? Is there a canteen? Are books available on the units or in a library? Can inmates work in the facility if they want to? Are there some programs for inmates who cannot work?

- If dormitories are used, are inmates properly screened for group living and are they used primarily for "short-timers," weekenders, trusties, and/or work release inmates? Can inmates secure their personal belongings in lockers?

With these minimal concerns provided, you should be looking at some new methods of inmate supervision designed to improve your security. The most recent innovation is direct supervision, which is compatible with the goals stated above. While its use may not be practical unless you can renovate the facility or build a new one, some programs of direct supervision can be operated out of existing dormitory settings.

C. Direct versus Indirect Supervision

The primary goals of security are to develop a facility that will (1) prevent escapes (2) ensure public safety (3) keep inmates and staff free from physical harm, and (4) establish and implement procedures that protect the staff and administration from negligence lawsuits. For these reasons it is important to know something about direct supervision and how it might be useful in jail operations.

Again, your principal concern is with a facility that meets both security and operational goals, such a facility being defined as follows:

> A functional facility operates consistently with its mission statement and provides ... a greater sense of safety for staff and inmates, less destructive (or "normalized") inmate behavior, minimal staff turnover through greater worker satisfaction, a physical plant which operates efficiently with minimal maintenance problems, and a more humane and positive environment based on the implementation of sound design concepts consistent with the standards of good practice of the field.[160]

The "state of the art" in inmate supervision has moved historically from what is known as a traditional form of supervision through more current direct supervision forms, with some mixture of the two styles of supervision. The problem in interpreting the language of these changes is that architectural terms are mixed with management styles. For example, "modular" design refers to distinct architectural units that "cluster" around a control booth. This design creates a supervision style that is remote, in that the officer is not "on" the unit with the inmates, but an officer designated as "rover" or "walker" may come onto the units briefly during each shift. Care must be taken to sort out these terms to see how architecture relates to inmate supervision.

Styles of Supervision. Traditional supervision took place in the older, corridor-style jails and prisons. Architects have come to call these jails "first generation" because they use "linear/intermittent" surveillance, that is, supervision of inmates is not continuous largely due to the architecture of the facility. A "second generation" or "remote supervision" form of supervision also has been identified. This design places the officer in a control booth from which the officer can see all the cells, not unlike the old circular prison, or "panopticon design," at Stateville, Illinois. In jails these are called "podular remote" designs because the units are smaller modular "pods." The "third generation" or "podular direct" supervision designs have eliminated the control booth and rely on direct and continuous contact supervision of inmates by officers in day room areas outside the cells.

Direct Supervision. The field of corrections has endorsed the management and design concept of direct supervision, which is intended to create more "normalized" prison and jail environments

---

160 Sechrest and Price (1985) 23.

through the use of "advanced practices." These designs and practices attempt to achieve a more humane environment, and rely more on classification, less use of concrete and steel, and greater control through staff management. Direct supervision is referred to as "podular/direct supervision," or "third generation design."[161] It was developed as "functional unit management" by the Federal Prison System in the mid-1970's and is used in its Metropolitan Correctional Centers and about a dozen jails around the country. It has been hailed as a major breakthrough for safe, cost efficient and effective operation of a correctional facility. However, its successes or failures have, for the most part, not been objectively evaluated.[162] For that reason alone its implementation must be carefully considered. Also, there is increasing evidence that crowding in a jail will defeat the effectiveness of the direct supervision approach. One study of officers' attitudes toward the change from traditional to new generation jails found change coming slower than expected, as discussed more fully below.

Some counties that claim to have used direct supervision with success include the Contra Costa County Detention Facility in Martinez, California; the Manhattan House of Detention for Men, New York City; Clark County, Las Vegas, Nevada; Dade County Stockade, Miami, Florida, Larimer County Detention Facility, Fort Collins, Colorado; and the Pima County Adult Detention Center in Tucson, Arizona. All Federal Metropolitan Correctional Centers and some correctional institutions operate on this model. Podular/direct jail design and management is defined as follows:

> In the podular/direct model each unit is staffed by one officer in direct control of 40 to 50 inmates. It is the responsibility of the officer to control the behavior of the inmates in his/her unit, keeping negative behavior to a minimum and reducing tension. In this model, the role of the management team is to structure the environmental forces so that correctional officers will be successful in proactive control.[163]

---

[161]William (Ray) Nelson, "New Generation Jails" Corrections Today April, 1983: 1; see W. Raymond Nelson, "The Origins of the Podular Direct Supervision Concept: An Eyewitness Account" American Jails Spring, 1988: 8-14.

[162]See James B. Wells, "Direct Supervision: Panacea or Fad? Does it Warrant Full Acceptance?" American Jails Spring, 1987: 46-49.

[163]Nelson (1983) 3-4.

This definition does not include the unsupervised dormitory. The design of the facility assumes single celling and the commingling of inmates in common day room areas most of the day under the direct supervision of a correctional officer.

In the more than 10 years of using the direct supervision model, much has been learned about this management approach in the shaping of environmental forces that can prevent negative types of behavior on the living units. Effective podular/direct supervision requires that all of the principles of management related to its operation to be in place.[164] Much of the effectiveness of direct supervision is attributed to the communication between officers and inmates.

In a 1987 article in American Jails, the Bureau Commander of the Pima County Adult Detention Center indicates that "[In examining] the direct supervision facilities in operation today, there can be no doubt that the concept is extremely successful."[165] He emphasizes the importance of implementing the eight principles of direct supervision that will make it work. These are modelled after those found in the NIC Publication Direct Supervision Models, in which eight "Principles and Dynamics of Direct Supervision Models" are elaborated upon.[166] These principles include (1) effective control of inmates in the facility, (2) effective supervision of inmates, inclusive of all forms of improved interaction, (3) the need for competent, trained staff, (4) concern for the safety of staff and inmates, (5) manageable and cost effective operations, (6) effective communication, (7) classification and orientation of all inmates, and (8) justice and fairness, i.e., just and fair treatment of inmates by staff.

Commander Davis emphasizes the need for leadership, feedback mechanisms, and evaluation of performance to provide effective supervision. He offers some advice for a manageable and cost effective operation that includes a four step problem-solving

---

[164]Nelson and O'Toole (1983) 7-18, and Ray Nelson, Michael O'Toole, Barbara Krauth, and Coralie G. Whitmore, Direct Supervision Models (Boulder, Colorado: National Institute of Corrections Information Center, May, 1984).

[165]Russell M. Davis, "Direct Supervision As An Organizational Management System," American Jails Spring, 1987: 50.

[166]Nelson et al. (1984).

strategy.[167] These four steps are (1) to define the real or "root" problem, (2) to examine that problem in relation to the other aspects of the organization, (3) to analyze the problem in terms of the eight principles cited above, and (4) to develop and implement a plan of action that will lead to the solution.[168]

Traditional Supervision. The direct supervision approach contrasts most directly with traditional inmate management practices known as "linear/intermittent surveillance." This type of supervision, still in use in the majority of jails (and prisons) can be described as follows:

> The design is generally rectangular, with corridors leading to either single or multiple occupancy cells arranged at right angles to the corridor ... management ... is oriented towards intermittent surveillance and supervision [requiring officers to] patrol to see into cells or housing areas. When in a position to observe one cell, they are seldom able to observe others; thus, while the inmates are not being directly observed they are essentially unsupervised.[169]

This design may work well in a maximum security unit or isolation unit where contact with dangerous inmates must be kept to a minimum. However, if crowded conditions have led to double celling this design can only yield management problems.

Remote Supervision. Podular/remote surveillance represents something of a compromise between traditional and direct supervision models. It is similar to the podular/direct approach in that inmate housing units are divided into small units or pods and as such represents a more recent development in facility architecture. Like linear surveillance, the design places the officer in an enclosed, secure control booth to observe all inmates from that one point, generally across a day room area. The difference is that the officer can see the doors of all cells without leaving the control booth. Contact with the inmates is provided through a grill window or speaker system:

> The podular/remote surveillance design facilitates a reactive management style, i.e., it is organized to react to inmate management problems rather than to prevent them.

---

[167]Nelson et al. (1984) 50-53.

[168]Nelson et al. (1984) 53.

[169]Nelson (1983) 3-4.

> From secure observational booths staff have minimal contact with inmates; they are only in a position to observe and to summon help to react to inmate misconduct within a pod.[170]

Control is enhanced by various types of security hardware and equipment, most of which is very expensive. Sight surveillance may be limited by stairways, columns or awkward viewing angles (usually to the sides).

This type of supervision is almost always supplemented by roving patrols of one or two officers who circulate throughout the facility, coming into each unit every two or three hours on an intermittent schedule. Under these conditions, nine inmates made their escape from the Baltimore County Jail in 1981 after over ten hours of sustained effort to defeat a security window in a cell. The window was not observable from the control booth due to a closed stairwell and a support column between the booth and the window. The "secure" windows are now covered with steel grates, welded in place at considerable cost.

Even backup systems are of no avail if the primary system can be deactivated, as shown in a recent Florida escape by a murderer and a burglar/child molester with 30 years to do in prison. These two inmates escaped from Cross City Correctional Institution near Gainesville, Florida, by tossing a copper wire attached to a rope over two power lines, which shorted the prison's electricity. In the available 30 to 40 seconds of darkness they clambered over 10- and 12-foot fences to freedom. To add insult to injury they used the "cool hand Luke" ploy of giving the bloodhound the scent of hot peppers, which caused swelling of the nose and put him out of action.[171]

D. Cost Comparisons of Supervision Models

Cost comparisons are available between the podular/remote designs (second generation) and the direct supervision designs (third generation). One such comparison changed the minds of the Dade County, Florida, County Commission, from construction of a second generation facility to adoption of a third generation facility design. After the architect conducted an extensive cost analysis comparing all three design and management approaches for the new detention

---

[170]Nelson (1983) 4-5.

[171]Miami Herald 29 Sept. 1987: 4BR.

center, the third generation, or podular/direct supervision approach showed improved operational performance, cost savings from reduced staffing, and a safer and more efficient facility to operate. Hypothetical designs revealed that a second generation 1,000 bed jail would cost $25 million to build and require 295 staff to operate the facility at an annual operational expense of $9.3 million. The third generation facility was more expensive to build at a cost of $37 million, but only required 172 staff positions and an annual operational budget of $6.2 million. The approximately $3 million savings a year in operating costs would pay for the institution in 12.5 years.[172]

All management and design principles of podular/direct operations were incorporated into the facility design in Dade County, and staff of the Dade County Department of Corrections and Rehabilitation have attended NIC training over a two year period in preparation for the proposed opening of the new facility in late 1988. Until the opening, staff have continued to use third generation management principles in a temporary dormitory structure called the "stockade."[173] Although this facility houses mainly minimum custody offenders, a recent article in the local paper claimed success for the "experimental barrier-free jail" in Miami: "Violence and vandalism are down. Discipline is honored. Walls are graffiti free. Officials are assured the concept will work."[174] As indicated above, there is every indication that it should work when the new facility is opened. However, a recent six month follow-up study of officers' attitudes toward the change from traditional to third generation jails in maximum security surroundings (in a Western state) found less dramatic changes than expected.[175] The change from traditional to podular direct supervision was found to improve job satisfaction, but

---

[172]"Comparative Analysis of Design Schemes," Dade County Stockade Expansion, Dade County, Florida (Miami: Harper & Buzinec, January 26, 1983); see also Stephen Horn, "The Cost Benefits of Podular Designed and Directly Supervised Correctional Facilities, February 16, 1984 (mimeo.).

[173]Randy Atlas, "Cost Saving Aspects of a Third Generation Detention Facility: A Case Study, The Dade County Stockade Expansion," draft for the AIA Design Resource File, 1984).

[174]Miami Herald 3 Aug. 1985: 3B; a departmental study found a four-fold reduction of incidents in the direct supervision unit compared to the conventional unit; cf. James Brannock, "Third Generation Study," memorandum, Dade County Corrections and Rehabilitation Department, January 29, 1987 (mimeo.).

[175]Linda L. Zupan, Ben A. Menke, and Nicholas P. Lovrich, "Implementing Organizational Change: From Traditional to New Generation Jail Operations," presented at the March, 1987, meeting of the Academy of Criminal Justice Sciences (mimeo.).

the changes in attitudes were not as great as expected. The change to direct contact may prove disruptive and can produce stress in correctional officers. A period of adaptation is suggested, even after training, which might last as long as six months.

The direct supervision (podular/direct) approach has received support from the National Institute of Corrections, the American Institute of Architects' Committee on Architecture for Justice, the American Correctional Association and the Commission on Accreditation for Corrections.[176] The concept is included in two new standards created by the ACA which state that "Written policy and procedure facilitate personal contact and interaction between staff and inmates" and, for new plant construction, "Physical plant design facilitates personal contact and interaction between staff and inmates."[177]

Some Cautions. Crowding will defeat the direct supervision design, as will poor training of staff in its implementation. The new facility should not be opened before staff are trained and ready to make the change to a new supervision style. Staff require a period of adjustment to this new form of supervision, especially where they are used to more traditional environments. Inmates may also have difficulty adjusting to the new environment. In one of the first such facilities inmate suicides went up as inmates found less crowding, more privacy in their cells, and greater movement in the facility. This resulted in the need for a better inmate screening system, which reduced the problem. Finally, political problems may arise if local officials are not fully aware of the type of supervision to be used. Direct supervision does not fit the vision of the lean and tough ("spartan") jail desired by some members of the community, including some judges and public officials.

IV. Community Programs

Many larger jails have work release programs, authorized by statute, for offenders sentenced to the facility (about 40% of the jails have such programs). The term "work release" is often used interchangeably with "work furlough," which has come to be more specific to special unescorted leaves provided for crisis situations, family deaths, and the like. Both types of programs share the same

---

[176]Nelson & O'Toole (1983).

[177]ACA Standards 2-5134-1 and 2-5171-1 (1984) 37, 41.

criteria for release on unescorted trips into the community. Work release programs are often operated out of minimum security facilities separate from the main pretrial facility. They allow inmates to spend their days outside the facility going to work or to school and returning to the facility at night. Such programs are particularly useful for employable offenders who must pay fines, restitution, or provide support for their families.

Critical to any type of release program is community support. Before attempting a release program it is suggested that a community advisory board be formed, or an existing advisory board approve of the concept. This may also be critical in finding a location for the program that is in, near or has good access to transportation to areas of employment. Community support becomes more critical if a serious incident occurs with one of the releasees. An entire program can be jeopardized by such an incident.

Community release programs require a special staff of counselors or employment specialists who can screen inmates for release, locate jobs, and see that inmates reach them successfully each day. Special accounting procedures are also required because working inmates are required to pay a fixed fee per day to the system for their upkeep, often returning millions of dollars to the taxpayers annually.

Work release programs are ideally suited to assisting offenders in finding jobs that they may retain after the jail experience and in easing their transition back into the community. The major problem with these programs is the transmission of contraband into the facility from the community, which requires that careful search procedures be implemented with immediate disciplinary action for violations. Security concerns are the principal reason it is important that this entire unit be separate from the maximum security population in the main jail.

Liability concerns may also exist for community release programs. At least some jurisdictions recognize that the correctional administrator's negligent failure to prevent harm to persons foreseeably subject to risk of injury by an offender makes the administrator liable to a party injured by the offender. This concept has been applied to allow third parties injured by offenders in release programs to sue program administrators.[178] Where such suits

---

[178] Doe v. United Social and Mental Health Services, Inc. 670 F.Supp. 1121 (D.Conn. 1987).

are allowed, risk obviously will increase as more dangerous offenders are admitted into minimum custody programs.

This problem is especially acute when drug dependent offenders are placed in pretrial or sentenced release programs, and often over half of the people on such programs have drug abuse histories. The possible return to drug use must be randomly monitored and violators must be quickly returned to the main jail. Such a program has operated very successfully for several years at the Montgomery County Pretrial Detention Center in Rockville, Maryland, which is described in chapter five.[179]

V. The Important Concerns, or What Must You Do?

Many experts concur regarding the negative effects of the traditional types of facilities and their related supervision problems. However, these facilities continue to be operated largely because these are the types of facilities most jail administrators have inherited. The debate on the merits of direct versus indirect supervision has little meaning if you are stuck with a small facility of traditional design, although if an annex or addition is planned a direct supervision unit may be the ideal choice.

Living with what you have requires that surveillance systems be improved through design changes, if possible, and through an evaluation of staff coverage. Concurrently, inmate screening and classification should be evaluated for possible improvements, and methods of communication — staff/staff and staff/inmates — should be improved as much as possible. As it becomes possible to renovate or build a new facility the newer designs must be considered in relation to what is known at the time of new facility planning.

County commissioners or city council members who feel the only way to ensure public safety is by using traditional methods of incarceration may wish to consider the construction of a facility that will allow for the use of both direct and indirect supervision units. In any case, their decision about the jail you must operate may depend on how they are influenced by local law enforcement and court officials, as well as by current public attitudes toward offenders (the

---

[179]Dale K. Sechrest and John F. Farrell, "Uses of Urinalysis in a Pre-Release Center," in Drug Abuse Testing: Successful Models for Treatment and Control in Correctional Programs (College Park, Maryland: American Correctional Association, 1981) 10-12.

"prevailing climate"). During the planning process it is wise to have available adequate facts and figures on the number and types of inmates (security classifications) to be managed in the new facility, the number and rank of staff needed, the type of design you favor, and the funds, staffing, and other resources necessary to build and operate the facility.

This confluence of interests — yours, local officials, the public, and criminal justice system representatives — often results in the adoption of a more current design that can be adapted to more traditional supervision in times of fiscal crisis or crowding. That is, living units are built with control booths that may not be used until needed. This is not sound planning. The types of supervision used will vary throughout the facility based on the security classification system, as traditionally done in the use of dormitories and segregation areas. The use of direct supervision can be beneficial to staff and administration, but cannot be done with "half-measures." If the operators of very small facilities (under 50 beds) must use traditional or podular/remote surveillance due to the limitations of staff, space, and budget considerations, they should be aware of its problems. These problems relate most specifically to inmate violence on the units when staff are not in full control of them. All jails should be implementing the principles of direct supervision in all areas of the jail.

No matter what the facility design may be, the administrator or supervisor will want to emphasize the development of the kinds of skills found in direct supervision. Training should emphasize communication and interpersonal skills, with training for all staff in order to prepare them to try new supervision models in all types of physical settings. For example, the new 852 single cell ($46,000 per bed) facility in Clark County, Nevada, created 48-cell modular units ("mini-jails") and trained officers in direct supervision methods, although it does not appear that all units are operated that way.[180]

---

[180]Gordon F. Yach, "Clark County, Meeting Design Challenges," Corrections Today April, 1986: 118.

CHAPTER FIVE: RIGHTS TO MINIMAL CARE AND PROGRAMS

I. Fundamental Rights

Beyond basic security and control, there are two levels of activity that must concern the jail staff. The first are the services that are required by law, and the second are optional programs that are desirable, or "nice to have," depending on facility size and resources. At a recent jail training meeting participants learned from each other that inmate programs are as important to small jails as they are to medium and large jails. The main differences for small jails were the greater use of part time personnel and less variety in programs available.[181]For large or small jails programs are seen as a major inmate management tool, as essential as basic services.

The first concern is with services required by law. The following are required for inmates:

Access to the courts and legal services

A reasonable degree of personal safety

Nutritional meals

Good medical care[182]

Safe and sanitary living conditions

Communication and visiting, both privileged (attorneys, clergy) and with the family[183]

Written rules and disciplinary procedures

Regular exercise

---

[181] Chuck Cadigan, "Programs and Small Jails,"A.J.A. Newsletter Summer, 1987.

[182]Surveys show that 77% of all jails have no medical facilities, but this does not preclude immediate access to services and staff training; see "Jail, The New Mental Institution," Cadigan 5.

[183]As indicated elsewhere, media contact is not required, but some jails have very successful procedures for allowing inmate access to the media.

The following services are desirable and recommended for inmates:

Work programs in the facility

Work release/study release programs[184]

Educational programs

Recreation/leisure activities

While higher standards are encouraged, and may be mandated by court orders in some jurisdictions, there are some minimum guidelines for the management of jail inmates. These guidelines apply whether they are pretrial detainees or sentenced prisoners. They are based on case law and national standards and are summarized as follows — not in order of preference — with commentary in subsequent sections:

- The abolition of strip cells to punish or restrain. The Supreme Court has said that pretrial detainees may not be punished, which means that any condition or restriction imposed must be "reasonably related to a legitimate governmental objective" — that is, rules cannot be arbitrary or purposeless.[185]

- The right of the inmate, upon arrival at the jail, to make a reasonable number of phone calls to counsel, a bondsman, and family members, and, thereafter, to make at least one weekly phone call.

- The right to search procedures that avoid unnecessary embarrassment or indignity to the inmate, to the extent possible based on security needs.

- The right to a rudimentary administrative hearing before the denial of privileges, such as visits, or placement in segregated cells.[186]

---

[184]Surveys show that 75% of all jails have no rehabilitation or treatment facilities or programs ; "Jails, the New Mental Institutions," Cadigan 5.

[185]Bell v. Wolfish 441 U.S. 520 (1979).

[186]Hewitt v. Helms, 459 U.S. 460 (1983).

- The right to confidential visits at reasonable times with one's attorney, including communication if in segregation (at least by telephone).

- The right to receive, free of charge if indigent, the necessities for communication with counsel and the courts (paper, pen, pencils, etc.).

- The right to contact with a representative of one's religious beliefs.

- The right to send unopened mail to one's attorney and receive unread privileged mail, although inspected in the inmate's presence, and to send and receive uncensored mail from family and friends, although it may be rejected with good reasons and inspected for contraband.

- The right to adequate nutrition and the essentials of personal hygiene, including soap, articles of feminine hygiene, cleaning materials, hot and cold water, a mattress, sheet, towel, blanket, clean clothing, a toothbrush, toothpaste, shaving supplies and the opportunity to shave regularly.

- The right, in the general population or segregation, to the basic amenities of daily living, including mail privileges, the necessities of communication (paper, pencils, etc.), normal toilet facilities, a sink and running water, a sanitary mattress, regular meals, access to a reasonable number of books and magazines and to a reasonable minimum amount of physical exercise. For segregated inmates, exercise is generally seen as one hour a day, seven days a week.

- The right to reasonable and appropriate medical attention, including:

  A general physical examination within a reasonable time after admission;

  The right to unimpeded access to a nurse or other health provider as soon as possible after making a medical complaint;

  Diagnosis and treatment of medical ailments by a physician or other person licensed to practice in the jurisdiction (e.g., physician's assistant under general supervision of an M.D.);

Medical coverage at all times by a health provider authorized under the jurisdiction's medical practice act;

Arrangements for prompt access to a hospital for emergency treatment;

Specialized treatment for medical problems (e.g. diabetes, asthma), including special diets;

A medically supervised detoxification program for drug abusers and alcoholics;

- The right to possess and receive literature (books and magazines) unless restrictions are necessary to further significant governmental interests related to the security of the jail. (See discussion of Bell v. Wolfish.)

While not absolute rights, that is, they may be restricted or denied, regular visits with family and friends are recognized as important in jail management. Where security permits it, they should be allowed. Also important is the right to express one's religious and political beliefs without interference, provided institutional order and security are not compromised.

II. Explanation of Rights

A. Access to the Courts and to Legal Services

Jail staff have a positive duty not to hinder inmates' efforts to question the legality of their confinement, to seek redress for illegal conditions of confinement, and/or to pursue remedies for civil legal problems. The facility must provide "meaningful access to the courts," which may include the provision of a law library or adequate assistance from persons trained in the law.[187] There are variations, as in Florida, where the 11th Circuit only mandated law libraries, not attorneys, stating that assistance from other (trained) inmates was satisfactory. Staff must transfer inmates to and from the court and make arrangements for written or verbal communications between inmates and the courts and their legal counsel.

---

[187] Bounds v. Smith, 430 U.S. 817 (1977); see also Collins (1986) 23-31.

The courts have upheld the right of inmates to receive attorney visits. However, some restrictions are possible, including the number of attorneys who may visit at one time, specification of the bar to which they belong, and prohibition of tape recorders. Attorneys may be denied visits at meal times or after 9:00 p.m.,[188] but minimum visiting hours can be required, such as 9 a.m. to 5 p.m. on weekdays and 9 a.m. to 8 p.m. on weekdays.[189] There should be an adequate visiting area for the attorney, and conversations must not be monitored, although they may be observed.[190] An attorney may be represented by a law student, law clerk, or other legal para-professional, although notice of the use of such an agent must be provided to facility staff.[191]

Inmates have the right to consult with other inmates, including "jailhouse lawyers," regarding their cases; however, this right does not validate the existence of jailhouse legal practitioners if adequate legal assistance is available, and specific restrictions may apply.[192] The jailhouse lawyer may provide help in the absence of "reasonable alternatives," may not be paid by other inmates, may not sign legal documents, and may be limited to specific times and places for providing such assistance. Assistance need not extend to jailhouse lawyers in other institutions.[193]

What legal assistance is required? There is some guidance from the courts as to how much legal assistance for offenders is enough. The provision of attorneys to assist pretrial offenders or convicted inmates to defend themselves in their particular cases is a function of the arresting jurisdiction. Assistance is usually handled through the office of the public defender, and questions in this area should be referred to that office. For pretrial inmates the standards are clearly higher than for convicted offenders. Jurisdictions must provide attorneys to offenders who are appealing their convictions where

---

[188]Miller v. Carson 401 F.Supp. 835 (1975) aff'd 563 f.2d 741 (5th Cir. 1977).

[189]Inmates of Suffolk County Jail v. Eisenstadt,360 F.Supp. 676 (Mass. 1973).

[190]Collins v. Schoonfield, 344 F.Supp. 255 (D.Md. 1972); Baker v. Beto, 349 F.Supp. 1263 (S.D. Tex. 1972); Adams v. Carlson, 488 F.2d 619 (7th Cir. 1973).

[191]Procunier v. Martinez, 416 U.s. 396 (1974).

[192]Palmer, 1985 101-102; see Johnson v. Avery, 89 S.Ct. 747 (1969), and Cruz v. Hauck, 515 F.2d 322 (5th Cir. 1975).

[193]Heft v. Carlson, 489 F.2d (5th Cir. 1973).

appeal is a matter of right,[194] although attorneys are not required where appeal is discretionary.[195] However, Whitebread and Slobogin indicate that most jurisdictions provide counsel to indigents at all appeals.[196]

Counsel appointed to represent an inmate in a criminal proceeding does not necessarily satisfy the jail's duty to provide "meaningful access to the courts" since the duty includes providing access to allow the inmate to pursue civil matters — such as suing the jail! Appointed criminal counsel typically will not provide voluntary representation in civil matters. The Supreme Court has not ruled that inmates have a constitutional right to lawyers to pursue civil matters.

As noted earlier, in 1977 the Supreme Court addressed the issue of legal assistance for convicted offenders in the case of Bounds v. Smith (1977), discussed in Collins (1986), chapter 3 and Collins (1987) at pages 19-20. The Court required prison authorities to provide prisoners with adequate law libraries or some other viable source of legal knowledge. The court did not rule that inmates have a constitutional right to lawyers to pursue civil matters. The "alternative means" of receiving assistance can include training inmates as paralegal assistants working under the supervision of attorneys, the use of paraprofessionals or law students, and voluntary, part time or full time attorneys working with legal assistance or public defender programs.[197] The provision of a law library is the best protection against the charge that inmates are receiving no legal assistance, and some help in using the library seems required. With these procedures in place, your legal assistance program will stand a good chance of being favorably evaluated by the courts. Collins discusses the need to provide "meaningful access to the courts" for the rich and the poor, but only if they are in jail.[198]

None of the alternatives to the law library appear to be as successful as the law library itself. Administrators of large jails

---

[194]Douglas v. California, 372 U.S. 353 (1963).

[195]Ross v. Moffitt, 417 U.S. 600 (1974).

[196]See Charles H. Whitebread and Christopher Slobogin, Criminal Procedure (Mineola, NY: The Foundation Press, 1986) 694-695.

[197]Palmer (1985) 118.

[198]Collins (1987) 20-21.

have opted for the purchase of a law library, usually spending about $30,000 to $35,000, with maintenance costs running at about 10 percent per year of the original investment ($3,000 to $5,000 per year).

Smaller jails have to be creative. They can make arrangements to use an existing library, although this practice entails security risks. Standards for Nebraska jails recommended a smaller law library for jails under 100 inmates and a full library for those over 100 inmates.[199]

While various organizations have published recommended law library lists, most such lists can be criticized as omitting key items, not being up to date (and hence missing new items or relying on documents no longer in print), or suggesting approaches, such as varying the size of the library and its contents with the size of the jail, none of which have been tested in court. Jail administrators should be very careful in relying on such lists, particularly if the list is more than three years old. Due to the need for various local reporters and procedural guidelines, it is best to confer with an attorney in your state to locate an acceptable list of publications. As a guide to discussing the content of such a library with an attorney, you may want to consider the following legal publications for a law library:

A leading law dictionary;

A simple book on criminal procedure;

A simple treatise on evidence or trial techniques;

A simple book on constitutional law;

A simple treatise on criminal law;

Rules of the United States District Court for your State, the State Supreme Court, the local district, county and municipal courts that have jurisdiction over facility inmates;

A current copy of your State Statutes;

---

[199]Nebraska Jail Standards (Nebraska State Bar Association Committee on Correctional Law and Practice, 1977) 124-125.

A list of all lawyers in the county with their phone numbers and business addresses;

A copy of any federal, state or local standards that are applicable to the facility, including laws relevant to the development of policy and procedures for the facility.

Any other suitable materials, such as a guide to the drafting of legal papers, relevant publications on criminal procedure, civil rights, prisoners rights, etc.

Your State's Supreme Court Reports; State Digest (West) or Regional Reporter or equivalent as approved by legal counsel;

Federal Supplement and Federal 2d Reporters (West), beginning in the mid-1960's; and,

Digest to United States Reports (U.S. Government Printing Office), Supreme Court Reporter (West Publishing Company), Supreme Court Reporter, Lawyers' Edition (Lawyers' Cooperative; Bancroft Whitney) or equivalent as approved by legal counsel.

Again, you must seek legal advice in developing the law library and/or in evaluating current holdings. Above all, do not have the evaluation of the collection done by a book salesperson. Their hearts may be in the right place, but their books will be on their minds and the collection may be hopelessly limited.

Finally, there must be a place to house the law library sufficient for the size of the collection, with sufficient space for expansion every year, and space for inmates to work that is based on potential usage. Tables should be provided to seat a minimum of six inmates at one time for a facility of 50 inmates. Lighting should be at least 30 foot-candles at table level. Access should be provided for at least 8 hours per day, including Saturdays, with at least three of these hours after 5:00 p.m. on weekdays to accommodate inmate day workers. The choice of providing typewriters and paper and copying for inmates who cannot pay for them, is yours, although they are recommended in national standards.

B. A Reasonable Degree of Personal Safety

Two major aspects of personal safety must be considered: (1) staff actions that may amount to "cruel and unusual punishment under the Eighth Amendment, and (2) the protection of inmates from assault by other inmates or staff. A reading of the Supreme Court case of Bell v. Wolfish (1979) is absolutely essential to an understanding of the constitutional view of detention facility operations. In this decision the Supreme Court blurred distinctions of the past between pretrial and sentenced inmates, indicating that restrictions on the rights of pretrial detainees would be judged for their constitutionality based on a "punishment" test. This test prohibited punishment for pretrial detainees and can be summarized as follows:

> ... actions will constitute punishment: (1) if there is an expressed intent on the part of correctional officials to punish; (2) if there is no rational connection between the rule or restriction and the purpose for the rule other than punishment (e.g., security reasons); or (3) where that other purpose is excessive in relation to the nonpunitive reasons given for the rule.[200]

While this is not an entirely clear test, it set the tone for the Court approving double celling under specific conditions, routine strip searches after visits, and unannounced "shakedown" room searches of a detainees cell outside his or her presence. (Other "reasonable" security concerns included a "publisher's only" rule with respect to hardback books and a regulation prohibiting the receipt of packages from family and friends.) Provided they are not excessive to the extent that they constitute punishment, these rules provide for the personal safety of everyone in the facility.

The second major concern is with the protection of the inmates from assault. As indicated earlier, "the number of correctional officers necessary to assure a constitutional level of inmate safety must bear some reasonable relationship to the total number of inmates.[201] The courts have been clear in stating that physical brutality, or acts that "shock the conscience" will not be tolerated in jails. Corporal punishment by staff, and inmate rape, extortion,

---

[200]O'Brien, et al. 65

[201]"Williams v. Edwards, 1977.

theft, and assault on other inmates are considered "cruel and unusual punishment" by Eighth Amendment standards, as is the use of trusty inmates ("barn bosses" or "building tenders") to supervise other inmates. While in civil rights actions a failure to protect must reflect "deliberate indifference" to the safety needs of the inmates (a failure that exceeds mere negligence), for the plaintiff to succeed,[202] the same failure to protect claim in many situations may be brought as a tort case in state court, where showing negligence alone will be the key to winning or losing the case.

Nonetheless, the courts have remained flexible in their interpretation of what may constitute a reasonable degree of personal safety in a given situation, appearing to approach problems of individual safety through a broad "totality of conditions" approach. This approach requires the court to consider all factors in determining the adequacy of conditions of confinement. For example, double celling is not unconstitutional unless in combination with other factors it yields a situation that may be intolerable. As recently as 1986 an Appeals Court in South Dakota stated that facilities should not exceed 95 percent of capacity and that in consideration of "all circumstances surrounding conditions of confinement" protective custody inmates should not be double-celled.[203] However, the requirement for single-celling was overturned on re-hearing and the case remanded to the District Court for further action.[204]

The courts or any observer of your jail operation could use the following as reasonable guides to assessing the personal safety of inmates in the jail, provided they could be accurately measured: reported use of physical force, weapons, restraints, and chemical agents; evidence of racial conflict, gang activity, and overuse of protective custody; confrontations of staff by inmates, and inmate to inmate conflict requiring medical attention; level of out of cell movement, including access to a dayroom, showers, and recreation and other program time.

The key elements in providing personal safety are an adequate classification system for incoming inmates combined with careful attention to staff selection, training, supervision and incident reporting procedures. These are addressed elsewhere in this book.

---

[202]Daniels v. Williams (1986) and Davidson v. O'Connor (1986).

[203]Cody v. Hillard, 799 F.2d 477 (8th Cir. 1986).

[204]See Collins (1987) 74-75.

Riots and Disturbances. A major concern with respect to the overall safety of the facility is the control of minor disturbances and major disturbances, takeovers, or riots. These disturbances may include hunger strikes, sit-down strikes, the setting of small fires, or more violent forms of aggressive action. Much recent attention has been paid to the causes of riots and disturbances. The American Correctional Association has published a book on the causes, prevention, and control of riots and disturbances, which is something of an update of an earlier publication done in South Carolina on collective violence in correctional institutions.[205]

Both publications deal extensively with conditions that may cause riots and disturbances, although the South Carolina publication surveyed institutions with riots as opposed to those without riots. They concluded that there is a greater potential for disturbances in older (substandard), maximum security prisons with greater design capacities (i.e., larger prisons), and where there is less warden-inmate contact, "more highly educated inmates and correctional officers," lack of meaningful and productive job assignments, inadequate recreational programs, and greater use of administrative and punitive segregation.[206] This listing is consistent with that developed for jails by Pappas. High on the list of factors related to disturbances are crowded conditions, correctional officer's negative attitudes toward inmates, poor disciplinary policies, poor food, excessive idle time, lack of ability to express aggressive impulses constructively, and a lack of incentives for conforming behavior.[207] The more recent phenomenon of inmate gangs is probably a greater contributor, but scant attention is paid to this in the 1981 ACA publication. Gangs are seen largely as a prison problem that began in California. However, it has spread to Illinois, New York, and Florida. There is no reason to believe that these gangs are not operating in the large, urban jails. The best solution has been the separation of gangs into different facilities, which may be difficult to do in most jails unless agreements can be worked out with other jurisdictions, local or state.

---

[205]William D. Leeke, Collective Violence in Correctional Institutions: A Search for Causes (Columbia, South Carolina: the State Printing Company, 1973); American Correctional Association, Riots and Disturbances in Correctional Institutions. College Park, Maryland: 1981).

[206]Leeke 32.

[207]Pappas 137.

A more recent publication provides a detailed survey of major elements of riots and disturbances.[208] A review of these materials indicates that poor management is most often at the heart of the problem of riots and disturbances, often accompanied by poorly selected and trained staff. A well-trained and led staff will communicate effectively with the inmate population and resolve the types of problems that lead to riots and disturbances.

Conditions for riots and disturbances are generally seen as either "predisposing" or "precipitating." Predisposing conditions include overcrowded conditions, poor food, too few staff, poorly-trained (incompetent) staff, long lock-up periods, and a host of attitudinal problems with staff and inmates. When these conditions persist without efforts to correct them, the possibility of a disturbance increases. The event will usually be triggered by a precipitating event, such as a fight between inmates or an inmate and an officer or a sudden change in routine. Recall that concern about a sudden change in routine was one of the reasons the Atlanta Penitentiary did not lock down after the Oakdale Mariel riots in November, 1987: "Bureau of Prisons officials believed that any attempt to lock down the bulk of the Atlanta prison 'would virtually assure some degree of rioting.'" For this reason they simply increased staff in key areas and maintained normal operations.[209] It did not work.

Fox defines five stages of the riot, four during and one afterward. These include an initial period of undirected violence followed by periods of organization, interaction with officials, surrender, and investigations after the riot.[210] Perhaps the most important of these stages is the investigation after the riot, at which time future policies will be developed and designed to prevent future occurrences.

Short of managing a facility that will reduce these conditions to a minimum, a plan for disturbances must be in place. Consistent with the fire plan for the facility, an emergency plan should be developed for handling disturbances, and staff must receive training in this important area. Fox advises discretion in handling riots, rather than negotiation or force. He recommends guidelines

---

[208]Michael Braswell, Stephen Dillingham, and Reid Montgomery, Prison Violence in America (Cincinnati: Anderson, 1985).

[209]Criminal Justice Newsletter Feb. 15, 1988: 2.

[210]Vernon Fox, "Why Prisoners Riot," Federal Probation, March, 1971: 9-14.

that will enable staff to react immediately based upon training and preparation. Fox notes that custodial action during the period of inmate disorganization could have prevented many riots.[211]

The plan for disturbances should include methods for containment, or isolating the disturbance to one area of the facility, followed by a plan for re-establishing control of the area.[212] All staff must be trained in the implementation of the plan. Appropriate outside agencies must be advised of the plan and their role in it. If no hostages have been taken and inmates are not being injured, this plan may simply allow inmates to "wind down." (If not, the rioters must be subdued through the use of force.) Negotiation to end riots and secure the release of hostages has become a well-developed area of expertise in the field. The ACA publication provides two sets of guidelines for hostage situations, one of which is contained in a model riot and disturbance plan.[213] Either individual staff members or a designated "squad" should be trained in such current procedures. Training topics include staff organization, negotiation with the inmates, clues about when to act, methods of handling the media, and what to do in the aftermath of the disturbance. Generally, a "wait and negotiate" posture is advised as long as hostages are not harmed and the inmates do not improve their situation. The most important thing to remember is that the inmates know that control will be regained.[214] Nonetheless, if inmates feel they either have no choice because conditions are so bad or they feel they have something to gain, they will be willing to riot and negotiate until some solutions are evident.

A riot or disturbance will place a moratorium on most areas of inmates rights, such as search and due process procedures for placement in isolation. The right to be free from unnecessary force or retaliation remains in place. Even after riots, the use of broad discretion in maintaining order does not allow the use of any amount of force once the threat of disorder has subsided.[215] When order is

---

[211]Fox 11.

[212]Pappas 137-139.

[213]American Correctional Association, "Riots and Disturbances..." (1981): Appendix B 40 and Appendix C 46.

[214]See Joseph Scanlon and Angela Prawzick, "Communications in Prison Crises: Taking Control," Corrections Today Dec., 1984: 20-24. Cf. Vernon Fox, "Managing Riots and Disturbances," Corrections Today Aug., 1982: 56.

[215]Inmates of Attica Correctional Facility v. Rockefeller, 453 F.2d 12 (2d Cir. (1971).

restored it is expected that regular disciplinary procedures will resume as soon as possible.

C. Food service

It is well understood that many of the disturbances and problems in a closed facility relate to poor food service. Next to choosing a chief of security, the most important decision you make as facility administrator will be in the choice of manager of your food service operation. American Correctional Association standards require "a staff member experienced in food service management" with the "resources, authority and responsibility to provide complete food service for the facility.[216] This is the minimum, even for a small facility. The manager must be familiar with menu preparation, procedures for serving food (cafeteria style, dayroom feeding, and cell feeding), sanitation, personnel requirements, budgeting and purchasing and accounting systems in order to determine the costs of meals per inmate. Generally, a thirty day menu cycle is used, although some facilities use six week cycles. Estimates of food requirements must be made on an ongoing basis, consistent with population size and composition. When juveniles are held in the facility, special attention must be given to their increased nutritional needs, both in quantity and quality.

Standards should be in place that ensure the quality and nutritional value of food, its preparation under clean and sanitary conditions, and the delivery of food that is palatable. Defective food carts as well as over-reliance on them may be a problem. Food carts have been purchased that will not fit through the doors of living units. Kitchens have been built so remote from dining halls that the food is cold when it gets there (especially when it must be moved outside in cold weather). Increased gastro-intestinal distress sometimes can be linked to unsanitary food service operations. Medical personnel should alert food service personnel to the possibility of this type of problem.

All food service personnel must be trained to understand the need for security in the kitchen and dining areas. Stolen utensils and cutlery can be dangerous weapons. Food theft by inmates and staff can pose a serious security problem. Inmates should be used in food preparation and service, but they should not be put in the position of supervising other inmates, and security must be maintained.

---

[216]ACA Standard 2-5233 (1981) 61.

The food service program can have a positive effect on the inmate population if attention is paid to providing some variation in type and service of food. Most facilities, for example serve special meals during holidays. The courts do not uniformly require facilities to meet the religious needs of inmates whose respective religions require that they not eat certain foods, such as pork.[217]. However, many facilities meet this need by finding acceptable substitutes. Special medical diets may be ordered by the courts and should be provided upon approval of medical staff. Snacks, or varied meals schedules, such as a Sunday late breakfast and early evening meal with a late snack, may also assist in facility management.

Several good food service publications are available and are listed in the Bibliography. These publications provide advice regarding menu preparation and examples of cyclical menu planning, and they provide information on the Recommended Dietary Allowances (RDA) of the National Academy of Sciences. Requirements for sanitation and storage of food must meet local health and safety laws, rules and regulations. A time-tested manual for facility sanitation was produced the U.S. Bureau of Prisons by Graham Walton, a U.S. Public Health Service Sanitary Engineer. This book is not in print; however, the National Sheriffs' Association also has a handbook available on the subject that covers very similar material.[218] The use of local health department officials as consultants in institutional sanitation is advisable, especially when they are required to do regular facility inspections.

Private contracting. Chapter six provides a discussion of private contracting at the levels of total facility operations or for ancillary services. Consideration may be given to the use of a contract food service, especially by administrators of small facilities, and it is one of the major areas of private involvement in justice facilities. It may be an efficient and cost effective method of providing food service and should be used where it can be truly cost effective. However, it can present problems. Security problems may arise with outside food service personnel working in the facility who

---

[217]See Rogers v. Scurr, 676 F.2d 1211 (9th Cir. 1982); this case denied Black Muslims pork-free diets; Kahane v. Carlson,527 F.2d 392 (2nd. Cir 1975) was specific in allowing orthodox Jewish inmates a pork-free diet.

[218]Graham Walton, Institutional Sanitation, A Manual of Environmental Sanitation, Prepared Specifically for the Use of the Sanitary Supervisors, Bureau of Prisons, 2nd ed. (Washington, D.C.: U.S. Bureau of Prisons, 1965); National Sheriffs' Association, Sanitation in the Jail (Washington, D.C., 1974).

do not understand the security concerns involved in working with inmates. Additional security in these areas and/or training of these staff may be required. A more recent innovation in some small jails has been the purchase of meals from fast food outlets. For a small, short term holding facility this may be nutritionally adequate and provide savings in food service costs. However, care should be taken to provide some variety in the food selected.

D. Medical Services: Managing Emergencies/Response Time

The U.S. Supreme Court has said that it is your legal duty to avoid "deliberate indifference to serious medical needs of prisoners".(Estelle v. Gamble, 1976). To meet this standard, you and your staff should be familiar with the American Medical Association (AMA) standards for jails. Developed by the AMA and approved by detention personnel, they are also part of the American Correctional Association standards for jails. The standards require the development of a four-minute response time to medical emergencies, a plan for detoxification of addicted inmates under supervision, and the proper supervision and management of mentally ill inmates.[219] The standards may require additional staffing, such as 24-hour medical coverage, and staff training in cardio-pulmonary resuscitation (CPR) and other first aid techniques. Many of these techniques will be as valuable for staff as for inmates. Your medical program supervisor should know about these standards and others of importance.

Some inmates are "malingerers" who use sick call to get out of other duties or to kill time. They sometimes anger and often frustrate staff — intentionally. This situation may lead to conflict between security concerns and the medical needs of inmates in your care. Such problems must be resolved before they lead to problems (and legal exposure) due to lack of attention to legitimate medical needs. These inmates might seriously be ill, and every possibility must be considered, lest an expensive suit be filed. A minimal screening at entry by a nurse, physician, or medical technician is well worth the investment to obtain basic medical information. Most facilities of any size have medical staff on duty or readily available 24 hours a day, and small facilities can contract with a local physician or clinic to achieve the same result. The minimum necessary to do the initial screening is a medically-trained correctional officer who is instructed

---

[219]ACA Standards (1981) 68-79.

to contact a physician, local clinic, or hospital if a problem is detected.

After admission to the facility, the most important first consideration in inmate medical care is unimpeded access to medical services. Security staff must never be allowed to turn down inmate requests for medical care. As stated in American Correctional Association and American Medical Association standards, access and treatment should be continuous. In one court case the prison health care system was held unconstitutional because access to primary care physicians was denied or substantially delayed by initial screening procedures and by inadequate recordkeeping.[220] In 1986 the staff of an 800-bed jail in Florida allowed an asthmatic woman to die in her cell because she was not allowed to keep the medication (an inhaler) that she needed to control her asthma. She was in jail for nonpayment of a minor debt. A staff member saw her lying on the floor at midnight and her replacement did not respond to the same situation until 6:00 a.m. the next morning, at which time she was dead. Policy and procedures that were in place were not followed. The deputies were fired, but the case is now in litigation. Such an incident causes legal problems to arise unless security and medical staff recognize and are trained in their duties in this important area.

The Mentally Ill. Mental cases are perhaps the most difficult to house and supervise in the jail. As the National Coalition on Jail Reform has expressed, the jail has become the "new mental institution" due to the lack of facilities to manage the mentally ill in the community. Most community mental health units do not provide 24-hour a day service, and many are not equipped to handle chronically mentally ill persons. Therefore, while transfer of these individuals out of the jail to other more appropriate facilities may be desirable, practically, these facilities do not exist.

What, then, is your duty to these individuals? Your first duty is to ensure the health and safety of mentally ill inmates while they are in the jail. This may include the use of restraints and segregation from the general population. Your next consideration is to try to get the most seriously mentally ill inmates into programs outside the facility, both for your good and for theirs. Short of keeping them safe while in the jail and trying to give them proper care, there is no clear constitutional requirement for treatment

---

[220]ACA Standards 2-5278, 2-5279 (1981) 74; see also Todaro v. Ward, 556 F.2d 48 (2nd Cir. 1977).

programs for people convicted of criminal offenses who are mentally ill. In medical and, by extension, mental health cases, however, the Gamble standard implies that something beyond "deliberate indifference to the serious medical needs of prisoners" is required. A more positive view is to face the problem squarely and develop programs for mentally ill offenders that can be conducted within the jail or at a specialized facility. As indicated elsewhere, some of these programs have been very effective.[221] Also, some of these offenders may have problems of drug addiction and alcoholism that will allow treatment in community programs and/or facilities devoted specifically to these problems.

Communicable Diseases — from Colds to AIDS. Chapter 4 of the National Sheriffs' Association Handbook on Sanitation in the Jail defines the traditional types of communicable diseases and the facility response to them.[222] These diseases range from the common cold to tuberculosis to hepatitis-B, which, although it is every bit as deadly, has now been overshadowed by AIDS — the Acquired Immune Deficiency Syndrome. There is evidence that crowded conditions alone will contribute to sickness rates in a detention facility or even a military barracks.[223] Good classification, sufficient space, and a good sanitation program will contribute greatly to a reduction in communicable diseases, since these diseases can be communicated either through human contact or through contact with infected water, food, or vermin. Despite current concerns about the AIDS epidemic, detention facility administrators have been dealing with communicable diseases, such as hepatitis-B, for many years and many of the same precautions apply to the management of inmates with AIDS.

Acquired Immune Deficiency Syndrome. AIDS differs from most such communicable diseases because it is generally fatal and there is no known cure. The most comprehensive document specific to AIDS in corrections is titled "AIDS in Prisons and Jails," which was updated in February of 1986.[224] It appears that this publication by the Na-

---

[221]See Joyce Jennings, "Mentally Ill Offenders," and Bill Curry, "Punishment or Treatment," State Legislatures 11:2 (February, 1985): 19-28.

[222]National Sheriffs' Association 15-18.

[223]See Bailus Walker and Theodore Gordon, "Health and High Density Confinement in Jails and Prisons," Federal Probation March, 1980: 53-57.

[224]Theodore M. Hammett, "AIDS in Prisons and Jails: Issues and Options," National Institute of Justice Research in Brief February, 1986.

tional Institute of Justice (NIJ) will continue to be updated; the full report can be obtained from the Institute (call 800-851-3420). Related NIJ reports are "AIDS and the law enforcement officer," and "Risk of infection with the AIDS virus through exposures to blood.[225] AIDS is a disease that breaks down the body's immune system, or its ability to fight disease, leaving the person with AIDS vulnerable to life-threatening illnesses that do not affect people with normal immune systems. There is some evidence that the AIDS virus can affect the central nervous system, thus causing mental and emotional disorders, but this area is not yet well-researched. The major concern is that this may be the case not only for persons with AIDS, but for individuals who test positive for AIDS antibodies, but do not have AIDS — the seropositives.

Prevalence

General Public. Recent data from the Centers for Disease Control showed more than 50,000 cases of AIDS in adults and children nationally through early 1988. Homosexual or bisexual males make up 66 percent of the victims; 16 percent are intravenous drug abusers, and 8 percent are both homosexual and IV drug abusers. Thus, 90 percent of all AIDS victims have a history of either homosexual/bisexual activities or intravenous drug abuse.[226] These, of course, are critical categories of concern in detention and correctional facilities. It is of particular concern because the portion attributed to intravenous drug abuse is expected to rise, and, if the facility is in a large urban area AIDS tends to be concentrated in such areas. New York and California account for 53 percent of all AIDS cases, followed by New Jersey, Florida, and Texas, with 19 percent.

Jails and Prisons. Hammett found 1,232 confirmed AIDS cases among inmates in 58 responding federal, state and local correctional systems as of October 1, 1986, a 72 percent increase from November, 1985 (455 cases).[227] Twenty-seven responding city and county jail systems were found to have 448 cases, up 44 percent from the November, 1985

---

[225]Theodore M. Hammett, NIJ Reports, (Washington, D.C.: U.S. Department of Justice, National Institute of Justice, November/December, 1987); Theodore Hammett and Walter Bond, National Institute of Justice AIDS Bulletin, October, 1987.

[226]Centers for Disease Control, AIDS Weekly Surveillance Report, August, 1987.

[227]Theodore M. Hammett, with assistance from Monique Sullivan and Taylor McNeil, AIDS in Correctional Facilities: Issues and Options, 2nd ed. with 1986 Update (U.S. Department of Justice, National Institute of Justice, May, 1987) xvi; Hammett (1986) 2.

number (311).[228] A more recent report shows 1,964 confirmed cases of AIDS in prisons as of October 1, 1987.[229] Hammett et al. point out that this 61 percent (averaged) increase is less than the 79 percent national increase for a similar period.[230]

As indicated by Collins, and reiterated by Hammett, the legal issues for detention facility administrators surrounding AIDS have not yet been fully litigated in the courts.[231] Courts have been considering cases for the general public, such as that of Todd Shuttleworth, who was fired by Broward County, Florida, in September, 1984, after being diagnosed as having AIDS. He was later reinstated as a county employee by a federal court with $190,000 in compensation. The court found a violation of Section 504 of the federal Rehabilitation Act of 1973, in that he had been denied equal protection of the laws and due process of law in his dismissal.[232] Subsequent to the case, the Florida Commission on Human Relations stated that AIDS is a handicap within the meaning of Florida law and that employment discrimination is illegal. (Mr. Shuttleworth died in 1987 after resuming employment.) A case in Massachusetts was won also based on handicap discrimination.[233] AIDS cases are becoming a legal specialty for such organizations as the Lambda Legal Defense and Education Fund in New York City, a law firm that specializes in gay rights law.[234] In San Francisco it is the National Gay Rights Advocates.[235] The American Red Cross has issued guidelines on AIDS that are used by some school systems. These guidelines indicate that children and staff members who have AIDS, i.e., are infected with the AIDS virus, may remain in school, unless a health review team or similar body determines that there is a risk to others. A recent publication, that has been widely distributed by the

---

[228]Hammett et al. (1986) xiv.

[229]Criminal Justice Newsletter Feb. 1, 1988: 7.

[230]Hammett et al (1986) xiv.

[231]Collins (1986) 15-22, Collins (1987) 10, 14-15, and 141; Hammett et al. (1986) 60-62.

[232]The Torch, American Civil Liberties Union of Florida, Winter, 1987: 1.

[233]The Torch 1.

[234]Roger Ricklefs, Wall Street Journal 7 October 1987: 37; this article discusses employment, testing, contagion, medical care, and children with AIDS.

[235]Ricklefs 37.

U.S. Public Health Service, is called "Understanding AIDS" and addresses the problem of preventing AIDS.[236]

AIDS Incidents in Jails and Prisons. Perhaps the most relevant case for facility personnel involved an inmate with the AIDS virus biting a federal prison system correctional officer in Minnesota. The inmate defendant was convicted of assault with a deadly weapon after biting two officers, breaking the skin on one of them. [237] The fate of the officers is not yet known, although the inmate got five additional years in prison. At this time there is no known case of transmission of the AIDS virus to correctional employees as a result of contact with inmates.[238] "Reasonable conduct" in handling inmates with AIDS related conditions (ARC) or with the HIV or "human immunodeficiency virus" — the "AIDS virus" only (and not the disease) — are not yet entirely clear, although progress is being made.[239] Courts in New York and Alabama have upheld segregation of inmates with AIDS, including disqualification for conjugal visits and work release programs. There are three major areas of concern: (1) prevention and control of the spread of the disease in the facility, (2) care and treatment of inmates with AIDS, and (3) staff reaction to the management of inmates with AIDS.[240]

Prevention and Control

The disease is a bloodborne disease, primarily transmitted through blood-to-blood contact, as through hypodermic needles or transfusions, or through semen-to-blood contact, the primary route for homosexuals. The best evidence to date indicates that AIDS cannot be communicated through casual contact — some type of fluid exchange must occur for transmission of the virus. According to the Center for Disease Control's Director for AIDS Activity, "No evidence supports AIDS transmission by casual contact, by the airborne route, by objects handled by people with AIDS, or by

---

[236]"Understanding AIDS," a pamphlet published by the U.S. Department of Health and Human Services, U.S. Public Health Service (Washington, D.C.: GPO 1988).

[237]U.S. v. Moore, ___F.Supp.___, 41 CRL 2484 (D.Minn. 1987), discussed in Collins (1987) 16.

[238]Criminal Justice Newsletter Feb. 15, 1988: 7.

[239]Hammett (1986) 7-8; other names used for the virus are HTLV-III, LAV, and ARV.

[240]Criminal Justice Newsletter Jan. 18, 1988: 3.

contaminated environmental surfaces."[241] Five years of study show that sneezing or coughing, swimming in public pools, using toilet facilities, shaking hands, hugging, or other casual contact at home, school, work, or in public do not spread AIDS. There is no evidence that it is spread through saliva (spitting), human bites, in urine or feces, or even through cuts or puncture wounds, although caution is advised. In doing CPR the use of masks and airways is recommended in order to reduce minimal risk even further.[242] Any contact with blood or body fluids is to be avoided, if possible. The danger from needlesticks and punctures is very small; infection from open wounds is even lower and only one case of mucous-membrane exposures leading to AIDS has been found. Nonetheless, Hammett and Bond strongly recommend the use of gloves, masks, and protective eyeware when dealing with HIV cases.[243] Officers conducting searches should exercise caution by directing inmates to empty their pockets and to use caution in probing unseen areas.

Clearly, the spread of AIDS through homosexual contact creates special problems for the jail administrator and staff. To the extent possible, homosexual inmates must be advised about the danger of AIDS. Where necessary to their health and that of others they should be segregated from the general population. Suspected drug users should also be segregated when they present a danger to other inmates.

Signs of AIDS include unexplained, persistent fatigue, unexplained fever, shaking chills, or drenching night sweats lasting several weeks, unexplained weight loss greater than 10 pounds, swollen glands in the neck, armpits, or groin lasting more than two months; pink to purple flat or raised blotches or bumps occurring on or under the skin, inside the mouth, nose, eyelids, or rectum (initially resembling bruises but harder than the skin around them); persistent white spots or unusual blemishes in the mouth, persistent diarrhea, and a persistent dry cough which has lasted too long to be caused by a common respiratory infection, especially if accompanied by shortness of breath.

---

[241]James W. Curran, Director, AIDS Activity, Centers for Disease Control, c. 1986.

[242]Hammett, AIDS and the Law Enforcement Officer: Concerns and Policy Reponses (Washington, D.C.: National Institute of Justice, 1987) 6; provides a guide to police officers regarding contact with individuals with possible AIDS infections.

[243]Theodore Hammett and Walter Bond, "Risk of infection with the AIDS virus through exposures to blood," AIDS Bulletin, National Institute of Justice, October, 1987.

Mass Screening. The issue of mass screening of HIV seropositives in confinement or elsewhere is not settled. A "seropositive" is a person who tests positive for AIDS antibodies, but not for the virus itself. Seropostive individuals may never develop AIDS or show any of the symptoms of AIDS; estimates are that 5 to 6 percent will develop end-stage AIDS, although more current estimates apparently go as high as one-third. Another 25 percent of the seropositives will develop the AIDS-related complex — ARC — wherein some of the symptoms of AIDS are found.[244] As Hammett points out, proponents of mass screening believe it is necessary to identify infectious individuals and target prevention programs, while opponents of mass screening argue that identification serves no purpose and would create a management problem. They feel that education is the best approach.[245]

Inmates who test positive for the HIV antibody ("seropositives") are generally not separated from the general population. The task of separation would be too great. Inmates with AIDS are, of course, segregated in medical quarters. They may also be candidates for additional security. An officer in Broward County, Florida, had an inmate with AIDS "spike" his coffee, and he has not suffered physical effects. Another was bitten by an AIDS inmate with no ill effects to date. The effects have been largely emotional with respect to the reactions of family and acquaintances to possible infection.

The American Correctional Health Care Association has taken a position opposing mandatory AIDS testing for prisoners as a waste of money and a diversion of resources from such tasks as AIDS education. Norman and Cotton quote the California policy recommendation regarding mass testing, indicating that testing should be done on a case by case basis on orders of a physician, and that the results of testing should be confidential; the recommendations also support AIDS education for inmates and staff.[246]

The initial Federal Bureau of Prisons policy was to test all newly-arrived inmates and those about to be released. A more recent

---

[244]Hammett 2.

[245]Hammett 4.

[246]Bonnie Norman and Barbara Cotton, "AIDS Antibody Testing of Prisoners,"American Jails Fall, 1987: 49.

decision is to test only five percent of the newly committed inmates, who will be chosen at random, with a retest after three months and at six month intervals thereafter "to determine the risk of acquiring the infection during confinement." This will be augmented with tests for inmates who exhibit predatory or promiscuous behavior, inclusive of those known to be homosexual.[247] The three categories noted above are used: (1) seropositives (HIV positive) but with no symptoms who remain in the general population, (2) persons with symptoms, the "AIDS-related complex" (ARC) group that are treated in a medical facility or can remain in the population, and (3) persons with AIDS, who are hospitalized. In October, 1987, the BOP had 33 inmates with "end-stage" AIDS out of a population of 44,000; 32 were intravenous drug users, and one was both an IV drug user and a homosexual. This dropped to 31 in November. An average of just over three percent of all federal inmates tested at different points in time (over 16,000) have been found seropositive.[248]

Care and Treatment.

The Eighth Amendment makes reasonable medical care a duty for the jail administrator, and it can be a very expensive duty. As Hammett indicates, however, "correctional systems have not been held responsible for ensuring the absolute safety of persons in their custody. Liability may stem from assault, for example, only if the officials knew, or should have known, of the risk to a particular inmate. [249] Caring for AIDS patients is not a duty for private medical providers. Many medical professionals will not treat AIDS cases, as has been vividly demonstrated in several jurisdictions. Some public agencies also have refused to take jail inmates. For example emergency services may refuse to take the inmate to a hospital. Arrangements must be made in advance of need for someone who will handle AIDS patients. For large jails the best resources are probably in-house; small or medium sized jail may not have resources available. In the latter case, transfer to a state facility may be necessary, particularly where a prison hospital is available.

In any case, the issue will quickly become one of who will pay for the treatment. AIDS cases are costly, possibly using the entire

---

[247] Criminal Justice Newsletter Nov. 2, 1987: 5.

[248] Criminal Justice Newsletter October 1, 1987, and November 2, 1987: 5.

[249] Hammett, (1987) 6; it is assumed Hammett is referring to Wood v. Strickland (1975) and the more recent cases of Daniels v. Williams and Davidson v. Cannon, which were decided in early 1986.

medical budget for one year for one case alone. The issue of cost is not easily resolved, and no doubt will await legislation and/or litigation. An alternative is to send the inmate home, if possible. But, as Collins suggests, this may constitute "deliberate indifference" to a serious medical need, even though the person is no longer a "prisoner."[250]

Staff Action and Reaction

For most staff the handling of AIDS and AIDS-related cases will be a matter of personal choice. The wise administrator will not force contact, but provide to staff all available information about the disease. Staff should be encouraged by administrators to surface their fears and concerns, and they should be provided the most current medical information regarding how the disease is communicated and how they may be protected from it. Clear and reasonable policies should be developed with staff participation in order to deal with the AIDS problem. As professionals, most detention staff have and will continue to deal with the problem based on their sense of duty, using precautions based on current knowledge or until advised otherwise.

What about the testing of staff for AIDS? Dale and Messing discuss the issue in the context of the right to privacy and what constitutes an unreasonable search.[251] They note that "reasonable suspicion" is sufficient to allow urinalysis and search of a staff vehicle.[252] Staff who feel they may have AIDS may volunteer for testing. But, if they are HIV seropositive can they be fired? Should they be removed from the jail or reassigned? The Shuttleworth case and others cited above indicate that if concerns arise on the part of other staff, re-assignment may be the best course of action, particularly if AIDS develops. Confidentiality of the information may also be good policy.[253]

For further information regarding accepted procedures and new developments in AIDS research, local health officials should be

---

[250]Collins 21.

[251]Michael J. Dale and Howard Messing, "Testing Jail Employees For Drugs and AIDS — Legal Implications," American Jails Winter, 1988: 6-8.

[252]McDonnell v. Hunter, 809 F.2d 1302 (8th Cir. 1987).

[253]Dale and Messing 8.

contacted. Also, there is a national AIDS hotline: 1-800-342-AIDS, and an information number at the NIJ: 1-301-251-5500.

E. Sanitary Living Conditions

Adequate sanitation is required by several court decisions, as well as by national standards. According to an 8th Circuit Court decision in Missouri, the jail must be cleaned on a daily basis and necessary cleaning supplies furnished to the inmates.[254] Four areas require attention: (1) a housekeeping plan for staff and inmates, (2) disposal of waste (sewage and garbage), (3) vermin and pest control, and (4) provision for laundering of clothing, linen, towels. Implementation of ACA or AMA standards will bring the facility into compliance in these areas.[255]

Inmates can be required to keep their living areas clean. A housekeeping plan is absolutely essential to the health of staff and inmates. Elements of a housekeeping plan are enumerated in the National Sheriffs' Association publication on sanitation in the jail.[256] The plan must include daily sweeping and trash removal, generous daily use of soap and water on showers, toilets, wash basins, and sinks, and weekly use on floors, walls, windows, and other cell and living areas. Smoking materials present problems of cleanliness; noncombustible receptacles should be provided and cleaned daily. Ongoing (daily) inspections of housing areas should identify foul odors (as generated by hidden food, human waste, etc.), clogged sewage systems, the existence of vermin and pests, and materials that might represent fire or safety hazards. Weekly inspections by staff outside the unit are advisable. Some jails provide incentives for keeping a clean living unit. In one such facility, all units had television sets, but the unit with the best inspection got the color television set for the week. During the NBA finals and the Super Bowl, competition became quite keen. Incentives should replace demands whenever possible in the jail.

The Handbook on Sanitation in the Jails provides technical guidance in areas of waste disposal and vermin and pest control.[257] In

---

[254]Ahrens v. Thomas, 434 F.Supp. 873 (W.D.Mo. 1977).

[255]ACA Standards, Sanitation and Hygiene (1981) 64-67.

[256]The National Sheriffs' Association, A Handbook on Sanitation in the Jail (1974) 8-12.

[257]See also Walton (1965).

a publication prepared for the Federal Bureau of Prisons, the authors state the following for jails:

> Any relaxation of control over waste, refuse, or personal filth may permit the spread of vermin. Cleanliness, construction, and chemistry are key words in vermin control. Cleanliness, including the proper handing and disposal of garbage, creates an unfavorable environment for vermin by limiting their food supply and breeding places. Construction involves exclusion of vermin through screening and ratproofing, for example. Chemicals — sprays, dusts, emulsions, and baits — help to control these dangerous pests. Some chemicals may be used by untrained persons, but others are exceedingly dangerous and should be handled only by professional exterminators. Advice as to the type of chemical that should be used and the method of its application may be obtained from local and state health departments.[258]

ACA standards require weekly sanitation inspections by qualified departmental staff and monthly inspections by a specialist in safety and sanitation.[259] Court requirements vary from 6 months to a year for public health department inspections.[260]

Inmates should not remain in their street clothing. Many new arrivals have body lice, and control must begin in the receiving area, inclusive of having their clothes sterilized and laundered. Jail clothing should be exchanged as necessary, consistent with work assignments, but no less than weekly, as recommended by ACA standards for bedding and towels.[261] One federal district court required a change of clothes available on a daily basis, another weekly for clothes and bedding.[262]

---

[258]Nick Pappas, ed. The Jail: Its Operation and Management (Washington, D.C.: United States Bureau of Prisons, 1971) 145.

[259]ACA Standard 2-5243 (1986) 83.

[260]Alberti v. Sheriff of Harris County, 406 F.Supp. 649 (S.D. Tex. 1975); Laaman v. Helgemoe, 437 F.Supp. 269 (D.N.H. 1977).

[261]ACA Standard 2-5252 (1981) 65.

[262]Mitchell v. Untreiner, 421 F.Supp. 886 (N.D.Fla. 1976; Campbell v. McGruder, 416 F.Supp. 100 (D.D.C. 1975, 554 F.Supp. 562 (D.D.C. 1982).

The courts have been clear about the obligation to provide inmates with showers (if not daily, at least three times a week) and the items necessary to personal hygiene, as have national standards. In Pugh v. Locke, the Alabama prison case that lasted for most of the decade of the 1970's, the Supreme Court left standing the Circuit Court order regarding functioning toilets and showers, with hot water available, and the need for the state to supply indigent inmates with soap, shaving gear, combs, shampoo, toothpaste, and toothbrushes.

F. Communication: Mail and Visiting

In order of importance, especially as it relates to problems of security and control, communication with the community is on a par with court and legal access and food service. Communication does not necessarily mean visits, but does include mail and telephone calls. While administrators have been allowed a great deal of latitude in controlling visiting, it is generally recognized as one of the most important programs to be offered in the jail, largely due to the calming effects of outside contact.

Regulation of visiting is both necessary and supported in law.[263] Visits can be limited based on the need for facility security and order. There is no standard for the number of hours and days of visiting required per week. American Correctional Association standards require visits limited only by "facility schedules, space and personnel constraints, except where there are substantial reasons to justify such limitation."[264] In the New York City jail case of Rhem v. Malcolm inmates requested three visitors per visit with a two hour daily minimum per week, which was denied by the Federal District Court.[265] However, one court found that a regulation permitting pretrial detainees one visit with family members for no more than 15 minutes per week too strict,[266] and another that one visit a week with two to five persons on an approved list was also too strict.[267]

---

[263]Block v. Rutherford, 104 S.Ct. 3227 (1984) and White v. Keller, 588 F.2d 913 (4th Cir. 1978).

[264]ACA Standard 2-5336, (1981) 89.

[265]Rhem v. Malcolm, 371 F.Supp. 594 (S.D.N.Y. 1974).

[266]Brenneman v. Madigan, 343 F.Supp. 128 (N.D. Cal. 1972).

[267]Tate v. Kassulke, 409 F.Supp. 651 (W.D. Ky 1976).

Administrators, therefore, do not have unfettered discretion to limit the number of visits, although they have considerable control over the conduct of visits (see Block v. Rutherford, 1984). The basis for an acceptable visiting schedule is as follows:

(1) Visitation for a minimum of nine hours per week, two hours of which must be on a week day after 6:00 p.m. and four hours on a weekend;

(2) A minimum of three visiting days per week;

(3) Regular visits of not less than one-half hour that may extend to two hours;

(4) Provision for additional visiting hours under special circumstances, and arrangements for visitors who must travel over 150 miles; and,

(5) Not counting authorized visits by persons providing services against regular visits — for example, court personnel, ministers, and medical personnel.[268]

The lower federal courts appear to agree that visiting time should be provided in the evenings.[269] Visits can be limited to the immediate family, but cannot be denied on racial grounds (woman visiting prisoner of different race). Privacy is not required, and conversations may be monitored, although this would not appear to be good practice unless some reason for such monitoring is evident.[270] Visits may be denied in the interests of order and security, particularly when contraband is brought to the facility. When visits are denied it is good policy to provide specific reasons for the exclusion to the inmate, who should be given an opportunity to appeal the decision. There is no constitutional right to contact visits,[271] although many minimum security sentenced facilities (annexes, jail farms, etc.) offer contact visits for inmates. There is no right to conjugal (family) visits, although release programs may allow family visits;

---

[268]Based in part onthe Nebraska Jail Standards (1977) 120.

[269]Jones v. Wittenberg, 330 F.Supp. 717 (N.D. Ohio 1971).

[270]Lanza v. New York, 370 U.S. 139 (1962).

[271]Block v. Rutherford (1984).

ordinarily, only state prisons usually offer these types of programs on the grounds. Inmates have no protected right to visit other inmates.

Searches. Issues of search at intake booking were discussed in chapter one. Strip searches of prisoners before and after visits allowing public contact are permissible.[272] The Supreme Court approved post-visit strip searches (not pre-visit) in Bell v. Wolfish (1979). Searches involving contact or probing body cavities were approved on a less than probable cause basis in Wolfish, but they can not be abusive. They should be done only by medically-trained personnel. Searches not requiring contact, i.e., strip searches or visual inspections, do not require medical assistance. Random drug testing of inmates has achieved approval in some lower federal courts; the major issue will probably be the reliability of such tests.[273]

Visitors. The rules regarding search of visitors must be clearly posted in the entry to the facility and in the visiting area. Visitors, like employees, have a reduced expectation of privacy when they enter the jail. However, the expectation is not so low as to allow intrusive searches without establishing reasonable suspicion. Searches of visitors should be confined to pat-down procedures and the use of metal detectors, unless "reasonable suspicion" exists that an individual is attempting to smuggle contraband into the facility.[274] As defined by Collins, reasonable suspicion must be "based on specific objective facts and rational inferences that may be drawn from those facts in light of experience," or simply facts combined with professional judgment.[275]

Where reasonable suspicion is the case, a strip search may be required as a condition of entering the facility. It may be as intrusive to require the subject to "bend and spread," although visual inspections usually suffice. Generally, such a search cannot be made against the person's will, if it is done prior to the visit. Requiring visitors to "consent" to strip searches as a condition of visiting, and, as part of a policy of strip searching visitors without probable cause, led to a $177,000 judgment against one sheriff, which was upheld by

---

[272]Hodges v. Klein, 412 F.Supp. 896 (D.N.J. 1976).

[273]See Collins (1986) 67-72.

[274]Blackburn v. Snow, 771 F.2d 556 (1st Cir. 1985); see Collins (1986) 60.

[275]Collins 61; Whitley v. Albers, 106 S.Ct. 1078 (1986).

an appellate court.[276] It is advisable to get approval of the officer in charge before conducting any search of a visitor. Under no circumstances should staff do a body cavity search of a visitor, even with consent. Move the visit to the non-contact area or terminate the visit.

The problem of searching becomes more difficult when the visitor has made contact with the inmate. When it is suspected that drugs have been passed from mouth to mouth a visit may have to be terminated immediately, the visitor dismissed, and the inmate searched. If evidence is sufficient to arrest the visitor, the appropriate procedures must be followed.

Space. When contact visits are provided an open room accommodating several visitors may be used. When the weather is good, an outside area may be used. An informal setting is considered beneficial. Non-contact visiting areas should use windows (security glazing) to improve visibility, rather than screens or other visual obstructions. Sound-powered telephones prohibit the exchange of contraband. As indicated above, attorney visits will require both contact and a private area for discussion. Conversations with attorneys may be observed but not monitored. (See Section II on visiting.)

Mail. Inmates have the right to send unopened mail to their attorneys, as privileged, and to send and receive uncensored mail from family and friends, although it may be rejected with good reasons and inspected for contraband. Procunier v. Martinez (1974) is the governing court case, which stated that mail regulations must further an "important governmental interest unrelated to suppression of expression," and that restrictions must be "no greater than necessary ... to the protection of the particular government interest involved." The interests protected are security, order and rehabilitation, and the restrictions need not show with certainty that adverse consequences would flow from the failure to censure a particular letter.

The problem of mail breaks down into "incoming" and "outgoing," "privileged" and "non-privileged," "packages," and "publications." Obviously, the major goals in examining mail are to prevent the introduction of contraband into the facility, to detect plans for illegal activity, principally escape, and discourage material that instructs in the commission of criminal activity. In a 1983 case a Federal

---

[276]Blackburn v. Snow (1985).

appellate court gave the following rules for rejecting correspondence sent by or to an inmate. Mail may be rejected when it contains (1) matter that is nonmailable under law or postal regulation, (2) information of escape plots, plans to commit illegal activities or violate institutional rules, (3) direction of an inmate's business, (4) threats, extortion, obscenity, or gratuitous profanity, (5) a code, or (6) contraband.[277] Following Martinez and Meadows, present case law supports reading, inspection, restriction, and/or rejection in the following circumstances:

General Mail (Not Privileged)

Incoming: Inspection is for contraband, money, or permitted personal property; reading is allowed for security purposes in high security facilities; rejection requires notice to the inmate and the author.

Outgoing: Reading is a questionable practice, but can be done if a danger exists, or threats or extortion have been made to the recipient; this practice is more likely to be done in a high security facility like a jail, and it is usually done on a random basis.

Privileged Mail

Neither incoming or outgoing privileged mail may be read by jail staff.

Incoming: If labeled "Special Mail" or "Privileged," which includes mail from attorneys, federal and state officials, other legal officers, and the news media, it is opened only in the presence of an inmate to determine if it contains contraband and to verify that it qualifies as privileged mail. (Signed receipts are sometimes used, but they are not required by the courts.)

Outgoing: If labeled "Special Mail" or "Privileged," it is not opened by staff and may be sealed by the inmate; should a valid reason to open the mail arise, it is treated the same as incoming mail.

---

[277] Meadows v. Hopkins, 713 F.2d 206 (6th Cir. (1983).

Packages:

Incoming: May be restricted entirely;[278] if not, opened and inspected prior to delivery (often limited to quarterly or special occasion); books from publisher only; packages from privileged correspondents may be inspected for contraband in the same manner as other privileged mail.

Outgoing: No clear rule, but subject to inspection for contraband prior to sealing, if not privileged.

Publications

Religious publications generally allowed; some justification needed to ban other materials based on a determination of whether it is "detrimental to the security, good order, or discipline of the institution or if it might facilitate criminal activity (see below)."[279]

While courts indicate that censorship or rejection of mail that "threaten the security of the institution" is appropriate, some courts are saying that a regulation written in such general terms is unconstitutionally vague or overbroad and that a regulation must be considerably more specific in indicating what types of publications threaten institutional security and, hence, should be banned.[280]

Another often overlooked aspect of mail censorship is the due process requirement that when mail is censored the sender and the inmate must be given the opportunity to appeal the decision to an official other than the person involved in the original decision to censor.[281] Collins notes that Martinez gives due process protections to the author of the letter, since the recipient may not, in fact, have seen the letter prior to its censorship.[282]

---

[278] Bell v. Wolfish(1979) and Jones v. Diamond, 594 F.2d 997 (1979), as amended; 636 F.2d 1364 (1981).

[279] Abbott v. Richardson, C.A. no. 73-1047 (D.D.C. 1984); Abbott v. Meese, 824 F.2d 1166 (1987).

[280] Martin v. Kelley, 803 F.2d 236 (6th Cir. 1986).

[281] Procunier v. Martinez, 416 U.S. 396 (1974).

[282] Collins (1987) 41.

The kinds of publications excluded in jails or prisons generally are those that threaten institutional security, which could include advocating or teaching criminal activity, methods of physical violence against others, or escape. These may include banning "sexually explicit homosexual and heterosexual magazines; non-explicit homosexual publications (i.e., gay rights material); publications that preach ethnic superiority, such as the newsletter of the American Nazi party; publications that advocate the unionization of prisoners, highlight instances of alleged abuse by prison officials, or state grievances of prisoners generally; journals that facilitate gambling by giving odds for the week's sporting events; self-defense publications such as Lethal Unarmed Combat; and instructional materials on electronics and radio."[283] Nude photos of family members or friends are also excluded. Review of magazines on a case-by-case basis rather than by title alone is the rule, generally within three weeks of their arrival at the facility. A recent appeals court case said Federal prison officials may not reject and return an entire publication if a portion of it is found to be objectionable.[284]

Correspondence lists have been upheld that may limit the number, type, and identity of persons corresponding with the inmate.[285] However, one Federal District Court did ban a limitation for pretrial inmates.[286]

Restrictions may include members of the inmate's family.[287] Business letters can be rejected.[288]

Indigent inmates are supplied postage in most jails. The federal system supplies postage sufficient to mail five pieces of first class mail per month. Privileged legal correspondence is mailed at government expense.

---

[283]Abbott v. Richardson (1984).

[284]Abbott v. Meese, 824 F.2d 1166 (D.C. Cir. 1987).

[285]O'Brien v. Blackwell, 421 F.2d 833 (5th Cir. 1970).

[286]Jones v. Wittenberg (1971).

[287]Corby v. Conboy, 357 F.2d 251 (2nd Cir. 1972).

[288]Stroud v. Swope, 178 F.2d 950 (9th Cir. 1951), and U.S. ex rel Wagner v. Ragen, 213 F.2d 294 (7th Cir. 1954).

Media Access. Access to the media has been limited in both state and federal prisons and in jails.[289] The media has no constitutionally protected right to interview specific individual inmates. Alternative methods exist for communication with the press without requiring detention facility administrators to allow interviews with inmates. These include use of the mails and the transmission of information through those with general visitation rights — family, friends, attorneys, clergy. The Federal Prison System has developed a policy for communication of inmates with the media that has appeared to work well. It requires approval of the inmate for the interview, and permission must be granted by the superintendent for the interview.

G. Written Rules and Disciplinary Procedures

The disciplinary system is undoubtedly one of the most difficult areas of detention facility operations. Inmates must be sufficiently aware of the rules so that they will be able to obey them or suffer the consequences. Order and security depend on discipline. However, the sometimes split second decisions of officers in situations requiring control are not easily understood outside the context of the incident. Therefore, incidents must be carefully documented and there must be a system in place for determining the guilt or innocence of the inmate or inmates who allegedly violated the rules. Finally, attention must be paid to conditions in the segregation units.

Documenting Incidents. A good rule is to document all incidents carefully, adding reports from witnesses. The Illinois Corrections Training Academy provides a wallet-sized reference to report writing:[290]

Ask yourself: Is a report necessary?

Am I the one who should write the report?

The seven essentials of the report:

1. Who? Identify the person or situation being reported.

---

[289]Pell v. Procunier (1974) dealt with state claims, Saxbe v. Washington Post Co., 417 U.S. 843 (1974) with federal claims; jail cases are Main Road v. Aytch, 522 F.2d 1080 (CA3 1975), and Houchins v. KQED, Inc., 438 U.S. 1 (1978).

[290]Illinois Department of Corrections Training Academy, Preservice Security Curriculum (Springfield, 1988).

2. What? The incident or conversation being reported.

3. When? The time of day, day of week, and the date.

4. Where? The location of the occurrence.

5. How? The order of events.

6. Why? Why you think the incident happened - subjective statement

7. Action taken - What have you done about the reported incident?

When you have completed the report ask yourself the following questions:

1. Is your report COMPLETE?

2. Have you been as CONCISE as you could be or do you just ramble on and on?

3. Is your report CLEAR? If others read it, will they know what you are talking about?

4. Is your report CORRECT? Have you reported the facts only? The reader knows when you are reporting what you think rather than the facts.

The Disciplinary System. A disciplinary system requires that a set of rules be made available to inmates along with an understanding of what sanctions are available. It requires a system for making up disciplinary reports for minor and major violations, a procedure for hearing these violations to decide on punishments, and a method for ensuring that punishments are carried out. One of the most important features of such a system, and one most often overlooked, is the management of the very minor offenses for which the inmate may be punished by a reprimand, loss of privileges or a brief (few hour) period of confinement to his cell — referred to here as "minor misbehavior." Ideally, writing up the inmate for a minor rule infraction or major violation should be a last resort. Disciplinary hearings are time-consuming and can be disruptive to the institution.

Minor misbehavior (such as cursing a staff member) may result in a reprimand or, as indicated above, some variation of the losses for any minor rule violation. More serious minor infractions are those that include loss of privileges, room (or unit) restrictions, loss of commissary, extra duty, and the like. The principal difference lies in who decides on the punishment. Minor misbehavior is decided upon by the unit officer, minor infractions by the senior unit officer or a unit committee in an informal hearing, and the major violation is decided by a facility-wide committee in a more formal hearing, as described below.

The principal concern of the courts is for the conduct of disciplinary hearings when needed for major rule violations and for the types of discipline given. That is, are the punishments used fairly related to the offense? Fairness is defined in terms of "grievous loss." Minor rule infractions involving less severe losses to the inmate are seen differently than those involving either additional time in jail (loss of gain time) or a "severe change in environment," such as disciplinary segregation.[291] The following situations are often defined as sufficiently serious as to require the imposition of full due process protections, or a major hearing:

> Violations that may result in any type of isolated confinement for more than 10 days;
>
> Violations punishable by indefinite confinement in segregation;
>
> Violations for which the punishment may increase the prisoner's sentence;
>
> Violations that may be referred to the district attorney for criminal prosecution.[292]

Loss of an institutional job is not considered grievous.

---

[291] Clutchette v. Procunier, 328 F. Supp. 767 (N.D.Cal. 1971).

[292] If the inmate is found guilty at an administrative hearing and punished he/she may also be tried in a court of law without being placed in a situation of "double jeopardy." See United States v. Hedges, 458 F.2d 188,190 (10th Cir. 1972). However, an administrative hearing after acquittal has been questioned, see Barrows v. Hogan, 379 F.Supp. 314 (M.D. Pa. 1974).

Full Due Process Protection. In the landmark case of Wolff v. McDonnell (1974) the Supreme Court defined the minimum requirements for a due process disciplinary hearing as no less than 24-hour advance notice of the hearing, right to receive a written statement of the evidence and reasons for the proposed discipline, and the right to call witnesses. There is no right to retained or appointed legal counsel, or to cross-examine witnesses, although the hearing board may allow it if it poses no danger. No written reasons for this denial are necessary. There need be no verbatim transcript of the hearing, although a written summary is required.

A concern not addressed clearly by the courts is the amount of time one can spend in prehearing detention while awaiting the hearing. ACA standards require that an investigation be undertaken within 48 hours of the time the violation is reported, charges given to the inmate within 24 hours of completion of the investigation, notice of the infraction given 24 hours in advance of the hearing, and the hearing held within 72 hours of the incident, excluding weekends and holidays.[293] Assuming the incident begins with the written report, the hearing should occur in a maximum time of nine days of the incident, inclusive of one weekend. An impartial hearing officer or board is considered important, as is the right of the inmate to be present, unless disruptive.[294] An inmate may choose to remain silent, but a "negative inference" regarding guilt may be drawn from this silence.[295]

The principal difference in practice between major and minor hearings is the makeup of the reviewing body and the formality of the hearing. Hearings on minor violations may be conducted by one senior officer on a unit.[296] Hearings on major violations may be conducted by a facility hearing board made up of three staff, usually an administrator, a custody officer, and a program staff member. Review of all disciplinary decisions is required in ACA standards, as is the inmate's right to waive various aspects of the hearing process, such as 24 hour notice.[297] An inmate disciplined in the facility may also be charged criminally without incurring double jeopardy; the

---

[293] ACA 2-5311 (1986) 55.

[294] ACA Standard 2-5318 (1981) 86.

[295] Baxter v. Palmigiano, 425 U.S. 308 (1976).

[296] ACA Standard 2-5319 (1981).

[297] ACA 2-5323 (1981) 86.

administrative hearing is to enforce discipline, while the criminal prosecution is to meet the purposes of the criminal law.[298]

The time allowed for punishment in segregation has not been resolved by the courts, with penalties ranging from 15 days to indefinite periods. ACA Standards, worked out with the U.S. Attorney General and consistent with the Attorney General's standards for prisons and jails, allow no more than 60 days in disciplinary segregation, with a 30 day review and approval by the facility administrator.[299] There is no difference for prisons and jails. The 60-day maximum raises problems for many facility administrators who feel these inmates are still dangerous after the 60 days and should be segregated from the general population. In these cases administrative segregation is used, for which the requirements are less stringent, and for which there are no specific time limits set by courts or national standards.

The decision on administrative segregation (or protective custody) is a classification decision for which the requirements of Wolff need not be met. The minimal due process standards for placement in administrative segregation found in Hewitt v. Helms are required.[300] The inmate must be provided a "nonadversary evidentiary review" — that is, an informal hearing — prior to such a transfer. He must be given "some notice of the charges against him and an opportunity to present his views to the prison official charged with deciding whether to transfer him to administrative segregation ... and the decisionmaker reviews the charges and then-available evidence against the prisoner" in order to make the decision.[301] One appeals court case found that an indefinite period of segregation did not amount to cruel and unusual punishment even though there was virtually no communication or association with other inmates; however, conditions provided satisfactory shelter, clothing, food, exercise, sanitation, lighting, heat, bedding, medical and psychiatric attention, and personal safety. There apparently was danger to the inmate from other inmates, and he was suicidal and escape-prone.[302]

---

[298] U.S. v. Smith, 464 F.2d 194 (10th Cir. 1972).

[299] ACA Standard 2-5313 (1986) 55.

[300] Hewitt v. Helms, 459 U.S. 460 (1983).

[301] Hewitt v. Helms (1983).

[302] Jackson v. Meachum, 699 F.2d 578 (1st Cir. 1983).

Depending on how the administrator write rules or policies, due process protections may be created for inmates where none otherwise might have existed. Under the concept of "state-created liberty interests," where a rule places substantive limitations on the exercise of discretion in a given area, it creates a liberty interest protected by due process and the Fourteenth Amendment. Thus, for instance, where the rule states that a particular decision will be made only upon the existence of certain conditions ("inmates will be placed in segregation only upon a finding that they are a threat to the security of the institution, an escape risk, or pending investigation of possible infractions ...") some form of due process review must accompany that decision. It is irrelevant under this method of analysis whether the decision is seen as disciplinary. What is critical is the presence or absence of limitations on discretion under the rule.[303]

Conditions of Segregation. Conditions of segregation have been addressed only minimally by the courts. It is not unconstitutional to use segregation provided sanitary conditions are maintained and the diet is equivalent to that of the general prisoners. ACA standards are more stringent regarding the conditions of segregation, including contact with others, exercise, and periodic review of the reasons for the confinement.[304]

H. Regular Exercise

Exercise must not be confused with passive recreation or leisure time activities. Exercise refers to rigorous physical activity in an indoor area, such as a gymnasium, or an outdoor area, preferably with both available. (Rigorous exercise in juvenile facilities is referred to as "large muscle exercise.") Exercise has increasingly become a concern of the courts, although primarily for offenders in segregation. ACA standards require a minimum of one hour a day, five days a week of exercise outside segregation cells, unless security or safety dictates otherwise.[305] The Supreme Court has not spoken clearly on this issue, although for Alabama they let stand a requirement for 30 minutes of outdoor exercise per day for inmates in isolation.[306] Lower courts vary

---

[303]See Collins (1987) ch. XI.

[304]ACA Standards (1981) 55-59.

[305]ACA Standard 2-5223 (1981) 58.

[306]Pugh v. Locke, 559 F.22d 283 (5th Cir. 1977).

from stating that New York City jails with 50 minutes a week of exercise is too little, while in Texas one hour outdoors three times a week is sufficient.[307] Certainly three hours a week is a minimum for inmates in either segregated or general conditions. A minimum of one hour per day, seven days a week will be legally adequate, but good facility administrators know the value of recreation and exercise in helping to relieve some of the tensions that can build up in a jail environment. As much recreation as possible should be arranged, limited only by staff and space constraints.

Passive leisure time activities should be available on an ongoing basis. These include television, radios, table games, a library, and somewhat more active games like pool and table tennis. Personal radios and television can be a problem, particularly if they are to be shared. Some system for selection of stations must be devised. Noise also can become a problem. To solve it, a Massachusetts jail, for example, required alteration of all personal radios and televisions by replacing the speakers with headphones, which ensured the listener's privacy and made the jail much more liveable.

I. Programs and Treatment

Do the inmates in your jail have a right to programs of rehabilitation or other types of treatment services? Do they have a right to work or develop job skills while incarcerated? What is your obligation to provide these treatment services? Certainly the lack of resources, trained personnel, and programs that work are logical constraints on providing programs for inmates. Also, the short stay of most inmates makes it very difficult to develop programs of rehabilitation, including employment skills training, that will be effective. Large jail systems that hold sentenced offenders for up to one year are more likely to have programs.

It is not at all clear that the Constitution requires correctional agencies to provide adequate or effective treatment or rehabilitation programs.[308] No court decision has held that there is a general right to programs of rehabilitation in correctional institutions. Inmates of the York County Prison in Pennsylvania

---

[307] Rhem v. Malcolm (1974); Alberti v. Sheriff of Harris Co., Texas (1975).

[308] Generally, see Sheldon Krantz, Corrections and Prisoners' Rights (St. Paul: West Publishing Company Nutshell Series, 1983) 190-194.

raised this issue in Padgett v. Stein.[309] The District Court said that provision of "meaningful rehabilitative treatment" is a social policy question that should be resolved by the legislative and executive branches of government, stating that lack of programs was not cruel and unusual punishment, and that it is not a duty of the jail to provide programs. The court did, however, include treatment services in its review of the following areas for minimal compliance: personnel, admission, orientation, rules and regulations, classification, housing (especially for juveniles), clothing, bedding, food services, personal hygiene, medical and health services, visiting, correspondence, work programs, library, religion, recreation, commissary, discipline and punishment, security, "extraordinary occurrences reports," investigations of deaths and notification, and sanitation and safety.[310] In another jail case a U.S. District Court said that rehabilitation must "be the overriding goal" of incarceration.[311]

This raises questions about the purposes of the jail — is its role simply incapacitation and punishment, and possibly deterrence? Some legislation, such as that in California, simply states that the purpose of prison is punishment. While this may be the case for prisons, programs still thrive in prisons. It is becoming increasingly clear that modern jails cannot function only as holding facilities. Where possible they can be very effective "first line" in directing offenders to needed services, although most services are very limited. Certainly the jail can use either a staff member or a volunteer to locate existing resources and arrange for some coordination in meeting the needs of some offenders in the jail. These include mental health centers, city or county health departments, county hospitals, drug abuse programs, Alcoholics Anonymous, Narcotics Anonymous, ministerial associations, and vocational services. Legal services and local educational and training opportunities should be included in this effort.

Work programs for inmates in the jail should be available, and usually are. These need not be and usually are not paid positions. Moreover, the Supreme Court has indicated that there is no constitutional requirement that prisoners be assigned meaningful jobs

---

[309]Padgett v. Stein 406 F.Supp. 287 (M.D. Pa. 1975); cf. Palmer on the right to rehabilitation programs 173-185 (Chapter 10).

[310]Palmer 629.

[311]Taylor v. Sterrett, 344 F.Supp 411 (N.D. Texas 1972).

based on skills and interests.[312] Sentenced prisoners can be assigned to do work for the benefit of the facility, including work release and other programs outside the facility in which inmates can earn wages to pay for their keep, provide restitution, pay fines, and/or support their families.

One of the more successful programs of prerelease is in Montgomery County, Maryland, and has been designated as one of six resource centers of the National Institute of Corrections. The Center houses up to 72 males and 12 females. Staff work closely with the main detention center in providing community release for offenders with six months left on their sentences. The Center provides work, counseling, drug treatment, recreation, educational opportunities, and medical and dental services. The commitment of the Center is to the offender and to the community, which demands strict supervision of releasees. Since about 40 percent have a drug problem, strict drug testing is used, as described earlier, with return to the main facility for violations.[313] Inmates contract with the Pre-Release Center and their performance is rated in order to advance through three program phases. Earnings are used to pay room and board, make support payments to their families, and pay required fines and/or restitution.

The Genesee County Sheriff's Department, located near Buffalo, New York, provides another example of how a local detention facility can balance the needs of the community and the offender. Genesee County is a county of about 60,000 residents which does not allow inmates to sit idle on the taxpayers money. Starting in 1982 a Community Service/Restitution Program was developed to address the needs of victims, offenders, and the community.[314] Offenders are placed on intensive supervision, put under house arrest, placed on community service in order to make restitution, and become involved in victim/offender reconciliation.[315] Over 800 offenders have been diverted to community service sentencing, providing 80,000 hours of service to 118 non-profit agencies. Thirty judges use the community service sentencing option, with 118 participating agencies.

---

[312] Newman v. Alabama, 559 F.2d 283 (5th Cir. 1977).

[313] Sechrest and Farrell 10-12.

[314] Genesee Justice, 1985-86 Annual Report, Community Service/Victim Assistance Program, Genesee County Sheriff's Department.

[315] "Genesee Justice, Instruments of Law, Order, and Peace," undated (c. 1986); Community Service/Victim Assistance Program, Genesee County Sheriff's Department, County Building No. 1, Batavia, New York 14020-3199, phone (716) 344-2550.

Ninety percent (95.3%) of the offenders involved have successfully completed their community service (707 of 742). Savings in jail and prison space are estimated at 65 years.

Genesee County also began a juvenile program with community assignments of eight to 250 hours of service. All 38 youngsters in the program so far have completed it. Another program addresses cemetery and school vandalism. A "Victim Directed Sentencing" program was instituted in 1983 that has intervened on behalf of 149 victims and their families to provide information, restitution, prosecution, and protection. A "Victim/Offender Reconciliation" program has also been initiated that is designed to ensure that offenders are accountable to their victims. Moreover, the sentenced population in Genesee county has dropped from 235 in 1981 to 186 in 1985. Both the numbers of defendants sentenced to the jail and state prison and the days served have been reduced. No suicide has taken place in the jail since 1981. Plans to build a new facility have been reduced by half the 2.8 million originally planned.[316] These Genesee County programs demonstrate how serving the interests of justice and the community can be done in detention environments. They show that these facilities can be more than jails, they can be proactive in bringing people — offenders and victims — back into the community.

---

[316]Instead of Jail, One County in New York Imposes a Sentence of Work ,Reparations or "House Arrest." Wall Street Journal 24 December 1983: 28.

CHAPTER SIX: CONTRACTING FOR SERVICES

I. Introduction[317]

There are several fundamental legal issues surrounding the question of "privatization," or the contracting of various portions of jail services to private service providers, up to and including the complete operation of the jail. This chapter addresses both, but a major current concern is the contracting of the entire jail operation to a private contractors. Issues relating to contracts for food service, medical care, laundry, and maintenance, are, with the possible exceptions of education, industries, and vocational training in state and federal systems, comparatively minor ancillary services in relation to contracting for the complete operation of a detention facility. The most controversial issue is contracting for the entire operation of jails by private firms. It has been opposed by the National Sheriffs' Association and other groups, especially unions.[318] Many of the questions raised involve the liability of the jurisdiction when it provides detention services through private contractors. Generally, the answer is that the county or city will not be able to avoid or diminish its legal responsibility for the care of inmates in the jail.[319] Issues of quality and accountability are management concerns whether contracting is for specific services or for entire facilities.

Much of what is said here would apply to other types of contracts just as they will also apply to the prison contracting situation. While the term "county" will be used throughout it also means municipal governments, to which most comments will also apply. While private operation of jails has some historic precedent legal and management issues in jail operation have changed so dramatically in the last 10 to 20 years that contracting issues or problems from the 19th century have little relevance in the waning decades of the 20th century.

---

[317]This chapter is adapted from Collins: Correctional Law 1986.

[318]John DiIulio, Jr. "Prisons, Profits, and the Public Good: The Privatization of Corrections," Research Bulletin No. 1 (Criminal Justice Center, Sam Houston State University) 2.

[319]Joan Mullen, "Corrections and the Private Sector,"N IJ Reports (Washington, D.C.: National Institute of Justice, May, 1985) 6.

There is no body of current case law dealing with the contracting of all jail operations to a private organization. Since there is then little immediate experience to draw on, it is not possible to identify and address all issues which may arise. It is possible, however, to identify and discuss some of the fundamental issues, one of which is simply recognizing the unknown aspects of contracting for jail services, and to try and identify these in the contracting process as much as possible. A related goal is to build into the contract enough flexibility to be able to address previously unidentified problems as they do arise.

II. The Power To Contract: An Uncertain Area

Recognizing the potential for substantial variation in law from state to state, some generalizations about contracting for jail services can be made. First, there are inherent constitutional limitations which probably prohibit a complete jail operations contract as being an excessive delegation of governmental powers. However, where government retains sufficient supervisory and monitoring authority and policy direction over the jail operation, an operations contract probably will pass constitutional muster, especially if there is specific statutory authority for contracting.

The necessity of specific statutory authority varies from state to state. Contracts for ancillary jail services (food, medical services, laundry, etc.) are probably valid, with or without specific enabling legislation. A recent publication of the National Institute of Justice addresses five issues in private contracting — the legality of contracting, labor relations, liability, use of force, and inmate rights.[320] The study was done by the Council of State Governments and the Urban Institute to develop guidelines for states and localities that want to contract for the entire operation of facilities. The authors conclude that such contracting can be done if State laws permit it, and most States are clarifying their laws in this area. They note that only 1,200 inmates are now held in secure private facilities, and only three of these are jails.

---

[320]Judith C. Hackett, Harry P. Hatry, Robert B. Levinson, Joan Allen, Keon Chi, and Edward D. Feigenbaum, "Contracting for the Operation of Prisons and Jails," Research in Brief (Washington, D.C.: U.S. Department of Justice, National Institute of Justice, June, 1987).

A. Total Facility Contract: Direct Precedent Lacking

There are virtually no reported court decisions which address the basic question of whether, and under what circumstances and limitations, a county can contract for its entire jail operation. Is specific statutory authorization needed? Even with a statute, are there ultimate constitutional limitations on the power to contract?

In the absence of directly applicable precedent, one turns for guidance to the general area of contracting for municipal services. There, one is struck by the lack of consistent court decisions. Virtually all of the case law in the area comes from state courts, so even where courts of different states may agree on a general principle, they may disagree on the application of that principle. Given the lack of any landmark decisions with nationwide applicability, any statements regarding the power to contract must be recognized as generalities. Advice regarding specific situations will require analysis of applicable state law (both statutory and constitutional) as well as examination of the charter of the municipal corporation which is considering a contract.

B. For What May Municipalities Contract?

With regard to the general question of the powers of local government to contract, the majority rule is that a municipal corporation may enter into contracts "which are proper and reasonably necessary to enable it to perform the functions expressly conferred upon it."[321] McQuillin, probably the leading treatise on municipal corporation law, states that implied power to contract exists as a necessary adjunct to the municipal corporation's abilities to carry out powers expressly granted the organization.[322] Thus, there is authority for the proposition that a municipality may enter into any contract it deems necessary in carrying out its expressly conferred powers. In another treatise on municipal law, Sands concludes that given a county's power to act in a given area, contracts in furtherance of the power are ordinarily viewed as ancillary to or subsumed in the basic grant of power.[323]

---

[321]McQuillin, Municipal Corporations, 3rd ed., sec. 29.05.

[322]McQuillin.

[323]Sands on Municipal Corporations, Sec. 22.03.

The principles from Sands and McQuillin suggest that even without specific statutory authorization, there is probably no legal problem regarding contracting for the provision of ancillary services in a jail — laundry, food services, medical services, maintenance, etc. In the controversy over privatization, there seems to be little or no question raised regarding the propriety of contracting for such support services. The more ministerial a task is, probably the more likely it can be contracted out.[324] A question then arises regarding what sorts of functions then can be seen as ancillary, especially when traditional custodial tasks are considered.

The privatization question lies on a continuum. Certain kinds of services which are integral to a jail (and which may well carry constitutional significance) can clearly be contracted. Other aspects of the jail probably cannot ever be delegated through contract to the private provider. Unfortunately, there is no bright line separating the valid from the void, and the probably irregular line which may exist is still shrouded in an opaque legal mist.

C. When Is Statutory Authorization Required?

The answer to this question is "it depends ..." on the state and the scope of the contract. If a statute does authorize a contract for jail operations, at least one basic issue is resolved. The remaining questions then generally relate to the mechanics of the contracting process. For example, who is authorized to contract on behalf of local government, is the contract in proper form, etc., and the omnipresent question of does the contract exceed the constitutional limitations that would exist in regard to a county's contracting away too much of a governmental service (even if general enabling legislation existed)?

An example of the uncertainty which exists in the absence of statutory authorization to contract for jail services is reflected in formal Attorney General opinions from New Mexico, South Carolina, and Tennessee.[325]

In New Mexico, the Attorney General interpreted a statute stating that the jails were under the "control" of the sheriff or jail

---

[324]Ministerial acts are distinguished from "discretionary acts" in the law. Ministerial acts are those that amount only to the performance of a duty in which the officer is left with no significant choice of his own. Discretionary acts are those that require personal deliberation and judgment; del Carmen (1985) 34.

[325]New Mexico AGO number 85-3; opinion of the Tennessee Attorney General dated June 20, 1984; opinion of the South Carolina Attorney General dated August 8, 1985.

administrator hired by the county commissioners to convey no authority to contract for the operation of the jail.

In Tennessee, general statutory language authorizing counties to "make all contracts necessary for the furtherance of any public works project," was read by the Attorney General to authorize jail operation contracts.[326] Tennessee statutes giving county officials supervisory power over jails were not seen as prohibiting a sheriff from employing a contractor to provide jailers and correctional officers for the maintenance of the jail. Tennessee opinion did note that while the private contractor could indemnify the county, county officials would remain ultimately liable for the operation of jails and work houses.

The South Carolina Attorney General reached a conclusion similar to that of the Tennessee Attorney General in an opinion regarding state contracting for prison operation. The state statutory duties to contract and supervise prisoners would not prevent a management contract so long as the state retained certain oversight functions. But even concluding that contracts for prison operation were consistent with state law, the South Carolina opinion adds a caveat, recognizing that a court could reach the opposite conclusion![327]

Despite the general assurances from McQuillin and Sands about implied authority to contract, the question of whether a specific county may contract for complete jail services in the absence of statutory authority remains almost unanswerable until appropriate courts decide the issue. To avoid confusion and uncertainty and the possibility of a contract being found void for want of enabling legislation, it is clearly preferable that enabling legislation be passed.

Few states have legislation which speaks specifically to contracting for jail operation. Typically, statutes regarding jail operation give authority to operate the jail to the sheriff or to the county or city, and are silent on the question of contracting.[328] Lack of specific legislative direction in this area may be due to the

---

[326]Tennessee Opinion 2.

[327]South Carolina Opinion 17-18.

[328]Kansas Statutes Annotated, 19-1901 et seq., Ill. S.H.A. ch. 75, Sec. 101 et seq., Cal. Penal Code 4000 et seq.

comparatively recent emergence of organizations interested in contracting for jail operation and should not necessarily be seen as a negative legislative statement on the contracting question.

At least two legislatures have passed statutes recently which authorize the private operation of jails. In Florida, a bill passed allowing county commissioners to "contract with private entities for the provision of the operation and maintenance of a county detention facility ... and the supervision of county prisoners."[329] The same act grants similar power to the Department of Corrections to contract for state facility operation, but only with specific legislative approval and specific appropriation.[330] The New Mexico legislature, in response to an attorney general's opinion discussed above which concluded that counties could not contract without specific legislative authority, took a more cautious approach in 1984. The legislature authorized two pilot projects, subject to Attorney General approval, prior to July 10, 1987.[331] All private jail operations are also required to post performance bonds, meet minimum training standards, as well as other specific statutory requirements.

While a lack of specific enabling legislation may leave contracting an open question, in some cases statutes may actually prohibit contracts. For instance, Washington statutes specifically prohibit contracts which "would have the effect of terminating classified employees or classified employee positions existing at the time of the execution ... of the contract." [332] There may be other nonstatutory impediments to contracting, such as existing union labor contracts. The NIJ publication specifically notes that state laws prohibiting strikes by public correctional officers "probably would not apply to private employees."[333] Clearly, this means that backup personnel must be available in case of a strike, work stoppage, or slowdown, and that contracts must require notice to the jurisdiction in advance of contract negotiations or termination.

---

[329]Chapter 85-3400 5, Florida Laws of 1985, F.S.A 944.105.

[330]Florida Laws of 1985.

[331]New Mexico Statutes Annotated Sec. 33-3-26.

[332]Revised Code of Washington 41.06.380.

[333]Hackett et al. 2-3.

D. Even With Proper Legislation, Is Delegation Excessive?

Assuming enabling legislation does exist, the question of whether the delegation of jail operation authority from the government to the private organization is authorized is answered. However, there remains the question of whether the authorized delegation is excessive under basic constitutional limitations.

The general statements of Sands and McQuillin regarding a county's contractual powers are limited, depending on the subject of the contract. Numerous cases hold that governmental and legislative powers (as opposed to proprietary powers) cannot be contracted, even with statutory authorization.[334] Without going into the rather murky distinctions between governmental and proprietary powers, suffice it to say that at least the "essence" of running a jail is a governmental function and probably cannot be contracted to a private organization.

But even the "can't contract governmental function" rubric is not absolute. Although the care of the poor and the sick is traditionally seen as a governmental function, the Alaska Supreme Court in 1963 approved a contract between the City of Ketchikan and a church organization for the operation of a public hospital. The court noted that the hospital did not lose its public purpose since the contract required care to be provided to all. While the contract allowed the religious order to adopt rules for internal operation (challenged as an illegal delegation of power), the court held that the power to lease the hospital for operation implies the power to delegate internal operational matters, since it would be impractical to do otherwise.[335]

A similar result has been reached by the Pennsylvania Supreme Court. [336] A contract between Philadelphia and two private universities to run the Philadelphia General Hospital was challenged. The City Charter called for the Department of Public Health to have general supervision over all city hospitals and for the board of trustees of Philadelphia General Hospital to direct and control its management. The Pennsylvania Constitution said that

---

[334]McQuillin 29.07; Pittman v. City of Amarillo, 598 S.W. 2d 941 (Tex. Civ. App., 1980).

[335]Lien v. City of Ketchikan, 383 P. 2d 721 (Alaska 1963).

[336]Robinson v. City of Philadelphia, 161 A. 2d 1 (Penn., 1960).

cities could not delegate to private corporations any power that would interfere with municipal improvement or property or which would allow the performance of any municipal function. Despite these limitations, the contract was approved by the court.

The contract left the board of trustees with the power to set standards for the hospital's operation and provided that the executive director of the hospital (a public employee) would still have "general supervisory" power. Because the operation had to satisfy the board of trustees, the court felt that the powers and responsibilities of the public agencies had not been unlawfully delegated and the contract was approved.

The principle that seems to emerge from the Lien (1963) and the Robinson (1960) cases is that if government retains enough of a supervisory or rule setting power or the ability to assure itself of satisfactory operation, a contract with a private organization which involves a governmental function will be approved. It is when a contract gives away so much of the municipality's power "as to embarrass and interfere with its future control over (the subject matter of the contract) as public interests may require," that the contract will be seen as void.[337]

By implication then a contract which deals with a governmental function (e.g., jail operations) but which does not"embarrass or interfere" with the municipality's future control over the subject of the contract is not necessarily void. Such a delicate balance was satisfactorily struck in both the Lien and Robinson cases.

E. What Is "Excessive" Delegation?

It seems clear that in some jurisdictions specific statutory authority is probably required for a major jail operations contract. Regardless of the statutory question, however, a contract that delegates too much of the county's supervisory duties over the jail and interferes with government's future control over the jail will probably be held absolutely void.[338]

---

[337]McQuillin, Sec. 29.07.

[338]McQuillin, Sec. 29.07.

Certain jail functions, if contracted, would clearly compromise the government's ability to act in the public interest in regard to jail operation. These would include, at a minimum:

> Exclusive power over the admission decision, particularly in the absence of the existence of any alternative facilities. If a dangerous felony suspect was refused admission into a jail because it was full (according to the contract), the government's ability to enforce the criminal laws and protect the public safety would clearly be prejudiced; and, the release decision and decisions which affect the date of release, e.g., granting or denial of good time.

Whether contracting for other jail functions, e.g., food, medical care, maintenance, etc., would "embarrass or interfere" with the county's governmental power to operate the jail becomes more debatable as one moves further away from the discretionary admit-release functions. Some kinds of contracts are implicit in jail operations. For instance, while the jailer has a clear duty to feed prisoners,[339] no one would suggest the government must produce its own raw food supply instead of purchasing it. Also, no one seems to suggest that contracting for food services is in some way unconstitutional. In fact, such food service contracts, with large corporations or local restaurants or individual citizens, are relatively common among jails and have been so for some time. On the other hand, classifying an inmate in or out of various levels of custody (increasing or decreasing degrees of liberty) is a more difficult question to answer.

While one is tempted to say the custodial aspects of a jail, including the use of force, represents basic governmental functions, the increasingly common usage of private security personnel suggests that even full police powers may be at least statutorily delegated to private organizations or individuals.[340]

In analyzing the question of how much power may be delegated and how much should be retained, the South Carolina Attorney General stated there needed to be ample guidelines for a

---

[339]Pugh v. Locke, 406 F.Supp. 318 (M.D. Ala. 1976) aff'd 559 F.2d 283 (5th Cir. 1977) cert. den. 98 S.Ct. 3144 (1978) stated that three wholesome and nutritionally adequate and properly prepared meals must be served to prisoners each day together with proper eating and drinking utensils, under the supervision of a food service manager at each institution, with the approval of a dietician.

[340]See Inbau, Aspen and Spiotto, Protective Security Law 20-24 (1983).

prison operation or a suitable reporting or monitoring system.[341] The South Carolina opinion also cautions that "the area of prison security would be particularly subject to close scrutiny by the courts, because that function embraces the very essence of governmental power.

F. Guidelines for Contracting

Given the uncertainty that exists about contracting, making specific statements about the legality of contracting for one function or another in jail is somewhat risky. With this in mind, the following guidelines are offered. These will be considered within the framework of four basic divisions of jail operations, each of which in turn contains many smaller components:

1. **Administration:** Management and policy setting, personnel (hiring, firing, training). budget, and recordkeeping.

2. **Security:** Inmate safety, key and gate control, perimeter security, contraband control,etc.

3. **Support Services:** Medical programs, food service, laundry, facility maintenance, etc.

4. **Programs:** Work release and other programs, such as visiting, education, recreation, religious activities, etc.

1. Administration

Obviously, ultimate jail policy is set at this level and cannot be contracted. Other sorts of administrative functions would appear amenable to contracting. These would include such things as clerical services, training, data collection, data processing, accounting, etc.

2. Security

Security is the essence of the jail function. It is security which keeps the inmates from wandering free in the community. Yet many "security" functions are almost entirely ministerial, such as opening and closing gates.[342] Because of such issues as use of force, clear statutory authority seems particularly advisable as a condition precedent to contracts for security functions.

---

[341] South Carolina Opinion, page 16.

[342] See del Carmen (1985) 34.

Even for security, however, the use of private resources is not uncommon. The use of private inmate transport services in the extradition area is quite common. California law allows the Sheriff to hire private security guards to supervise prisoners held in hospitals.[343]

As in disciplinary procedures, the key to a security contract appears to be the excessive delegation question: has the county retained enough supervisory and policy control so that the contract does not potentially embarrass the county in its ability to maintain necessary jail services?

Under the test to determine if the activity would "embarrass or interfere" with the basic operation of the jail, only classification would appear to present potential contracting problems. Since jail classification is primarily a security function, it must be approached more cautiously with respect to contracting.

3. Support Services

Many support services, some of major constitutional significance, are commonly contracted without particular question or controversy, e.g., food and medical services. Perhaps the one support service which presents serious concern is that of disciplinary procedures, especially when they may involve the length of an inmate's term. Actions which are directly part of an inmate's "punishment," as length of stay would be, are clearly part of the essential governmental function of the jail. Delegated disciplinary procedures would have to be examined very carefully, especially to the extent government employees did not retain ultimate authority over sentence length.[344]

4. Programs

From a legal standpoint, this is perhaps the easiest division to evaluate. Virtually all types of inmate programming can be contracted. Indeed, much already is — work release, drug and alcohol treatment, and religious activities, for example. Many such

---

[343]California Penal Code Sec. 404.

[344]One notes, by perhaps imperfect analogy, the relatively common practice of courts using private attorneys as "pro tem" judges under proper safeguards and with proper enabling legislation, State v. McNairy, 20 Wash. App 438, 580 P. 2d 650 (1978), consent of parties to use of a pro tem judge required.

programs do not touch constitutionally significant areas and, therefore, civil rights liability exposure is comparatively slim. However, especially when constitutionally protected interests are involved, close supervision of contractor policies and practices will be important, e.g., mail handling and delivery. Being a relatively ministerial function, mail services would appear easily "contractable." Yet if mishandled, mail issues can involve rights of both the prisoner and the free-world correspondent. As indicated under security, classification is the one area that may represent difficulties.

G. Summary

Because of the inconsistency between court decisions in the area of municipal corporate contracting, there is no clear "yes or no" answer to whether a jail operation may be contracted in its entirety without specific legislative authorization. Even with such legislation, it is not clear how far a private contractor may go in assuming complete operation of the jail. However, certain general principles can be stated:

> In the absence of statutory authorization, a county's power to contract for complete jail operations is, at best, suspect and may be condemned as an unauthorized delegation of the county's powers. Therefore, having clear statutory authorization is certainly advisable.[345] Clear and comprehensive legislation can address and answer many questions (beyond the basic authority issue) which otherwise may remain somewhat unsettled until addressed by a court, e.g., what powers to use force do private jailers have?

Even with legislative authority behind it, a contract may go too far. To avoid the "excessive delegation" issue (if this is possible), an operations contract would have to be drafted in a way so as to preserve the essence of the governmental function for government officials. It would have to assure that the public's interests in maintaining the jail, by holding the pretrial detainee, punishing the sentenced offender, etc., are not delegated to the private provider. Additionally, the contract should assure that the county retains

[345]Pure legalities aside, legislative consideration of the privatization issue may also help address, in a public forum, the philosophical and policy questions which are so much a part of the privatization controversy.

clear supervisory and monitoring powers. This will allow the county to continue to assert policy control over jail operations and also to identify problems and assure their prompt correction. The degree to which contract makes the private provider simply the administrative extension of the county government, leaving ultimate authority in the hands of the government, the more likely it is that the contract will pass judicial scrutiny.

III. Liability in Contracting

A properly drawn contract can probably eliminate liability exposure in some situations and, through contractor insurance, reduce monetary exposure in other areas.

Will a correctional services contract shield a county from liability exposure to inmate litigation? A great deal has been said about liability and ultimate responsibility, some of which can be best described as argumentative nonsense. The NIJ publication notes that there has been no court test of contractor liability under 42 U.S.C. 1983, but that neither contractors nor the jurisdiction will be shielded from civil liability; however, contractual specificity can apparently reduce governmental exposure.[346]

If properly drafted, a contract can remove some, but not all, liability exposure from the county altogether, and it can also erect an insurance-type barrier of protection from other forms of liability. In any event, the government will, of course, pay for liability protection as the contractor's insurance costs are passed on to the agency as part of the contractor's overhead expense.

A fundamental point regarding jail contracting and liability is that a county may be able to eliminate and/or reduce its actual liability exposure to some extent through contracting for correctional services; however, the jail inmate's ability to sue for violations of their constitutional rights will not be reduced. At best (or worst, depending on one's point of view), the identity of the defendants will be changed.

A. Contractor Actions Will Be State Action.

Contracting operations to a private operator will not cut off potential liability for violations of the Civil Rights Act, 42 U.S.C. Sec. 1983,

---

[346]Hackett <u>et al</u>. 3.

either for the government or for the contractor. Operation of the institution, or operation of a significant program in the institution, is typically seen as being "under color of law," even if done by a private provider. Therefore, the provider, and possibly the government, are exposed to civil rights liability or constitutional violations.

Where a power delegated to a private provider is one "traditionally reserved to the state" or traditionally the exclusive prerogative of the state, the acts of the private provider are seen as "state action" for liability purposes, as indicated in Medina v. O'Neill 589 F.Supp. 1028 (S.D. Tex. 1984).[347] This is sometimes referred to as the "public function" test.[348] Medina is significant because it demonstrates how liability can flow from the private provider back to the contracting government agency. In Medina, Immigration and Naturalization Service (INS) employees, who issued detention orders for a group of stowaways, were found liable for unconstitutional living conditions maintained in a private facility in which the stowaways were held. A second issue involved the killing of one inmate and wounding of another by a private security guard. In both instances the federal defendants shared liability with the private company. The test, drawn from a 1982 case, Rendell-Baker v. Kohn, stated that the relevant question was not simply whether a private group is serving a "public function" but whether "the function performed has been 'traditionally the exclusive prerogative of the State.'"[349] Detention was seen to come squarely within this test.[350]

Acts of private security guards taken in concert with police or pursuant to customary procedures agreed to by police can constitute state action.[351] Similarly, where private parties can substitute their

---

[347]589 F.Supp. 1028 (S.D. Tex. 1984); Ancata v. Prison Health Services, Inc., 769 F. 2d 700 (llth Cir.) 1985.

[348]See Rolando V. del Carmen, Potential Liabilities of Probation and Parole Officers, 1985 184-186, for a discussion of four tests of government liability and responsibility; also see Ira Robbins, "Privatization of Corrections: Defining the Issues," Federal Bar News and Journal 33(5) May-June, 1986: 196-197.

[349]457 U.S. 830 (1982).

[350]See also del Carmen, (1985) 184-185 and Robbins (1986) 196. The facility discussed in Medina was an improvised holding facility maintained by a shipping company, and not one of the major INS facilities that have been contracted out to one of the leading private prison corporations.

[351]El Fundi v. DeRoche, 625 F. 2d 195 (8th Cir. 1980).

judgment for state officials regarding a state act, state action exists.[352] In these cases the courts may apply the "joint action test," where private defendants are seen as joint participants with state officials.[353]

Therefore, the private jail service provider generally is cloaked with enough attributes of the state to expose the provider to potential liability under the Civil Rights Act. In at least some circumstances liability will extend beyond the provider to the government agency ultimately responsible for providing jail services.

In what may be a very significant pair of decisions, the Fourth Circuit Court of Appeals has ruled that where "a professional (a medical doctor in the two cases), acting within the bounds of traditional discretion and judgment, does not act under color of state law, even where ... the professional is a full-time employee of the state." In other words, the court is saying that where a professional like a medical doctor acts like a doctor and not part doctor and part correctional official, the doctor cannot be sued under the Civil Rights Act. It remains to be seen if this holding is adopted by other circuits, but to the extent that it becomes the law of the land (or even parts of the land), it suggests careful scrutiny be given to the role of professionals in the jail.[354]

B. Municipal Liability is Not Automatic

Assignment of liability to a government does not automatically flow from a finding of private provider liability in the civil rights area. To be liable in a civil rights action, a defendant must be personally responsible for the violation.[355] Since most counties indemnify their employees for most types of civil rights litigation, individual liability has the effect of being county liability, at least for monetary purposes. But where liability arose from the isolated acts of individuals employed by the corporation, liability would stop

---

[352]Jones v. Eagleville Hospital and Rehabilitation Center, 588 F.Supp. 53 (E.D. Pennsylvania 1984), citing Lugar v. Edmonson Oil Company, 457 U.S. 922 (1982).

[353]del Carmen, Potential Liabilities of Probation and Parole Officers, supra, 1985: 184-186.

[354]West v. Atkins, 815 F.2d 993 (4th Cir. 1987), reaffirming the holding in Calvert v. Sharp, 748 F.2d 861 (4th Cir. 1984).

[355]Rizzo v. Goode, 423 U.S. 362 (1976), Padway v. Palches, 665 F. 2d 965 (9th Cir. 1982), Webster v. Huston, 689 F.2d 1220 (5th Cir. 1984).

with those individuals and/or the corporation, unless it could be shown that the government agency was in some way directly linked with the critical activities. The so-called "vicarious liability" civil rights cases demonstrate ways in which such a link can be forged.[356] For instance, a failure to train can be the basis for supervisory liability where the supervisor took no direct part in the actions which actually violated the plaintiffs civil rights if it can be shown that the supervisory failure to train led directly to the violation. Other supervisory failures can also be the basis of vicarious liability where an affirmative link between the failure and the ultimate violation can be shown. These include such things as failure to supervise, failure to direct, negligent hiring, negligent retention, etc.[357]

A municipality itself, as opposed to municipal employees, can be found liable where a violation is found to result from a custom or policy of the municipality.[358] More than a single incident is needed to constitute a policy or custom.

The policies or customs of a`private corporation acting pursuant to government contract in at least one case were seen as policies of the government. Thus, as found in Ancata, a civil rights violation alleged to have been caused by policy of a private medical service company contracted to provide medical services in a jail also exposed the county to liability.[359] However, liability was not found under a "respondeat superior" theory but on the basis that the county cannot delegate liability for unconstitutional policies it allows others to set for it.

Under the reasoning in Ancata, policy or custom of the private provider could probably be attributed to the county. Alternatively, the county could be found liable for failure to supervise. Under either analysis, a violation arising from a policy or custom of the provider will expose the county to liability. Under this reasoning, municipal liability could also be established in situations where the county failed to monitor the contractor properly and thus failed to detect and correct constitutionally impermissible activities

---

[356]See Chapter III.

[357]See Oklahoma City v. Tuttle, 105 S.Ct. 2427 (1985).

[358]Oklahoma City v. Tuttle, supra.

[359]Ancata v. Prison Health Services, Inc., 769 F.2d 700 (llth Cir. 1985).

which, while not reflecting written company policy, occurred with sufficient regularity to constitute a "custom."

But many jail or prison suits do not arise from supervisory failures or improper policies or customs. Instead they result simply from unforeseeable actions of individuals, where no affirmative link can be drawn between the actions of the primary defendant and management, let alone through management of a private corporation to a government agency. Thus, where responsibility starts and stops with the individual employee, the liability buck should stop at the contractor level. If government is not automatically liable under the Civil Rights Act from unconstitutional actions of individual government employees, it is hard to see how automatic.liability would attach for actions of a contractor's employee. This was recognized by the llth Circuit in the Ancata decision cited above, when the court noted:

> ... if a constitutional tort committed by an employee of Prison Health Services was not a result of the policy or custom of the entity, then the county would not be liable.[360]

In some civil rights litigation, as well as in some tort litigation, there is the potential that liability will attach both at the corporate level and also at the government level. In these cases the government can still be shielded from at least the monetary aspects of liability and the direct costs of litigation. This is done by requiring the contractor to defend all cases that arise from the contract operation and to hold the government harmless for those cases in which monetary liability is found and/or in which attorneys fees are awarded. A concomitant to the hold-harmless clause would be a requirement that the corporation carries sufficient insurance to absorb damages or attorneys fees. Remember, however, no such insurance type shield would appear available for injunctive relief if the injunction reached the government, as it probably would.

The indemnify/hold-harmless situation with total facility operation contracts is in marked contrast to the practice in contracts between correctional authorities and halfway houses, which is a common type of "privatization" in the field of corrections. In this situation, where typically a small, private (often nonprofit) organization is operating a work release facility, liability is

---

[360]Supra, at 705, n. 8.

generally either shared equally between contractor and government or the government attempts through formal or informal means to protect the contractor from liability exposure.

Thus, a government agency that elects to contract out its entire jail operation might be found liable along with its private corporate contractor. However, a hold-harmless and insurance requirement in the contract should protect the government from having to actually expend any funds directly to satisfy the court award or the costs of defense (save those funds attributable to the contractor's insurance costs).

Finally, if a privately run corrections facility can be operated better than a government run facility, the number of losing lawsuits should decrease. Indeed, even the number of suits filed should decrease since a well run facility typically will generate less litigation that a poorly run facility. If a contract limits the population in a facility to its rated capacity, the types of suits which arc the by-products of crowded jails should decrease. This of course does not solve the county's overcrowding problems, but merely moves them somewhere else.

C. Real Costs of Litigation: An Incentive for Contractor Performance?

There may be another incentive for improved correctional practice which comes from the liability/insurance/litigation defense area. Litigation costs to the private provider would be clearly identified as a cost of doing business, whether paid through insurance or otherwise. Any reduction in litigation should reduce these costs. However, as noted by George and Camille Camp, the government agency's legal costs may not be seen by the corrections agency as a cost of doing business, since such costs often are included in the budgets of other agencies, typically the Attorney General or the County Attorney.[361] Even if the dollars may ultimately come from the corrections agency, the FTE's (personnel positions) in many cases do not. Legal costs are probably never included in the "per diem" costs quoted by governmental agencies as their costs of running a prison or jail.

Over 95 percent of inmate litigation results in a judgment for defendants. Money saved by a reduction in litigation becomes

---

[361]See The Real Costs of Corrections (South Salem, New York: Criminal Justice Institute, April, 1985).

potential additional profit to the private provider. To the government agency, such "savings" may either be completely unapparent (if they affect another agency budget) or may simply disappear as an unspent appropriation at the end of a fiscal period. Therefore, the private provider may have more incentives than government not only to reduce losing litigation, but also to take steps to reduce all litigation.

D. Summary

Contracting will not diminish the extent to which the U.S. Constitution protects the jail inmate. It may affect who the proper defendant should be. The government will share liability for constitutional violations caused by policies or customs of the provider but not for violations caused by independent actions of contractor employees. Even where liability attaches to the county, insurance and hold-harmless requirements in the contract may protect the county from the monetary costs of that liability.

IV. Contents of the Contract

The requirements of the contract may determine its success or failure in protecting you from liability and/or monetary losses. As important as the contract is, it is not possible to address here every subject that should or could be addressed in a complete services contract. In fact, local laws and statutes will require specific provisions that will necessitate your use of legal assistance. The generic issues that should be addressed in virtually every correctional services contract can be discussed, however.

A. Stating Performance Criteria

One of the most often heard concerns about privatization has focused on the profit motive and a fear that the corporation will cut corners by operating at the lowest possible cost in order to increase profits. Another is a fear that inmates will be exploited. Absent some form of performance criteria in the contract, coupled with conscientious monitoring to allow early identification and correction of problems, this concern could well become reality. The county will get (a) what it demands and (b) what it pays for.

As a way of minimizing liability exposure, as a way of minimizing disputes regarding performance expectations, and as a matter of general policy, it is recommended that any correctional services contract require adherence to at least some set of recognized national standards. This should be the case whether the entire operation of some ancillary services are being contracted.

To what performance criteria will the contractor be held? Will they be the American Correctional Association (ACA) standards, other national standards, such as those of the American Bar Association, or state standards? What about the medical standards of the American Medical Association and the American Public Health Association? The parties, through the contract, must set out and understand performance standards or criteria for the contractor. These criteria, wherever possible, should be objective standards. However, it is recognized that completely objective criteria are not always possible and in some situations, not necessarily desirable.

The criteria adopted as performance standards may vary and will be a matter of negotiation between parties. Obviously ACA Standards are a comprehensive, widely accepted set of standards which could provide at least a starting point for such negotiations. There is some evidence that the ACA standards are being accepted in some courts and legislative bodies, either in whole or part.[362]

B. Monitoring and Auditing the Contract

What is expected of the contractor? What form will the agency's monitoring efforts take? What right of access to the facility, and to records, does the government retain? What self-auditing or other reporting requirements are imposed on the contractor?

There may be a tendency, once a service is contracted out, to assume that the contractor will take care of any problems that may arise. A "contract it and forget it" attitude is a grievous error, especially in correctional services contracts where there exists so little experience with the private sector's operation of correctional programs and where the government remains ultimately responsible for the care of the persons in the facility.

---

[362]See Atlantic County Jail, Mays Landing, New Jersey; Ippolito, et al., v. Howell Docket No. 78-0911 (D.N.J., July 11, 1980). The facility agreed to obtain accreditation from the Commission on Accreditation for Corrections as a condition of the consent decree and is currently under contract with the Commission. State cases are cited in Dale Sechrest and Ernest G. Reimer, "Adopting National Standards for Correctional Accreditation," Federal Probation (June, 1982): 18-25.

Critical to a successful correctional services contract is aggressive monitoring by the contracting agency. Such monitoring must focus on evaluation of current performance, not after-the-fact performance audits.

Just as jail administrators have duties under the Civil Rights Act to monitor jail operations and can be found vicariously liable where a failure to monitor contributes to a violation of inmate rights, so also would they have a duty to monitor the ongoing performance of a private contractor. A failure to monitor could also easily be found to be a "custom or practice" of the county, thus exposing the county directly to liability.

Insufficient monitoring could also be condemned as an excessive delegation of government power and thus be a basis for a court to void a contract altogether.

C. Dispute Resolution

How will disputes be addressed, especially regarding issues which are not specifically identified in the contract? The contract should include some form of mediation, arbitration or other informal means for dispute resolution lest every disagreement wind up in court.

D. Penalties for Non-Performance

What sanctions exist for non-performance? If termination of the contract is the only sanction the government may find itself without an effective tool to deal with performance deficiencies which do not warrant termination.

E. Training to Standards

How will the government agency be assured that performance standards will be met unless provider staff are properly trained? Inadequate training is a likely area for the government to be drawn into litigation through the concept of vicarious liability. Where and how will the provider train its staff? Are local or state corrections training academies available to the private sector?

F. Retaining the Failure Option

The best laid plans...often go astray. Likewise, the best corporate hopes sometimes wind up in failure and bankruptcy court. A county considering contracting for jail services must anticipate what it will do if the corporation fails, or gets out of the jail business, or delivers such poor service the county decides to cancel the agreement. Bankruptcy of a private prison did happen as recently as early 1986 in Pennsylvania. "Center 268," a 55 bed facility that housed prisoners from the District of Columbia, was forced into bankruptcy "after a week-long fiasco involving prisoners from out of state [the District], extensive publicity, court orders, and passage of legislation placing a temporary moratorium on private prisons in the state."[363] Questions were raised about the power of government to delegate its power to punish and the authority of the jurisdiction to hold inmates from one state who are transferred to another. At the time of its closing, Center 268 was reportedly losing $5,000 per month. Center employees are suing both the state and a community group that opposed the prison for lost wages.[364]

Particularly if the corporate failure is abrupt, as it may be, how will the county continue to provide jail services? Where will necessary staff come from, let alone the expertise to run a jail? What if the corporation actually owns the facility? The answers to these questions should be in the contract. The contract could provide, for instance, that the county may have use of the corporate owned property beyond any premature termination of the agreement. However, this and the other questions must be addressed clearly in the contract.

If the county is without the ability to maintain jail services because the corporation fails or the corporation refuses to allow the county to resume operation of the jail, the contract could well be found to be an improper delegation of a government function and therefore void.

G. Relations With Local Law Enforcement

Who will pursue escapees? If the contract is with the chief county law enforcement officer, this question is easily answered. But, if the key local law enforcement agencies are not party to the contract, will they cooperate in escape or riot situations? Responding to these issues may require collateral contracts plus a close examination of

---

[363]"Private Prison Goes Bankrupt," Public Employee, 51(4) May-June, 1986: 27.

[364]"Private Prison Goes Bankrupt"; the news accounts of this incident suggest it was a predictable result from a poorly planned contract, quickly executed and entered into without the level of care and planning that should go into any such contract, especially one involving the movement of inmates across state lines.

relevant escape statutes. The NIJ publication says that once an escaping inmate has left the property of the facility public law enforcement officers are responsible.[365]

H. Summary

Numerous other potential contract content areas could be identified, but rather than try to continue to list specific issues for a possible inclusion in an operations contract, a general recommendation may be better. The contract drafting effort must try to identify all aspects of jail operation, including those which may involve third parties, and ask if they can be done privately and, if so, how they will be done.

V. Drafting the Contract

Remember, before deciding on any type of contract, several decisions must be made relative to the type of service to be contracted, inmates to be affected, public reaction, and the like. Performance criteria must be drawn up, and the procedures must be in place to allow bidding on your contract. Skillful development of a contract requires close and thoughtful interaction between administrative authorities and legal counsel, preferably legal counsel knowledgable about government contracting, local statutes, and the needs of a detention facility. As noted at several points in this chapter, the contents of the contract are of tremendous importance to its success or failure in two significant respects: (1) a carefully drafted contract stands a much better chance of successfully overcoming a challenge to the contract's underlying legality, and (2) a well drafted contract provides a much better vehicle for the county to monitor and assure that contract services are properly provided and to move quickly to remedy any deficiencies that may develop.

In the context of this section, reference to the "contents" of a contract has two meanings:

> (1) The subject areas contained in the contract — the performance requirements, monitoring requirements, fiscal expectations, etc.
>
> (2) The actual language — the wording used in the drafting of the agreement.

---

[365]Hackett et al. 3.

The agency (the administrative authority) must identify both what is desired from the contractor ("complete operation of the medical system ...") and what is required of the contractor (self audits, reports, staffing levels, training schedules, etc.). Legal counsel must determine if there are any impediments to contracting and how they can be removed or avoided. Counsel must also help identify the general subject areas, or issues, that need to be addressed in a contract. These subject areas are specified in the NIJ publication, inclusive of the legal issues, policy and program issues, contract provisions, and monitoring.[366] Many of these areas are relevant to contracting for ancillary services. Having identified the general subject areas to be addressed, attention next must be focused on drafting the contract in an understandable and precise fashion.

Administrator and counsel should continue their collaboration through the negotiating process. Particularly in a complete services contract situation, the drafting process would try to address as many potential problem areas as the parties can identify and include a workable process for resolving problems which are not anticipated or addressed in the contract. Since correctional services contracts are for the most part untested in practice a carefully drawn contract can provide a roadmap for getting through much of the unknown.

A practical problem may arise in developing a jail contract. The county's main source of jail expertise, its chief jail administrator, may be less than enthusiastic about developing a contract for the operation of the facility by a private contractor. This may also be true for others with a vested interest in the jail. Should this situation develop, the county should look for consultant assistance in the contract development and negotiation process. Such help may be available through the National Institute of Corrections, from a state standards and inspection unit, or through potential private consulting groups. For contracts covering ancillary services this may be a problem only where specific staff may be affected.

The drafting of a correctional services contract can in a sense be compared to the drafting of a consent decree in a major conditions of confinement case. The rights and duties of the parties are set out in detail. The all too common problem of agencies agreeing in consent decrees to more than they can deliver, often because they failed to think through the implications of their original commitments,

---

[366]Hackett et al. 3.

suggests a lack of close collaboration between administrator and counsel in drafting contexts. This drafting problem suggests the value of a model correctional services contract.

VI. Conclusions

Contracts for correctional services are not without potential legal problems. However, short of a county trying to completely turn over the jail to a private company, the legal problems all appear to have solutions. The particular solution will depend in large part on the applicable state statutory and constitutional law. In some cases, the solution will require state enabling legislation. In all cases, the solution will probably be helped by such enabling legislation.

Ultimate success of any correctional services contract, and especially one for major correctional services, will hinge on the drafting and monitoring of the agreement. Can we legally do what we want to do? Does the contract contain the proper mechanics for what we want to do? Are we committed to seeing that the services described in the contract are in fact that which are delivered? If these challenges are met, contracting for services can achieve its goals. Moreover, for jurisdictions considering contracting for the entire facility, the question of whether privatization is an asset or liability to corrections should be answered fairly.

CHAPTER SEVEN: PLANNING THE NEW FACILITY

I. General Considerations.

A. Getting Help

Planning a new facility is a rare occurrence, often happening just once in a career. This is the opportunity many have waited for — the chance to build the facility "right," to correct past errors, and have a facility that is secure and operationally trouble-free. Experience shows that this may not always happen. Why not? In the past there was little good help available, and now that it is, many jurisdictions persist in not using it. Such help can assist in clearly stating the goals of the new facility, be these goals primarily incapacitation and punishment or oriented toward programs in the community. In the past ten years architects have formed the Committee on Architecture for Justice of the American Institute of Architects. They attend seminars on jail standards and practices and now work closely with detention practitioners in the planning, design, and operational development of new facilities. Practitioners are also becoming more involved in the planning process. Still, in the building phase, construction is often poorly monitored, products touted by vendors are difficult to test or compare and sometimes fail, and building materials and components are sometimes substandard. These problems must be confronted and solved.

Under most conditions, you will have to seek help outside your jurisdiction in the planning, design and construction of your new facility. Most localities build jails too seldom to benefit from the prior knowledge of the process by local or even state sources. While the situation is improving, it is often difficult to find people who understand fully the problems involved. Also, several useless or outdated books have been written on correctional facility planning.

Get some good advice on what is currently being done to build correctional facilities. Some of the best help is available through the National Institute of Corrections (NIC) Jail Center. Assistance is provided through consultation and participation in its program on Planning of New Institutions (PONI), which has been applied in over 100 jurisdictions throughout the United States.[367] The PONI program

[367] Planning of New Institutions, Information and Application Packet, A Systematic Response to Correctional Planning Problems. U.S. Department of Justice, National Institute of Justice, May, 1986.

works within the framework of what Farbstein et al. call the "participatory planning model.[368] This model requires a "project planning team," that works with a citizen's advisory committee, as described below for the PONI program, and with the criminal justice agencies involved in the process. The planning team and the advisory board work in task forces to implement the various stages of planning, design, and construction of the facility. The task forces have three to five members, some of whom may be specialists who are not part of either group but will assist the task force in gathering and analyzing data and studying alternatives, and in the selection of architects and consultants, site selection, and facility programming and design review. Above all, however, none of these planning steps will work without a project coordinator or project manager who is dedicated full time to the process. The construction of a new facility is important enough, and surely expensive enough, to warrant such an investment.

The NIC PONI program augments the first phase of the participatory planning process. There are three phases to the PONI program.[369] The **first phase** is a one-day community meeting held with local officials who have the principal responsibility for the design and construction of the new facility. It is required for the process to continue. At this meeting, critical social, legal and planning issues are addressed by a team of NIC Jail Center consultants experienced in community planning for jail design and operation. Topics addressed are the scope of the undertaking, legal issues, community values and goals, the exploration of alternatives, data needs, sharing of expertise, the need for participation by all segments of the community, and the presentation of a rational planning method. The goal is to interact with participants and begin the planning process. It is critical at this stage to include judges, prosecutors, public defenders, law enforcement administrators — the sheriff and/or the chief of police, county and/or city administrators, probation/parole representatives, representatives of community programs — alcohol, mental health, etc., critical decisionmakers on the city council and county commission, and some representation from the general citizenry, inclusive of church and civic groups. Representatives of the media should also be involved in the planning

---

[368]Farbstein/Williams & Associates, Corrections Planning Handbooks, Chapter 2.1.

[369]John R. Firman calls it the "Criminal Justice Collaborative Planning Model" in "Criminal Justice System Planning in the 80's Using the Collaborative Model," a paper presented to the Committee on Architecture for Justice of the American Institute of Architects, June 1, 1984.

process. Ideally, this group will not exceed 15 persons. Due to its emphasis on involving a wide base of decisionmakers, this model is referred to by NIC as the "Total Systems Planning Model."[370]

The **phase two seminar** builds on the content and outcomes of the first phase. It is a five day program held in Boulder, Colorado, for a jurisdictional team of six members. It emphasizes operational philosophy and architectural programming, design impacts, staffing, and state-of-the-art design. The primary goal is to develop necessary skills for the planning process, inclusive of developing a collaborative working relationship and teaching participants about the developmental, planning, and action plan processes.

Phase three involves the provision of technical assistance in areas such as staffing analysis and training in making the transition from the old to the new facility. It may include on-site assistance or other types of support, such as recommendations about other sources of help.

B. PONI's Five Main Phases of Work

The five main phases of work addressed by the NIC are (1) pre-architectural, (2) site selection and planning, (3) architectural design, (4) construction, and (5) occupancy.[371] Some of the tasks addressed in the seminar are total system planning, the development of a mission statement, economic feasibility, programming (facility uses), site analysis, bidding, etc. The three basic architectural models and related inmate management styles discussed in Chapter IV are presented. Various "scenarios" are developed to show how ideas will actually work in practice; that is, "how will booking work? food service? work release?" Most importantly, construction costs as well as long term costs (facility life cycle) in relation to design are addressed. One of the most important aspects of cost is the staffing analysis, which was discussed in Chapter III, and is a major PONI topic. Also addressed are financing alternatives, and new and innovative construction techniques that may provide greater speed of construction without a loss of quality.[372] Finally, project management

---

[370]"Criminal Justice Planning Process: A Total Systems Model," Transfer 14: National Clearinghouse for Criminal Justice Planning and Architecture (Washington, D.C.: U.S. Department of Justice, Law Enforcement Assistance Administration, reissued May, 1977).

[371]See Sechrest and Price (1984, 1985).

[372]See Dale K. Sechrest, Nick Pappas, and Shelley J. Price, "Building Prisons: Pre-Manufactured, Prefabricated, and Prototype," Federal Probation March, 1987: 35-41.

is addressed. A major failure of many construction projects (in and outside criminal justice) is in the construction phase, which is discussed more fully below.

C. Additional Sources of Help

Other sources of information are available in this area from the National Institute of Justice. A source of information on facility construction has been created within the National Institute of Justice called the Construction Information Exchange that publishes two documents: a National Directory of Corrections Construction, and a Construction Bulletin.[373] Information on construction will be available from agencies who will volunteer it, with the goals of better and more efficient construction to meet the demands of crowding. The Construction Information Exchange is also conducting post-occupancy evaluations using a mail questionnaire.[374] Comparisons of the experiences of other jurisdictions will be made based on these reports.

In 1985 the National Institute of Justice published a report on the planning, design, and construction of correctional institutions. The report was done by research staff of the Commission on Accreditation for Corrections and included telephone interviews in 18 states with vendors, architects, and owners of new correctional facilities. Site visits were conducted at four newly constructed facilities.[375] One of the most difficult problems found by the study was the problem of political influence on the planning, design, and construction process. Construction involves money, and the location of facilities means jobs. In one jurisdiction, correctional facilities that were designed to be operated in an urban, industrial environment were placed in counties far removed from the sources of their markets. These facilities are recognized in that state as a monument to the inability of corrections professionals to influence the political process. In more than one instance for the sites studied it was found

---

[373]Charles B. DeWitt: "Florida Sets Example with Use of Concrete Modules" (Washington, D.C.: National Institute of Justice, March, 1986), p 1; See "New Construction Methods for Correctional Facilities" (Washington, D.C.: National Institute of Justice, March, 1986); and, "California Tests New Construction Concepts (Washington, D.C.: National Institute of Justice, June 1986); Stephen A. Carter, Lowell Nordquist and Polly Reno, Evaluation of Pre-Manufactured Housing for Correctional Purposes Carter-Goble Associates, Inc. (Washington, D.C.: National Institute of Corrections, February, 1984).

[374]Construction Information Exchange, Facility Survey [c. 1986].

[375]Sechrest and Price (1985b).

that work was overpriced and shoddy, and that some work was never completed at all.

Cooperation between all actors in the planning phase of the construction process is critical to the success of new facility construction. For the local jail this includes the collaborative involvement described as part of the NIC's program for planning new institutions (PONI).

The paper by Sechrest and Price provides a flow chart of the planning, design, and construction process that stresses continuity from start to finish. For example, a key descisionmaker should be appointed at the start of the project who is committed to remaining with it to its completion. A written plan should be developed that includes a description of project roles and tasks, an organizational chart indicating channels of communication, and clearly stated timelines that are communicated to all participants. The planning process:

> "... refers to all activities that occur following the decision to build through the completion of construction documents. Basic elements of the planning process include: the use of studies and information defining needs of the correctional system and the new facility; preparing the preliminary budget request or scope statement; and developing the architectural program."[376]

Failure to follow these steps tended to result in extended project schedules and cost overruns. The planning process may take two to three years before construction begins, although one jurisdiction completed the process in less than a year. A major concern in planning was making accurate cost estimates for the facility; half the facilities surveyed went an average of 39 percent over the initial budget.[377] The development of accurate estimates of facility staff was another major problem area, particularly regarding the numbers of correctional officers needed. Unfortunately, it is not uncommon for a jurisdiction to commit itself to a new facility with no analysis of the facility's staffing requirements, only to find as the new jail nears completion that staffing costs will exceed the jurisdiction's ability to pay. It is sometimes not well understood that the best and strongest

---

[376]Sechrest and Price (1985b) 43.

[377]Sechrest and Price (1985b) 43.

materials available do not insure a secure facility. Detention facility operators with many years of experience understand that 90 percent of security is invested in staff selected and trained in supervision. This point must be made early and often, and the facility must be designed physically to make the best use of staff. The staffing analysis plan should be done at the earliest point in the process when the project scope is being considered (schematic phase).

Costs of maintenance and daily operations were often underestimated because they were not carefully considered in the early part of the planning process. Facility siting was often seen as a difficult area due to the problems inherent in locating a facility for criminal offenders in the community. As a politically sensitive matter, it is a major contributor to time delays in the planning stage. As noted by Richard McGee, a veteran correctional administrator, the community does not benefit from facts and logic regarding the placement of the facility — it is an emotional and political matter.[378] The question of sitting is covered more fully in III.A. below.

The planning process becomes more explicit as the "architectural program" for the facility is developed. This is sometimes referred to as the "pre-architectural" phase of the project. The architectural program should tell the designer exactly what is expected of the facility in terms of functional and operational requirements — movement patterns, staffing required, security details, programs and services planned, overall space needs, housing configurations, equipment and maintenance needs, and the like.[379] In short, it should state the overall operational philosophy. Staffing is particularly important and should be done by someone other than the architect, preferably by someone with specific expertise in this area who is independent of the jurisdiction and the architect.

It is at the planning stage that the jurisdiction should be clear about the mission of the jail. This should not be left to the architect by default. As indicated for the PONI process, much information needs to be gathered to assist in the planning process, including population projections, who should go to jail and for how long, and what kinds of alternatives are available — for example, weekender programs, pretrial intervention using suspended sentences

---

[378]Richard McGee, Prisons and Politics (Lexington Books, 1981).

[379]See the California Corrections Planning Handbooks; cf. William M. Pena, et al., Problem Seeking: An Architectural Programming Primer (Boston: Canners Books International, 1977).

to try program options, community service, restitution, the use of county probation, and possibly the use of one of the newer in-house supervision programs with electronic monitors.

Finally, the selection of the architect/engineer is critical to a successful project. Unfortunately, this process is often controlled through legislation or political processes that limit involvement by the user of the facility. The proposed facility administrator should insist on being part of the process of selection. The American Institute of Architects indicates that "the agency-based selection system" is the best for all concerned.[380]

At the time of appointment of the architectural firm, questions should be raised in several areas, such as the scope of its work, the method of payment, and potential liability for errors. A primary concern, for example, is the extent of its liability for the completed work in relation to your need for compliance with national or local standards in the construction of the facility. One of the problems in thc planning and design of a new facility is confronting the diverse and seemingly inconsistent sets of codes and standards that will apply to a such construction. These range from local building codes and standards, through regional codes (BOCA, Southern, etc.) to national professional standards, which may or may not be enforced. Much may depend on the courts and the "evolving standard of decency" mentioned earlier. At the least you will be expected to build consistent with the best knowledge and practice available at the time of construction. Some of this knowledge and these practices have been presented in the earlier chapters. In any event, it is critical that throughout the entire process you retain the right to make decisions about these issues and other matters related specifically to the planning, design, and construction of the facility. If you do not, you and your successors will pay dearly for your inattention for many years.

---

[380]American Institute of Architects, Selecting Architects for Public Projects, A Guide for Local, State and Federal Officials (Washington, D.C.: American Institute of Architects, January, 1982).

II. Planning a New Facility: What Must You Do?

A. Use Existing Resources

Use the National Institute of Corrections program for the Planning of New Institutions (PONI). Employ an architect with experience in this area, and there are some good ones. The American Institute of Architects Committee on Architects for Justice may be contacted regarding their members, many of whom have current experience in detention facility design. Check the references of any architect or consultant that you consider with persons for whom he or she has worked. You will be tempted to do business locally because you know the people involved, and statute may even require you to do so, as is the case in many jurisdictions. In this case, don't be the "good old boy" who offers on-the-job training for the local architectural firm in jail design. Get the local firm to team up with a national firm that has done this type of work and bid it together. They will benefit and you and your successors will be far more likely to have a facility you can live with for 30, 50, or perhaps 75 years.

As with the purchase of new equipment, it is advisable to hire a consultant or an architect (or firm) who has had major responsibility for the design of one or more modern correctional facilities. Visit the facility designed by the architectural firm you want to hire, and visit other facilities that express different design characteristics and supervision models as explained in Chapter IV. It will be money well spent. Remember at all times that the architect can be helpful, but will be bound by "what you want," which, for a variety of reasons, may not match the latest "state of the art" in the business. Tell the consultants and architects exactly what you want, listen to their responses, and then tell them your decision; otherwise you may get what they want.

Once construction begins, consider the use of a construction manager to oversee construction of the facility. A construction manager or firm can monitor the work at each stage of the process in order to prevent poor or substandard work. For example, many of the problems of construction relate to subcontracting, a practice that often results in the use of substandard materials and equipment. The construction manager should be able to ensure that the exact specifications for materials and equipment are met, and that the construction is completed on schedule.

Like the architect, the construction manager should be very familiar with correctional facility requirements and have a good record in construction management for other jurisdictions. Unless your general services department has demonstrated expertise specific to correctional facility construction, try to limit their involvement to helping principally in those areas that do not involve the design or operational aspects of the facility. For example, they might be most helpful in the bidding process, developing materials and equipment specifications, and in inspecting the facility at various stages of completion.

In the final analysis, there is no guarantee of success in detention facility construction, only degrees of satisfaction. There is no ideal design, or prototype, and there are no absolute answers in planning or design. There is a need for careful review of all variables which must be coordinated in planning the facility. The planning process must be applied with equal rigor to the selection of prototype or pre-manufactured designs as it is to the development of any other design.[381] This responsibility cannot be left to the vendor, the architect, or an agency too far removed from detention practice. A design should be selected only when it meets the requirements of the jurisdiction — that is, your requirements!

Avoiding Problems. To assist in the evaluation and selection of designs, whether conventional, pre-manufactured, or prefabricated component facilities are used, the following are critical in evaluating the design:

- the actual costs and/or savings in dollars and time in relation to meeting your needs (the user), both in initial construction costs and in projected long term operating costs

- the total square footage for the facility, inclusive of support space

- compliance with applicable local and state codes, including zoning, fire, health, and environmental requirements.

Where pre-manufactured housing units are used, especially temporary trailers, they should be considered temporary structures or

[381]See Dale K. Sechrest, Nick Pappas, and Shelley J. Price (1987).

as support facilities. Their primary use should be for short-term detention in the community or as temporary additions to existing long-term facilities. Long term use of these facilities in high security facilities will lead to their swift deterioration with the resulting security problems and code violations.

B. Costs

Estimating the costs of constructing a new facility can be very difficult. To have money allocated for the new facility, often a request must be made for the money before the design is completed. Ideally, money would be made available for a feasibility study prior to presenting the total costs of the facility to the governing body, i.e., commission or board of supervisors. Moreover, it should be clear to the funding body that these construction costs, or "first costs," do not include the operating costs of the facility, which generally are ten times first costs over the life of the facility.

A planning handbook prepared for the California Board of Corrections provides an example of first cost estimation for a 300-bed jail.[382] This estimate is done prior to more detailed consideration of the design and before actual specifications are prepared or bids received. The figure is for planning and comparative purposes. Their procedure begins by simply multiplying local costs per square foot by a size estimate (about 400 square feet per bed) to get current construction costs. This is followed by adjustments for inflation and the addition of other costs, such as architectural fees, testing, furnishings, equipment, administrative costs, site development, and contingency fees.[383]

The California planning handbook also provides methods of estimating operating costs, to include personnel, services to be provided, maintenance costs, and the like.[384] Personnel account for as much as 70 percent of annual operating costs, which means that the need for each post must be carefully considered. This is followed by annual maintenance costs at about 20 percent of operating costs, with the remaining 10 percent for inmate care (food, medical, laundry, etc.). Future personnel needs must also be considered in projecting

---

[382]Board of Corrections, State of California, Corrections Planning Handbooks, (Prepared by Farbstein/Williams and Associates, 1981).

[383]Farbstein/Williams, Handbooks.

[384]Farbstein/Williams, Handbooks.

costs, as well as inflation and possible emergency needs. As indicated earlier, the current AIDS epidemic in jails and prisons has led to extraordinarily high medical budgets that were not predictable. The report also presents some strategies for limiting operating costs, such as reducing overall space, improving staff efficiency through design, using energy efficient technology, using mechanical systems that have low maintenance and repair costs, and using better quality materials.[385]

C. Political Considerations

Unfortunately, political considerations rather than professional judgment control the design of a new facility in the majority of cases. Many hard line local residents, politicians, law enforcement personnel, prosecutors and judges want a secure facility that will meet only the minimum constitutional requirements. This is sometimes referred to as the "spartan" jail — very secure, clean, no amenities, and designed to send the message that "crimes in our community will be severely punished." Other citizens see the jail as the place to intercept errants and guide them to a more satisfactory and law abiding life. They will want pretrial intervention programs, drug treatment programs, education and work release, restitution and community service programs, and other types of meaningful activities for the inmates. Involvement of all of these groups in the initial planning project and development of the mission statement may reduce much of the more negative and potentially damaging political and philosophical influences on the process.

In a community with a facility of less than 50 beds it will be difficult to meet a wide range of program needs in the facility, although many may be met through community agencies. Some services and programs are required, however, and others are optional. Those that are required are discussed in Chapter IV and must be implemented. As the size of the facility increases, or if it is possible to develop a separate minimum security or prerelease center, it will be possible to consider more sophisticated programs.

III. Specific Considerations in Construction

Additional considerations specific to the planning, design, and construction of a new facility are given here, with appropriate references.

---

[385]Farbstein/Williams, Handbooks 6.

A. Siting: Locating the Facility

As indicated earlier, locating a jail in a community is often seen as a problem due to the fact that it leaves offenders in the community. In contrast to long term state or federal sentenced facilities, however, it is imperative that the jail be located in the community near the courts and various local police agencies. Questions that arise from citizens include the impact of the facility on property values, the local economy, public safety, and local law enforcement services, and the community generally.

A study completed in mid-1987 for the National Institute of Corrections has addressed some of the problems of correctional facility siting. Although the study only included two jails (and five correctional facilities), the conclusions are encouraging with respect to the construction of local jails and provides much useful information that can assist administrators in gaining adequate sites for jails.[386] The study found no evidence that any of the facilities they studied had significantly harmed property values in the areas around the facilities, based on real estate studies, nor had they endangered the public safety.[387] Law enforcement officials agreed that there had been no increase in danger to the communities around the facilities. Community surveys showed that the neighborhood quality of life and safety had not declined as a result of the facility being placed in it.[388] There was some problem with the fact that jails are often in urban areas with high crime rates, which makes it difficult to determine how much the facility might be contributing to them. The impact on the economy of the local community was, "not surprisingly," positive, based on studies of household income and employment.[389] Most importantly, when residents were informed about the facility's positive contribution to the local economy and queried about benefits and disadvantages, they generally took a more positive view of the facility.[390] Media involvement in the siting

---

[386]Kathleen Shea Abrams and William Lyons, Impact of Correctional Facilities on Land Values and Public Safety (Miami: FAU-FIU Joint Center for Environmental and Urban Problems, Florida International University, July, 1987).

[387]Abrams and Lyons 4-5 and Chapter 4, "The Impact of Property Values" 97-99.

[388]Abrams and Lyons 5-6 and Chapter 6, "The Impacts of Correctional Facilities on Public Safety" 172-173.

[389]Abrams and Lyons 5 and Chapter 5, "The Impact of Correctional Facilities on the Local Economy" 145-146.

[390]Abrams and Lyons 7.

phase as well as in ongoing facility operations was seen as critical to judgments about the facility.

One of the most important parts of the report is that which deals with the administrator's role in approaching and using the media and in approaching the legislative and judicial branches of government. The state legislature must be regularly informed of the impact of its sentencing laws on local jail populations, and local judges and prosecutors must understand the impact of their decisions on jail populations. Methods to do this include regular reports; however, some local jurisdictions and states have begun to create sentencing boards that evaluate the status of the system on a monthly or semi-annual basis to determine how resources can most effectively be applied across all areas of the criminal justice system.

Local and state zoning laws directly influence the location of new correctional facilities of all types.[391] There must be a way for you to deal with zoning laws when new facility sites are needed. Local detention administrators and county officials in some growing jurisdictions often designate areas for jails and other types of public safety facilities years in advance of need. In this way they can aggregate such facilities in areas in advance of real estate speculation and possible challenges to their use for public safety purposes.

The placement of hazardous waste facilities is used in the FAU/FIU report as an example of how community involvement in the siting process can be effective when both informal and formal communication is emphasized. A related factor of importance is the public's confidence in the officials destined to operate the facility.[392]

B. Cell Size and Occupancy

Nearly 70 percent of local jail residents share their cells with other inmates and are housed in cells and dormitories that provide less than 60 square feet per person. About 60 percent of federal and state prisoners share cells and two-thirds have less than 60 square feet per cell/dormitory. Sixty-two percent (62%) of all inmates were housed in cells, with the remaining 38 percent in dormitories.[393] The current

---

[391]Abrams and Lyons 273-274.

[392]Abrams and Lyons 337-338.

[393]American Prisons and Jails, Volume I, (1980) 61.

national standards of the American Correctional Association as applied in accreditation, require the following cell sizes for detention facilities (ACA, 1981):

Existing Detention Facilities

Single cells of 60 square feet of floor space per cell when inmates are locked in less than 10 hours per day (2-5111);

Single cells of 70 square feet of floor space per cell for inmates confined over 10 hours per day (2-5111, 2-5115)

New Detention Facilities

70 square feet of floor space per cell for all inmates confined in the facility (2-5138)[394]

Dormitories in jails or prisons require 50 square feet per inmate and no more than 50 inmates per dormitory. Cell space is measured from interior wall to interior wall, less the space occupied by plumbing chases and columns. It includes the space occupied by beds, desks, plumbing fixtures, closets, and entrances and exits; dormitory space is measured from interior walls, less areas restricted to access and egress and excluding bathrooms or showers. Space includes that occupied by beds, desks, closets, chairs and partitions, but does not include separate dayroom space.

C. Space Considerations

Very few detention facilities have enough space to meet current needs. Several areas are of special concern, unless general crowding is the rule.

Intake. One of the most critical areas is the intake area where the greatest amount of inmate movement occurs. Movement creates security problems, and space must be available for holding inmates being processed into the facility. Intake areas must include space for searches, showers (and other hygiene precautions), medical exam-

---

[394]American Correctional Association Standards (1981, 1986) for prisons require 60 square feet of floor space for single cells in existing and new facilities when confinement is less than 10 hours per day (2-4129) However, for confinement of over 10 hours per day 80 square feet of floor space is required (2-4135).

inations and attorney visits. They should also include space for the temporary holding of persons attempting to make bail or other forms of community release. Where feasible, consideration should be given to the development of a separate building for intake processing. A modular structure or even a trailer might be used for initial screening of misdemeanants and less serious offenders, with more serious offenders being processed in the main facility. This avoids having to mix minor arrestees with general population detainees and reduces problems resulting from the limited strip search problems that such mixing creates. Remember, minor offenders (misdemeanants, certain types of felonies, etc.) cannot be strip searched without reasonable suspicion that they may represent a danger.

Storage and Service Space. For unknown reasons, jail designers and planners often do not include sufficient storage space for clothing, bedding and inmate property. Inmate property should be sent home as soon as possible, but space must be provided sufficient to give each inmate a minimum of about nine square feet of storage outside the cell area. Space for the storage of inmate records is often not sufficient, and old records can take up considerable space. In one facility the padded cells were closed down and being used to store old records, which may represent a fire hazard to the local inspector. Laundry space and machine capacity for laundry are also frequently neglected, as is space for haircuts and dayrooms, recreation areas, and classrooms.

So what do you do? Obviously, storage needs and service area requirements should be addressed when planning a new facility. If this has not been done, facilities must convert existing space, which often results in the loss of office space or other functional areas. In this case it may be more desirable to use prefabricated structures for some offices and for dayrooms, classrooms, recreation areas and service areas. These facilities have a varied life span, however, depending on use, upkeep, and weather conditions, that must be carefully evaluated against other types of additional construction.[395] Also, security for these structures must also be given careful consideration, especially when they are separate from the main facility and/or are of traditional linear construction.

Jail Annex. One method of easing crowding is to provide a lower cost minimum security facility, sometimes called an annex, prerelease or work release center, or "jail farm," that will accommodate many of

---

[395]Dale K. Sechrest, Nick Pappas, and Shelley J. Price (1987) 39.

these inmates. To do so the population must be evaluated to determine how many inmates might qualify for less than maximum security confinement, especially inmates sentenced to the facility (see classification section in chapter four). Since these inmates are not state prison candidates, many are not "serious" offenders and can be placed in less secure facilities. With the increasing need to manage weekenders, given momentum by periodic campaigns against drunk drivers, drug dealers, nonsupport cases, and the like, a minimum security annex is almost a necessity, even in the small jail. In larger systems it may also be a suitable alternative for older inmates. In any case, these facilities can be used for community programming, such as work or educational release and other alternative programs that may benefit the offender and his/her family. These types of programs are discussed in "Supervision of Inmates." Unfortunately, new jail planning sometimes overlooks the minimal custodial requirements of this portion of the jail population, leading to the existence of more costly high security beds than are needed for this population.

Handicapped Access. An important concern is the management of handicapped inmates and visitors, including the deaf, blind, and wheelchair handicapped. Federal laws govern physical access in facilities receiving Federal funds. These laws were discussed in chapter four. Confined persons with handicaps or disabilities that interfere with major life functions must be either accommodated in a special area of the facility or placed in an alternate facility. The jail annex suggested above might be quite appropriate to this task.

D. What Criteria Do You Use?

Standards created by practitioners are perhaps the most comprehensive source of information for use in planning, design, and construction of a new facility. You will have to consider these professional standards along with local and regional codes, regulations, and licensing requirements that address construction, building, sanitation and fire safety conditions. Professional standards have been adopted by consensus of approving bodies such as the American Correctional Association, the Commission on Accreditation for Corrections and the National Sheriffs' Association. As indicated above, these standards may exceed court requirements as found in the Supreme Court cases of Bell v. Wolfish (1979) and Rhodes v. Chapman (1981) and others. However, the standards, in whole or part, have been adopted in several court decisions, and they will probably gain increasing authority over time in such areas as security, fire safety, medical services, sanitation, and conditions of isolation. For these reason you will have to give them careful consideration in new facility planning and design. While cell size and occupancy (single versus double cells) may not rise to constitutional requirements, the standards are a sound yardstick for measuring the "totality of conditions" in a detention facility, especially as crowding may affect such conditions.

Persons operating police lockups or holding facilities should be aware that the Commission on Accreditation for Law Enforcement Agencies accredits these types of facilities.[396] The American Medical Association also conducts a separate accreditation program for medical services in jails. The American Correctional Association also has a program for certification of specific areas of performance.

Many architectural firms that know the criminal justice field have researched national standards and codes to determine how they may apply to your proposed facility. Ultimately, you will have to make a choice about which standards to use, and an architect familiar with the standards as well as local codes will be an asset. Remember, when initial building costs ("first costs") are compared with long term operating costs there is no question that "building up" to the highest reasonable standards will pay long term dividends. These dividends will be of two types, both mentioned earlier: (1) reduced overall operating costs and (2) less potential legal liability. For example, there is some evidence that the costs of double-celling inmates may exceed the initially higher costs of building single cells. Double cells and dormitories create operational problems that require more staff, and staff are very costly. Double, triple, and gang cells require more staff, they are harder on staff, and they may lead to greater violence and the resulting litigation.

While the Supreme Court has not accepted the concept of single- celling outside the context of the "totality" of conditions, it has left open the possibility of requiring it. The most recent example is Cody v. Hillard (1986), in which the appeals court said "Double-celling ... resulted in crisis management with respect to the maintenance of ancillary support facilities such as food services, laundry services, medical services, plumbing and electrical wiring. [it] ... has resulted in an overloading of services such as the work, recreation and school programs ... we conclude that the district court did not err in banning double-celling both in the general population

---

[396]The Commission on Accreditation for Law Enforcement Agencies publishes a Commission Update; their address is in the references at the end of the book.

and in protective custody cells."[397] As indicated earlier, however, this portion of Cody was overturned on a re-hearing.

E. Hardware and Equipment Selection

The testing, selection, operation and maintenance of durable, efficient and cost effective hardware and equipment is a continuing problem in the renovation of existing facilities and the construction of new facilities. Facilities are found with no reinforcing bars in high security areas, such as control centers. Traditional building materials (screws, hinges, etc.) lead to security problems, as do the awkward placement of control panels and communication devices. Window glazing (glass) may be placed in a frame that is poorly attached to the facility structure. In one instance, inmates would lift out their entire steel doors, frame and all, in order to go into their dayroom at night to watch television. One need only look at the notorious escape of serial killer Ted Bundy from a Utah jail through a false ceiling to envision the types of problems involved in poor construction. After he escaped he killed again.

A large part of the problem of equipment selection involves communication with vendors. Experienced detention facility staff are often not able to communicate their needs to vendors of security materials and equipment. The bid, for example, may specify that the buyer select "maximum security" or "detention quality" fixtures and furnishings. There are no standardized definitions for these terms that are related to their performance characteristics. A related problem is when bid procedures require that a particular product or its "equal" be used. The component used may not meet facility needs but will be accepted for lack of sufficient information or careful review of specifications.[398]

In too many cases inferior material, hardware and equipment are used by contractors or their subcontractors, many of whom are aware that they are illegally installing inferior equipment. They do it because they are not being held accountable. Prevention of this type of fraud can be avoided through the use of a full time project manager, dedicated to your facility, who will inspect work at every step to ensure quality work and expeditious completion of tasks. County engineers and inspectors may not have the time or expertise to devote to this level of oversight, although they may supplement a

---

[397]799 F.2nd 450, (8th Cir. 1986).

[398]Sechrest and Price (1985) 57.

project manager. An alternative is to use an established and reputable construction management firm, which will require careful checking of credentials and track record. The costs of retrofitting the facility with new equipment or renovating poor construction are well in excess of the costs of careful scrutiny during the initial installation.

A 1987 publication by the National Bureau of Standards (NBS) may be of some help in equipment selection, although it laments the lack of existing performance standards for equipment and systems in correctional facilities. Prepared for the National Institute of Justice, it is entitled Standards for Building Materials, Equipment and Systems Used in Detention and Correctional Facilities[399] Citing the "expensive lessons" learned by correctional officials during the recent era of new construction, the goal of this publication was "to develop guidelines, test methods and the technical bases for standards to assist in the selection, application, and maintenance of building materials, equipment and systems used in detention and correctional facilities."[400] In the first year of what appears to be a multi-year effort, the report provides performance data on building materials, equipment, and systems used in correctional facilities and provides a review of existing standards used in facility design and construction.

The NBS report provides 26 useful pages of technical data on materials, equipment and systems and an Appendix B — Brief Descriptions of Selected Standards for Materials, Equipment, and Systems. Several technical reports are referenced, including those done by the NBS, the National Fire Protection Association, the American Society of Testing and Materials (ASTM), American Society of Heating, Refrigerating & Air Conditioning (ASHRAE), and others. Many of these standards were used in the formulation of American Correctional Association standards for detention facilities. These technical data are accompanied by a set of recommendations regarding those aspects of facility materials, equipment, and systems requiring future study. Pending future research, this new resource provides a starting place for the proper examination of construction materials, equipment, and systems used in new construction.

[399]Robert D. Dikkers and Belinda C. Reeder, (Washington, D.C.: U.S. Department of Commerce, National Bureau of Standards, November, 1987).

[400]Dikkers and Reeder 1, 3.

F. Secure Construction Does Not Insure Security

As indicated earlier, the best and strongest materials available do not insure a secure facility. Detention facility operators with many years of experience understand that 90 percent of security is invested in staff selected and trained in surveillance:

> Most materials, hardware and equipment can be overcome by inmates under conditions of poor surveillance and inspection. For this reason the failure parameters of these items must be known; i.e., their capabilities in relation to their use. Since [as noted by national standards], inmates in high and medium security in jails must be observed at least every 30 minutes by a correctional officer, the security materials, hardware and equipment must retain its integrity and function for this interval or longer, generally with a safety factor of twice the anticipated need.[401]

Many, if not most, escapes are foiled by staff who conduct frequent and careful inspections of the facility coupled with thorough searches of inmates and their living areas. These procedures also assist in reducing serious incidents at the facility.

G. Opening the Facility

The final step in building the new facility is opening it to inmates, at which time security hardware and procedures will receive their real test. The National Institute of Corrections has a program called "How to Open New Institutions" (HONI) that can be useful at this time.[402] It is referred to as "transition" to a new facility, since the move is from an old facility to a new one. This program is provided by NIC and should be attended prior to opening the facility to inmates. Five "transition principles" or guidelines are given in a Resource Guide, stressing involvement by staff and taking advantage of the opportunity to make positive changes during the transition. Task forces are recommended, which, again, may be of little use in a small facility transition, but nonetheless provide guidance to the

---

[401]Sechrest, Dale K., and Shelley J. Price, Correctional Facility Design and Construction Management (Washington, D.C.: National Institute of Justice, 1985) 57.

[402]The following is derived from "How to Open a New Institution, Resource Guide" (Boulder, Colorado: National Institute of Corrections Jail Center, c. 1987).

tasks required. The important point is communication, which is a good management principle in any situation.

Resistance to the "task force" process is discussed, with the apparent solution lying in full involvement of the transition "team." Important to any move are logistics — establishing a timetable for movement of inmates, equipment, etc. — and orientation and training. Orientation and training means seeing that personnel understand how to run the new facility, especially new equipment or existing systems that will change in the new facility.[403] There is a discussion of "scenario development," which is discussed in the Resource Guide. As discussed earlier, scenario development should have occurred at the pre-architectural stage. Doing so prior to opening should just be a review. Scenario development means that staff must think through how each operation ("function or activity") will be carried out in the new facility, such as reception, booking, food service, recreation, and the like. In planning and opening a new facility, it is a critical exercise that must be integrated into regular training schedules and reflected in practices well in advance of the move. It should lead to the development of better operational policies and procedures, including decisions about staff scheduling and coverage. The Resource Guide includes a section on policy and procedures development. The process should result in the overall improvement of operations at the new facility. It should be noted that scenario development is a management task that can be helpful at any time in improving facility operations, even without new construction or renovation.

Coordination of the move with the architect and/or contractor is critical, including the time of "acceptance" of the new facility. The actual move, including its timing in stages, is critical. Most new facility occupancies stage the transition so that a small staff group comes into the facility first followed by a small group of trusty inmates who "test" the facility for weaknesses, then more staff and inmates are gradually moved into the facility until the all functions are operational and the transition is complete. With all orientation and training in place this gives staff a chance to work out the "kinks" in operations before becoming fully operational.

Sometimes things do not go well. Nothing will be of help if the facility has not been designed with staffing in mind, or if safety violations preclude occupancy. In a $47 million, 840-bed jail recently opened, 18 safety deficiencies were found that would increase the

---

[403]NIC 4.

danger of suicides and assaults among inmates. Among these were metal grills over air-conditioning ducts that were too widely spaced; poor observation of up to half the cells from control booths due to glare on windows; towel racks that could be used for hangings; shields in front of toilets in the booking areas that blocked the officers' view of certain sections; and wire mesh fences in the recreation areas that were not strong enough. Sound levels were disturbing for both staff and inmates. Fortunately, a staged transition allowed staff to discover some of these problems and find remedies prior to full occupancy.

A satisfactory facility opening depends on good initial planning, the use of competent help in all phases of design and construction, control over the design and construction phases, careful evaluation of hardware and components, and negotiation within the political process to provide a secure facility with programs that meet both community and inmate needs. Sound knowledge of the inmate population — present and future — along with a clear perception of the mission of the facility will aid greatly in building a facility that will meet these needs.

CHAPTER EIGHT: REACHING FOR PROFESSIONALISM

The goal has been to show how to operate a good detention facility both by improving operating procedures consistent with good practice and by conforming to legal definitions of an inmate's rights. It is suggested that rather than wait for the courts to decide issues of good practice, the good administrator will seek out and define good practice. "Jails" must become "community detention facilities" in the sense that they move away from the role of just holding offenders for the courts to the provision of new forms of community programs. Diversion from the criminal justice system must become an additional goal of the detention facility.

In order to meet these goals, much more information on good detention facility operations is now available. The National Institute of Corrections operates training programs through its National Corrections Academy and provides technical assistance to facility managers through its Jails Division. National standards and an accreditation program are available through the American Correctional Association. The National Sheriffs' Association conducts audits that follow closely the ACA standards. There are other sets of standards for medical services and health care services. Model community programs, such as those in Genesee County, New York, and Montgomery County, Maryland, are available for adoption. Such programs not only meet offender needs, but they meet citizen needs, such as arranging restitution and having detention staff work with victims, providing both understanding and restoration to victims and offenders.

The courts generally do not address administration, facility management, fiscal procedures, personnel requirements, training hours or content, recordkeeping, research and evaluation, program monitoring, and community relations. Professional administrators who address these areas will reduce litigation. These concerns must be addressed before any court orders regarding an inmate's rights can be implemented. If these procedures are in place, and executed well, court orders may not be necessary. For example, the Denver County, Colorado, Jail had ten of eleven suits dismissed by a federal magistrate (with the eleventh settled out of court) because the magistrate felt that accreditation using nationally accepted (ACA) standards rendered the complaints invalid. The time required to respond to each suit dropped from 275 hours to 16 hours, a considerable savings in time and money.[404]

"Professionalism" means being trained and capable of high performance in a specialty, or "worthy of the high standards of a profession."[405] A professional does not look over his or her shoulder constantly to see what the courts want, or what must be done. The professional knows what to do and works with people trained to know what to do under ordinary conditions and in emergency situations. The professional informs the legislatures and the courts about good practice and makes requests for the resources necessary to achieve high standards of performance. It is anticipated that this book will provide additional support for these professionals and all individuals who strive to improve the operation of local detention facilities.

---

[404]Robert H. Fosen and William Lucas, "Why Jail Accreditation," The National Sheriff August-September, 1983: 10.

[405]Webster's New World Dictionary, College Ed., 1957.

REFERENCES

GENERAL

Franklin, Marc A. Torts, Sixteenth Edition. Chicago: Gilbert Law Summaries, 1984-85.

Kerle, Kenneth E., and Francis R. Ford. The State of Our Nation's Jails, 1982. Washington, D.C.: National Sheriffs' Association, 1982.

Mullen, Joan. American Prisons and Jails, Volume I. National Institute of Justice. Washington, D.C.: U.S. Government Printing Office, 1980.

O,Brien, Edward, Margaret Fisher, and David T. Austern. Practical Law for Correctional Personnel. St. Paul, MN: West Publishing Company, 1981

ASSISTANCE, STANDARDS, AND GUIDELINES

American Correctional Association,
4321 Hartwick Road L-208
College Park, Maryland 20740
(301) 699-7600

Standards for Adult Local Detention Facilities, 1981a.
Guidelines for the Development of Policies and Procedures, Adult Local Detention Facilities, 1981b.
Correctional Standards Supplement, October, 1984 and January, 1986.

American Jail Association
P.O. Box 2158
Hagerstown, MD 21742
(301) 790-3930

Commission on Accreditation for Law Enforcement Agencies. Standards for Law Enforcement Agencies. 4242B Chain Bridge Road, Fairfax, Virginia 22030: 1984.
(703) 352-4225

National Commission on Correctional Health Care
Box 3500
200 North Racine,
Chicago, Illinois 60614

Standards for Correctional Health Care (1987)

National Sheriffs' Association
1450 Duke St.
Alexandria, VA 22314-3490
(703) 836-7827

Handbook on Jail Administration, 1974
Handbook on Jail Security, Classification and Discipline, 1974
Handbook on Sanitation in the Jail, 1974
Handbook on Jail Programs, 1974
Handbook for Jail Architecture, 1974.
Handbook on Inmates' Legal Rights, rev ed., 1987.
Food Service in Jails, 2nd ed., 1988 (by Marilyn B. Ayres)
Guidelines for Planning a Detention Facility, 3rd printing, November, 1986
Jail Audit Manual, 3rd printing, January, 1987
AIDS: Improving the Response of the Correctional System, Fall, 1986.

Nebraska State Bar Association Committee on Correctional Law and Practice. Jail Standards (Proposed). February, 1977.

National Institute of Corrections
Jail Center
P.O. Box 9130
Boulder, Colorado 80301
(303) 497-6700

CRS, Inc.
P.O. Box 234
Kents Hill, Maine 04349
(207) 685-9090

Publisher of the Detention Reporter

AIDS: ACQUIRED IMMUNE DEFICIENCY SYNDROME

National AIDS hotline: 1-800-342-AIDS
National Institute of Justice Information Number 1-301-251-5500

DesJarlais, Don, and Dana E. Hunt. AIDS and Intravenous Drug Use. Washington, D.C.: National Institute of Justice, Feb., 1988.

Hammett, Theodore M. AIDS in Prisons and Jails: Issues and Options. Washington, D.C.: National Institute of Justice, Feb., 1986.

Hammett, Theodore M., with assistance from Monique Sullivan and Taylor McNeil. AIDS in Correctional Facilities: Issues and Options, 2nd ed. Washington, D.C.: National Institute of Justice, May, 1987.

Hammett, Theodore M., and Walter Bond. Risk of Infection with the AIDS Virus Through Exposures to Blood. Washington, D.C.: National Institute of Justice, Oct., 1987.

Hammett, Theodore M. Precautionary Measures and Protective Equipment: Developing a Reasonable Response. Washington, D.C.: National Institute of Justice, Feb., 1988.

Musto, David F. "AIDS and Panic: Enemies Within." Wall Street Journal 28 April 1987.

Rowan, Joseph R. A Pro-Active Prevention Program for Same-Sex Rapes and AIDS in Jails. American Jail Association Newsletter, Spring, 1986: 7.

CONTRACTING

McQuillin, Municipal Corporations, 3rd Ed. 29.05
Sands on Municipal Corporations, Sec. 22.03.
Camille and George Camp, The Real Costs of Corrections, South Salem, New York: Criminal Justice Institute, April, 1985.

INMATE MANAGEMENT

Nelson, William (Ray). "New Generation Jails." Corrections Today, April, 1983.

Nelson, William (Ray), and Mike O'Toole, "New Generation Jails." Correctional Information Series, Library Information Specialists, Inc. December, 1983. [xerox]

PERSONNEL

Benton, F. Warren. Planning and Evaluating Prison and Jail Staffing. Washington, D.C.: National Institute of Corrections, 1981.

California Youth and Correctional Agency, Board of Corrections. Corrections Planning Handbooks. Prepared by Farbstein/ Williams and Associates. Sacramento, California: Board of Corrections, 1981.

Federal Prison System. Staffing Guide for the Federal Prison. Washington D.C.: Federal Prison System, 1980.

Institute for Public Policy Analysis, Work Schedule Design Handbook. Washington, D.C.: U.S. Department of Housing and Urban Development, 1978.

NEW FACILITY CONSTRUCTION

Abrams, Kathleen Shea, and William Lyons. Impact of Correctional Facilities on Land Values and Public Safety, FAU-FIU Joint Center for Environmental and Urban Problems, Florida International University, July 1987.

Atlas, Randy. "Cost Saving Aspects of a Third Generation Detention Facility: A Case Study, The Dade County Stockade Expansion," draft for the AIA Design Resource File, 1984 [xerox]; see also, Randy Atlas, "Violence in Prison, Environmental Influences." Environment and Behavior, 16 (May, 1984).

Camp, George, and Camille, "Stopping Escapes: Perimeter Security." Construction Bulletin, U.S. Department of Justice, National Institute of Justice, August, 1987.

Carter, Stephen A., Lowell Nordquist, and Polly Reno. Evaluation of Pre-Manufactured Housing for Correctional Purposes. Columbia, South Carolina: Carter-Goble Associates, Inc., February, 1984.

DeWitt, Charles B. "Florida Sets Example with Use of Concrete Modules," U.S. Department of Justice, National Institute of Justice, March, 1986.

____, "New Construction Methods for Correctional Facilities," U.S. Department of Justice, National Institute of Justice, March, 1986.

____, "California Tests New Construction Concepts," U.S. Department of Justice, National Institute of Justice, June, 1986.

____, "Ohio's New Approach to Jail and Prison Financing," U.S. Department of Justice, National Institute of Justice, July, 1986.

____, National Directory of Corrections Construction. U.S. Department of Justice, National Institute of Justice, August, 1986.

Dikkers, Robert D. and Belinda C. Reeder. Standards for Building Materials, Equipment and Systems Used in Detention and Correctional Facilities. Washington, D.C.: U.S. Department of Commerce, National Bureau of Standards, November, 1987.

Farbstein, Jay. Correctional Facility Planning and Design. Florence, KY: Van Nostrand Reinhold, 1985.

Friedman, Jay. "Costs, Projecting for Construction," Corrections Today, April, 1985 106, 108, 112.

Kimme, Dennis. "The Nature of New Small Jails: Report and Analysis." Champaign, IL: KIMME Planning and Architecture, prepared for the National Institute of Corrections, October, 1985.

Mullen, Joan, Kenneth Carlson, and Bradford Smith. American Prisons and Jails, Volume I, National Institute of Justice, 1980.

Pena, William M., with William Caudill, and John Focke. Problem Seeking: An Architectural Programming Primer (Boston: Canners Books International, 1977.

Price, Shelley J., and Dale K. Sechrest, "Continuity in Design and Operation," Corrections Today, April, 1986.

Sechrest, Dale K., and Shelley J. Price. Correctional Facility Design and Construction Management. National Institute of Justice. Washington, D.C.: U.S. Government Printing Office, 1985a.

Sechrest, Dale K., and Shelley J. Price, "Planning and Decisionmaking in Correctional Facility Construction." Federal Probation, December, 1985b.

Sechrest, Dale K., Nick Pappas, and Shelley J. Price, "Building Prisons: Pre-Manufactured, Prefabricated, and Prototype." Federal Probation, March, 1987.

State of California, Board of Corrections. Corrections Planning Handbooks, prepared by Farbstein/Williams and Associates, 1981. Board of Corrections, 600 Bercut Drive, Sacramento, CA 95814. Telephone (916) 445-5073.

CASE LAW

Abbott v. Meese, 824 F.2d 1166 (D.C. Cir. 1987)
Abbott v. Richardson, C.A. no. 73-1047 (D.D.C. 1984).
Adams v. Carlson, 488 F.2d 619 (7th Cir. 1973).
Ahrens v. Thomas 434 F.Supp. 873 (W.D.Mo. 1977).
Alberti v. Sheriff of Harris Co., 406 F.Supp. 649 (S.D. Tex. 1975).
Alberti v. Heard, 600 F.Supp. 443 (S.D. Tex. 1984).
Ancata v. Prison Health Services, Inc., 769 F. 2d 700 (llth Cir. 1985).
Baker v. Beto, 349 F. Supp. 1263 (S.D. Tex. 1972).
Baxter v. Palmigiano, 425 U.S. 308 (1976).
Bell v. Wolfish, 441 U.S. 520 (1979).
Blackburn v. Snow, 771 F.2d 556 (1st Cir., 1985).
Block v. Rutherford, 104 S.Ct. 3227 (1984).
Bounds v. Smith, 430 U.S. 817 (1977).
Brenneman v. Madigan, 343 F.Supp. 128 (N.D.Cal. 1972).
Brewer v. Perrin (Mich App. 1984).
Campbell v. McGruder, 416 F.Supp.100 (D.D.C. 1975), 554 F.Supp. 562 (D.D.C. 1982).
Clappler v. Flynn, 605 F.2d 519 (10th Cir. 1979).
Clutchette v. Procunier, 328 F.Supp. 767 (N.D.Cal. 1971).
Cody v. Hillard, 799 F.2d 477 (8th Cir. 1986).
Collins v. Schoonfield, 344 F. Supp. 255 (D.Md. 1972).
Cooper v. Pate, 378 U.S. 546 (1964).
Corby v. Conboy, 357 F.2d 251 (2nd Cir. 1972).
Cross v. Powers, 328 F. Supp. 899 (W.D.Wis. 1971).
Cruz v. Hauck, 515 F.2d 322 (5th Cir. 1975).
Daniels v. Williams, 106 S.Ct. 662 (1986).
Davidson v. Cannon, 106 S.Ct. 668 (1986).
Davis v. Zahradnick, 600 F.2d 458 (3th Cir. 1979).
D.B. v. Tewksbury, 545 F.Supp. 896 (D.Ore. 1982).
Doe v. McFaul, 599 F.Supp.1421 (D.Ohio 1984).
Doe v. United Social and Mental Health Services, Inc., 670 F.Supp. 1121 (D.Conn. 1987).
Douglas v. California, 372 U.S. 353 (1963).
El Fundi v. DeRoche, 625 F.2d 195 (8th Cir. 1980).
Estelle v. Gamble, 429 U.S. 97 (1976).
Garcia v. San Antonio Metropolitan Transit Authority, 105 S.Ct. 1005 (1985).
Gates v. Collier, 501 F.2d 1291 (5th Cir. 1974).

Griffin v. Smith, 493 F.Supp. 120 (W.D.N.Y. 1980).
Heft v. Carlson, 489 F.2d (5th Cir. 1973).
Hendrickson v. Griggs, No. 2C 84-3012 (N.D. Iowa, April 9, 1987).
Hewitt v. Helms, 459 U.S. 460 (1983).
Hodges v. Klein, 412 F.Supp. 896 (D.N.J. 1976).
Hutto v. Finney, 437 U.S. 678 (1978).
Inmates of Attica Correctional Facility v. Rockefeller, 453 F.2d 12 (2nd Cir. 1971).
Inmates of Suffolk County Jail v. Eisenstadt, 360 F.Supp. 676 (Mass. 1973).
Ippolito, et al., v. Howell, Docket No. 78-0911 (D.N.J., July 11, 1980).
Jackson v. Meachum, 699 F.2d 578 (1st Cir. 1983).
Johnson v. Avery, 89 S.Ct. 747 (1969).
Jones v. Diamond, 636 F.2d 1364 (5th Cir. 1981)
Jones v. Eagleville Hospital and Rehabilitation Center, 588 F.Supp. 53 (E.D. Pa. 1984).
Jones v. Wittenberg, 330 F.Supp. 707 (N.D.Ohio, 1971).
Kahane v. Carlson, 527 F.2d 392 (2d Cir. 1975).
Laaman v. Helgemoe, 437 F.Supp.269 (D.N.H. 1977).
Lanza v. New York, 370 U.S. 139 (1962).
Lien v. City of Ketchikan, 383 P. 2d 721 (Alaska 1963).
Lugar v. Edmonson Oil Company, 457 U.S. 922 (1982).
Martin v. Kelley, 803 F.2d 236 (6th Cir. 1986).
Meadows v. Hopkins, 713 F.2d 206 (6th Cir. 1983).
Medina v. O'Neill, 589 F.Supp. 1028 (S.D.Tex. 1984).
Miller v. Carson, 401 F.Supp. 835 (1975) aff'd 563 F.2d 741 (5th Cir. 1977).
Mitchell v. Untreiner, 421 F.Supp. 886 (N.D.Fla. 1976).
Monell v. New York Department of Social Services, 436 U.S. 658 (1978).
Monroe v. Pape, 365 U.S. 167 (1961).
National League of Cities v. Usery, 426 U.S. 833 (1976).
Newman v. Alabama, 559 F.2d 283 (5th Cir. 1977), modified 438 U.s. 781 (1978).
Nolan v. Scafati, 430 F.2d 548 (1st Cir. 1970).
Novak v. Beto, 453 F.2d 661 (5th Cir. 1971).
O'Brien v. Blackwell, 421 F.2d 833 (5th Cir. 1970).
Oklahoma City v. Tuttle, 53 LW 4639 (Supreme Court 1985).
O'Lone v. Estate of Shabazz, S.Ct. 107 (1987).
Owen v. City of Independence, 442 U.s. 622, 100 S.Ct. 1398 (1980).
Padway v. Palches, 665 F.2d 965 (9th Cir. 1982).
Pell v. Procunier, 417 U.S. 817 (1974).
Pittman v. City of Amarillo, 598 S.W. 2d 941 (Tex. Civ. App., 1980).
Procunier v. Martinez, 416 U.S. 396 (1974).

Pugh v. Locke, 406 F.Supp. 318 (M.D.Ala. 1976), aff'd 559 F.2d 283 (5th Cir. 1977) cert. den 98 S.Ct. 4144 (1978).
Redmond v. Baxley, 475 F. Supp. 1111 (E.D.Mich. 1979).
Rhem v. Malcolm, 371 F.Supp. 594 (S.D. N.Y. 1974).
Rhodes v. Chapman, 452 U.S. 337 (1981).
Rizzo v. Goode, 423 U.S. 362 (1976).
Robinson v. City of Philadelphia, 161 A. 2d 1 (Penn. 1960).
Rogers v. Scurr, 676 f.2d 1211 (9th Cir. 1982).
Ross v. Moffitt, 417 U.S. 600 (1974).
Ruiz v. Estelle, 679 F.2d 1115 (5th Cir. 1982).
Salinas v. Breir, 695 F.2d 1073 (7th Cir. 1982), cert. denied, ___ U.S. ___ (1984).
Sanders v. Chatham Co., 728 F.2d 1367 (11th Cir. 1984).
Schall v. Martin, 467 U.S. 253 S.Ct. (1984).
Smith v. Sullivan, 553 F.2d 373 (5th Cir. 1977).
Smith v. Wade, 103 S.Ct. 1625 (1983).
Stroud v. Swope, 178 F.2d 950 (9th Cir. 1951).
Swansey v. Elrod, 386 F.Supp. 1138 (N.D.Ill. 1975).
Tate v. Kassulke, 409 F.Supp. 651 (W.D.Ky. 1976).
Todaro v. Ward, 556 F.2d 48 (2d Cir. 1977).
Turner v. Safely, 107 S.Ct. (1987).
United States ex rel Wagner v. Ragen, 213 F.2d 294 (7th Cir. 1954).
U.S. v. Moore, ___ F.Supp. ___, 41 CRL 2484 (D.Minn. 1987).
U.S. v. Smith, 464 F.2d 194 (10th Cir. 1972).
Webster v. Huston, 689 F.2d 1220 (5th Cir. 1984).
West v. Atkins, 815 F.2d 993 (4th Cir. 1987).
White v. Keller, 588 F.2d 913 (4th Cir. 1978).
Whitley v. Albers, 106 S.Ct. 1078 (1986).
Williams v. Department of Justice, 433 F.2d 958 (5th Cir. 1970).
Williams v. Edwards, 547 F.2d 1296 (5th Cir. 1977).
Wood v. Strickland, 420 U.S. 308 (1975).
Wolff v. McDonnell, 418 U.S. 539 (1974).

NAME INDEX

INDEX